Street Player

Street Player

My Chicago Story

Danny Seraphine
with Adam Mitchell

John Wiley & Sons, Inc.

Published by John Wiley & Sons, Inc., Hoboken, New Jersey
Published simultaneously in Canada

For general information about our other products and services, please contact our Customer Care Department within the United States at (800) 762-2974, outside the United States at (317) 572-3993 or fax (317) 572-4002.

Wiley also publishes its books in a variety of electronic formats. Some content that appears in print may not be available in electronic books. For more information about Wiley products, visit our web site at www.wiley.com.

Library of Congress Cataloging-in-Publication Data
Seraphine, Daniel, date.
  Street player : my Chicago story / Danny Seraphine with Adam Mitchell.
    p. cm.
  Includes index.
  ISBN 978-0-470-41683-9 (cloth); ISBN 978-0-470-62534-7 (ebk);
  ISBN 978-0-470-62571-2 (ebk); ISBN 978-0-470-62573-6 (ebk)
    1. Seraphine, Daniel, 1948– 2. Drummers (Musicians)—United States—Biography. I. Adam X. II. Chicago (Musical group) III. Title.
  ML419.S463A3 2010
  782.42166092'2—dc22
  [B]   2009045970

Printed in the United States of America
10 9 8 7 6 5 4 3 2 1

To Rebecca, who led me out of the darkness with all her love, trust, and companionship over the past fifteen years. I could not have made it without you.

To my children, Maria, Kris, Danielle, Ashley, J.D., and Taryn, who have always been there for me and loved me unconditionally.

To my grandchildren, Katie, Gabriel, Sofia, Kaden, and Sarafina, who give me renewed joy and hope that the best is still ahead.

Contents

Photo galleries start on pages 89 and 217.

Introduction

The red and white lights of the ambulance flashed against the trees in the yard, throwing leaf pattern shadows against the face of the house. In each burst of light, I saw the coroner as he exited the front door and carted Terry Kath's body down the walkway. There were police everywhere by then. One of the officers came up and pointed in my direction. He wanted me to move aside to clear a path.

Stepping out of the way, I watched as the coroner passed. Suddenly I found myself fighting off the urge to reach out and stop him from taking Terry away. I wiped at the tears welling up in my eyes, but it made no difference. Everything around me remained blurry and distorted. I looked on as the coroner came to a stop at the back of his van and forcefully swung its rear doors open.

An hour or so after Terry had killed himself, the coroner and paramedics attempted to stuff all six feet and two inches of him into a plastic body bag, only to find out there wasn't enough room. His giant snakeskin boots (size 12) were left sticking out of the end. I couldn't stop staring at them. Over the years, along with his bright grin and happy-go-lucky personality, those cowboy boots had become his trademark.

My mind wandered. I thought back to the first time I had seen Terry's vibrant smile. It was the day I joined Jimmy Ford and the Executives, a band he and Walt Parazaider were already playing in. Despite the fact that I was a sixteen-year-old drummer and they were both more experienced players, the three of us hit it off and were inseparable from then on. On that day, Terry, Walt, and I set out on the ultimate musical journey. We went on to grind it out in Chicago's club circuit in the early days as members of groups like the Missing Links and the Big Thing. Together with our bandmates Jimmy Pankow, Lee Loughnane, Robert Lamm, and Peter Cetera, we eventually picked up and moved from our hometown of Chicago to the West Coast to chase after our dream. We were determined to make a name for ourselves.

And together we did. Our group, Chicago, went on to become one of the best-selling American bands ever.

I remembered the times Terry and I locked eyes onstage after we broke big and opened for rock legends like Janis Joplin and Jimi Hendrix. I recalled watching him blaze through his guitar solos at festival shows in front of a hundred thousand screaming fans. Finally, I thought back to the last time I had seen Terry. It was weeks earlier at my house for a summer cookout. He was alive, but not well, and more strung out than ever. The coke and booze had taken their toll on his body and mind.

"I'm going to get things under control," Terry had assured me. "If I don't, this stuff is going to kill me."

His words echoed in my head as I realized I would never lock eyes with him onstage again. I would never catch another glimpse of Terry smiling back at me.

Our journey was over.

After they loaded Terry's body, the coroner shifted the van into gear. It soon inched down the driveway and out onto the street. I shuffled after the truck, staring at its flashing lights as they burned white dots into my field of vision. As much as it hurt my eyes, I couldn't bring myself to look away.

I should have done more, I told myself. *We all should have done more.*

Terry deserved a better exit from this life.

There were too many questions and no answers. The only thing certain was that Terry Kath, a guy I had considered my brother and musical soul mate since we were teenagers, was gone forever. The van continued down the block and disappeared around the corner. As soon as the sound of its engine fell away, there was nothing but silence. I stood alone in the driveway, wondering where it had all gone wrong on that dark Los Angeles night.

1

Back to Chicago

From the time my parents brought me home from Oak Park Hospital in the late summer of 1948, I was a wild child with a constant need for movement. I had a tendency to run toward the flame.

The sound of a fire engine siren was the first thing to catch my ear. Whenever one of the trucks came screaming through our neighborhood of New Little Italy, I waddled out the front door after it as fast as my short legs would take me. My mother was usually able to catch me before I made it to the street, but occasionally I slipped out without her noticing. One time I was found by a Chicago police officer almost a mile away from our house! Needless to say, my parents were horrified.

New Little Italy was an overflow of sorts for Chicago's Little Italy, a twelve-block stretch around Taylor Street. It was a typical Italian neighborhood: the houses were on the small side and packed close together. Families could smell what their neighbors were cooking in the kitchen and hear what they talked about at the dinner table.

My father, John Seraphine, met my mother, Mary, shortly after he returned home from a stint as an MP in the army during World War II. In the summers, my mom and dad took me and my older sister, Rosemary, on trips to beautiful Cedar Lake about an hour and a half outside of Chicago. We went on Wednesdays because it was my father's only day off from his job driving a bread delivery truck. Since it was the middle of the week, our family had the camp mostly to ourselves. We spent the scorching summer afternoons at the beach making sand castles and splashing around in the lake. It was our only escape from the sweltering summer heat. There was also a pavilion nearby with a dance floor where music boomed out of a jukebox throughout the day. I remember how the twelve-bar blues of Bill Haley and the Comets' "Rock Around the Clock" echoed up into the trees and carried out over the water. It was a nice family getaway from the bustling city streets.

My nervous energy drove my parents crazy. I was stubborn as hell. It got so bad they couldn't sit at the picnic table with their friends playing gin rummy for five minutes without me disappearing. They decided the only option left was to wrap a rope around my waist and tie me to a tree in the lakehouse yard. When I was in my playpen, they slid a section of chicken wire over it to make sure I didn't climb out. Their methods might have been a little over the top, but it was the only way they could be sure I wouldn't make a run for it.

Fortunately, there were more than enough family members to help keep an eye on me around our neighborhood. My mother grew up one of twelve kids, and my father had six brothers and sisters. Most of them lived close by, and we all got together regularly at my grandma Filomena's house on the corner of Grand and Narragansett to celebrate every holiday and birthday. With the size of my family, there was no shortage of occasions. The women brought over their best dishes for our huge Italian meals— homemade ravioli, spaghetti and meatballs with marinara, and chicken Vesuvio, which was served right on the bone with potatoes, a Chicago specialty. My mother always cooked up a batch of her famous lasagna, which I could never get enough of. There was a running competition to see who was the best cook, but nobody could beat my grandmother's homemade deep-dish pizza topped with her delicious sausage and peppers. As long as she was around, the title was hers.

My grandmother didn't speak much English, but she did the best she could. She was a strong lady who had single-handedly raised twelve children after her husband, my grandfather Michael, died. When I was young, her boisterous personality and heavyset frame sometimes scared me a little. But whenever I'd start crying, she was the first to calm me down. She'd call me by her nickname for me, Danootz. "What's the matter, Danootz?" she would ask, picking me up into her arms.

By the time I was eight, I had found the perfect outlet for my never-ending energy: my mom's cookware. While she fixed dinner, I sat on the faded linoleum in our kitchen banging away on over-turned pans, colanders, and saucepots with a set of her wooden mixing spoons. I loved the sound each one made—the high-pitched ting of the frying pan and the low bass thump of the mixing bowl.

My mother's pots and pans were the closest thing to having my own drum kit. I came up with the idea from watching my uncle Dominic play drums with his band at family parties. During the set breaks, he sat me on his drum stool to get a better look. My feet didn't come close to touching the floor, but I still wanted to be exactly like Uncle Dominic one day. I remember my family saying he was only a part-time drummer because making a living playing music back then was simply unheard of. It was considered "pie in the sky," as they used to say.

My whole family had a deep love for music, especially my mom. Whenever my father didn't have a Chicago Cubs game on the radio, she tuned the dial to Lawrence Welk. The songs were truly an escape. They allowed my mother's mind to wander to a place far from her routine existence as a housewife. Together, we spent the long afternoons listening to her old forty-five records of classic crooners like Vic Damone, Frank Sinatra, and Dean Martin. Early on, my mother saw the passion I had for music.

After her father died, she had led a hard life. She was left to help my grandmother take care of her younger brothers and sisters. I can't imagine what kind of a struggle it was for my mother.

I loved to see her face light up as I drummed on her pans while she fixed dinner. She got such a kick out of it.

"You sound so good, Danny," my mother told me as I pounded away. "I just know that one day you're going to be a famous drummer." My playing had become her soundtrack as she cooked dinner.

My father wasn't as thrilled with the new activity. After returning home one night from a long day of work, he remained in the doorway staring at me. The expression on his face couldn't have been a clearer cue to stop with my banging. I looked up at him from my setup on the floor.

"This is what you have Danny doing while I'm out driving the truck all day?" he asked my mother, sliding into a chair at the kitchen table. He pulled off his baseball cap and scratched the back of his head. I was already having trouble in school. The nuns were telling my parents I could hardly read. The last thing he wanted to come home to was the sight of me sitting on the floor banging on pots.

"Have you seen how well he does it?" my mother asked. "At least I can keep an eye on Danny in here, and he's not out wandering the streets."

My father got quiet and ran a finger over his mustache. He didn't want to admit it, but he knew she had a point.

"I want to enroll Danny in lessons and buy him a real drum set," she continued. "I saw one down at the music shop."

"What? Do you know how much those things cost? Where would we get the money?" my father snapped.

"I'll take care of it. I've been setting a little something extra aside for the past few months and it might be enough," she explained.

"Well, what are you asking me for if you've already made up your mind? You always do what you want no matter what I say," he told her, getting up out of his chair. He grabbed a slice of bread from the counter and made his way into the living room. As soon as he was gone, my mother looked down and gave me a knowing wink. I smiled back up at her and returned to pounding on the pans.

My mother was a real handful. She was headstrong and opinionated, two traits I inherited from her. She didn't hold her tongue for anyone and regularly nagged my father. Being the gentleman that he was, my father stayed calm and cool. It was his nature. He had come from a poor immigrant family and also led a hard life. His father, who I was named after, died when he was young and my dad was forced to drop out of school at sixteen to help support the family. Despite the hardships of his childhood, I never once heard my father say a bad thing about anyone. Ever.

My mother made good on her promise to start me playing drums. I graduated from my set of pans to a rubber practice pad she bought down at the music shop. The mixing spoons were traded out for my first set of oak drumsticks and I sat in my bedroom for hours practicing until my forearms were sore and my hands ached. I drummed along to my mother's classics as well as to my sister Rosemary's hip new forty-fives by Elvis Presley. I couldn't get enough of songs like "Heartbreak Hotel" and "Hound Dog."

Once I got bored with the practice pad, my mother helped me put together an actual set. I started with a Slingerland snare and then added a bass drum and cymbal. She enrolled me in private drum lessons after school with a teacher named Mr. Spranzo, who walked me through all of the basics, including seating and positioning and hand technique. I rode my Schwinn bicycle down to the local music store where he had a practice room in the back and went through the routines on a practice pad. My left hand was weaker than my right, but he told me that was typical of most beginning drummers. Not long after my lessons began, Mr. Spranzo moved, and I didn't like the guy who took his place. It was fine with me because I had grown tired of the lessons anyway.

I set up a space for my drums in our basement and practiced along with Gene Krupa, Sandy Nelson, and Cozy Cole records for hours. Those musicians became my heroes. The albums sounded amazing, especially Cole's *Topsy Part II* and the soundtrack for *The Gene Krupa Story*. There were kids whose parents had to force them to practice their piano or accordion, but I couldn't wait to get down to the basement after school and get behind my kit. It was the only thing I thought about all day.

My banging didn't sit well with my older sister, Rosemary. She hated me drumming in the house. Whenever she reached her boiling point, she would whip open the basement door and shout at me to keep it down. Being the snotty-nosed little brother that I was, her outbursts only made me play harder. Rosemary was a straight-A student and the perfect daughter. I got a real kick out of messing with her.

My sister wasn't the only one who was annoyed with my playing. The neighbors weren't thrilled with the racket either. The houses on our street were practically on top of one another, so the sound of my drums didn't have far to travel. My banging shook the foundations of a couple houses in each direction.

One afternoon, a guy named Stanley showed up at the basement window above where I was sitting behind my kit. He was an old, crotchety neighbor who always had a sour look on his face, probably because he worked nights and found it impossible to get a wink of sleep during the day. As he stood there shaking a clenched fist at me, I glared through the window and chucked the middle finger back at him. Old Stanley almost blew a gasket.

Within seconds, there was a pounding at our front door. I tiptoed up the basement steps to hear what was going on.

"Do you know what your son just did to me?" I heard Stanley ask my mother. "He flipped me off!"

"Well, Stanley," my mother answered, "Danny has a right to play, so stop picking on him!"

There was no response from Stanley. How was he going to argue with her? That was my mother for you. She had my back no matter what the circumstances. Even though Stanley's visits became a routine occurrence, I could never do any wrong in my mother's eyes. My father, on the other hand, was a different story. He thought I was wasting my time. What future was there in playing the drums? In his mind, I should have been upstairs studying.

By the time I was eleven, I had mastered a mean version of the Surfaris' hit song "Wipe Out" in my basement. While attending St. Priscilla's Middle School, I tore through the tune onstage at the talent show. I practiced for weeks and even added my own twist, coming up with a cool drum solo to throw on toward the end. My inspired performance attracted plenty of attention from the girls in the front row.

"Go, Danny, go!" the girls shouted from their seats.

This drumming thing just keeps getting better, I thought to myself.

Soon afterward, I connected with a couple of other kids at school, an accordion player named Rosario Duca and a guitarist named Ken Gorski. Rosario was an Italian immigrant from the old country who looked like a European movie star with his slicked-back hair and navy blue blazer. Ken had his blond locks whipped up into a pompadour and could play all of the Ventures' songs on his new Fender Stratocaster guitar. The three of us spent afternoons practicing at Rosario's house down the block or in my parents' basement. If my playing alone annoyed Rosemary, having the band over sent her into the red.

What we came up with was some type of hybrid of pop and accordion music. We gave the Top 40 hits of the time a whole new style. Although it may have sounded interesting, I'm not sure we did songs by popular performers like Chubby Checker much justice.

"Come on-a baby-a, and do-a the twist-a," Rosario would sing with his thick Italian accent.

Our jamming was short-lived, though. I then began hooking up with other kids in the neighborhood to play with once in a while, but nothing constant came together. We made it as far as learning a few songs and performing at a middle school dance, but that was about it. Our families supported us by going to the few shows we played, but they were usually the only people there. To make up for the lack of an audience, they applauded as loud as they could at the end of each song.

Between practicing in my basement and playing the occasional school dance, I started hanging out in Shabbona Park off West Addison Street. It was only a short walk from my house. There I met a couple of boys named Rick Bracamontes and Mike Sells, who I thought were the coolest kids around. From the start, Rick and Mike were impressed with how well I could curse. It was a talent I had picked up over the years of eavesdropping on my uncle Pete and uncle George while they were talking with my father.

After I finished one of my obscene rants, Mike clapped me on the shoulder. "Wow, you really know how to *swear*, man!" he gushed.

Our lives revolved around the park. During the summer break from school, the three of us spent our days strutting around trying to look as cool as possible. I also began sneaking into my mother's purse and stealing her Viceroy cigarettes to smoke. Everyone knows you can't look cool without a cigarette dangling from your lips, right? When we weren't chasing down girls and copping a feel of them in the bushes, we were vandalizing the park restrooms and blowing up toilets with cherry bombs. It was easy. Light the wick, flush the thing down the toilet, and *boom!* One night, we blasted three toilets clear off of their pedestals. Within seconds, the park attendant rushed toward us with his arms flailing. The other guys took off running, but I didn't make a move. I was too cocky and arrogant to run. As far as I was concerned, we were just blowing off a little steam. What was the big deal?

"I'm calling the cops!" the attendant yelled.

"Go right ahead," I told him, lighting up a cigarette.

The guy took my advice, because the next thing I knew, two Chicago policemen came out of nowhere and hauled me down to the station. My mother and father couldn't understand what was getting into me. My mom had my uncle Pete, who was also a World War II veteran, come down to pick me up from the police station later that night.

"What's the matter with you?" he growled, stuffing me into his car. "You better not pull any shit like this again or the last thing you'll have to worry about are cops coming for you. You'll have me to deal with!"

My father didn't have the personality for discipline, so my mom brought in Uncle Pete anytime she thought I needed straightening out. Not that it did any good. I continued getting into trouble, especially with the nuns at St. Priscilla's. They were a bunch of mean old grumpy hags who didn't hesitate to slap you around to keep you in line. Corporal punishment may have been looked down on in the public schools, but Catholic schools were another story. It was open season.

One day, a lady named Sister Moore dragged me out of the classroom by the neck for goofing off in the back with a few of the other boys. Once we got out into the hall, she grabbed me by the shoulders and slammed me up against the wall. I exploded in a fit of rage and pushed her back as hard as I could.

"Get off me, you old bag!" I shouted.

Sister Moore lost her balance and fell down a short flight of stairs a few feet away. Most of the kids lived in complete fear of the nuns, especially Sister Moore, who was about six feet tall. The look of shock on her face when she got up from the foot of the staircase was priceless. I have a feeling no student had ever stood up to her like that before.

When my parents were called in for an emergency meeting at the school, my mother was beside herself. She was realizing I wasn't her sweet little boy any longer. Luckily, I was a talented athlete on the boys' basketball team at the school and my coach put in a good word with the nuns. Because of my mother's emotional pleading and the urging of my coach, I was allowed to stay at St. Priscilla's. They probably let me graduate just to get me the hell out of there.

When I moved on to St. Patrick's High School out on Belmont Avenue, the fierce side of my personality continued to rear its ugly head. Being on the short side for my age, I got picked on by the older kids from the moment I stepped into the schoolyard. I surprised a lot of them because I never backed down. The more I fought, the tougher I got, and I quickly developed into a wiry street fighter. I became the poster boy for a defiant teenager.

At the same time, I also started getting interested in cars, especially my dad's '58 Chevy. My father got up at the crack of dawn every day, so by the time he got home from work he was exhausted. After he lumbered back to the bedroom to take his nap, I'd grab his keys from the kitchen counter and take off in the car. I'd pick up Rick and Mike and we would buzz the neighborhood a few times.

But my fun didn't last long. As I crept up the street one night, I caught sight of my father standing out at the corner of our driveway with his arms crossed tightly in front of him. There was going to be no talking my way out of this one. I was screwed. My dad rarely lost his temper, but when he did it wasn't pretty.

"Okay, okay," I said stepping out of the car. "I deserve it. You can just—"

Whack!

He slugged me a good one to the side of my head. I couldn't run in the house fast enough. My parents grounded me and warned me never to even think of trying a stunt like that again. I was one of those kids who never got away with *anything* and had to become a fast talker out of necessity. I was always scrambling to try to get myself out of a jam.

It wasn't long before I got into another fight at school, this time with one of the brothers at St. Patrick's. It was almost a carbon copy of my run-in with Sister Moore back at St. Priscilla's. Unfortunately, St. Patrick's wasn't as forgiving and decided to kick me out altogether. They didn't want to listen to anything my parents or I had to say.

Despite getting kicked out, my marks were so awful at St. Patrick's that I needed to go to summer classes at the Steinmetz School before I could transfer. Of course, I paid no attention to the teachers there either. My focus was on a pretty little thing named Elsie, a cute brown-haired girl who sat in the row next to me. From the moment we met, we started spending most of our time together. I had messed around with girls before, but I finally lost my virginity to Elsie. We couldn't get enough of each other.

Shortly after I turned fifteen, Elsie told me she was pregnant. I had no idea how to react. I was a carefree corner kid. How could I possibly support a child? I wasn't in any position to get married and become a father. Elsie didn't want to hear anything I had to say and decided to have the child on her own. In the end, I had to come to terms with the fact that I just didn't love her enough to stay with her. From that point on, the only contact I had with Elsie and the baby, a girl she named Maria, was through her family attorney. I was allowed to see Maria once and that was it. When I asked Elsie's lawyer when I could speak to her again, the guy told me, "She said she hates you, Danny. It wouldn't be a good idea." In the end, my only option was to stay out of the picture to avoid ugly confrontations.

All the kids had something to prove hanging out in Shabbona Park. Everyone wanted to be known for being a tough badass. In our neighborhood, if you didn't have respect, you didn't have anything. Somebody would mouth off, and before you knew it, two guys were tumbling around in the grass beating the hell out of each other. Overall, you could say I took as much as I gave. One day, I got caught by a sucker punch and was in the middle of having my ass handed to me by a much bigger kid when a guy named Tom Padula came to my rescue. He landed a left hook that nearly took the other kid's head off. I had known Tom since grammar school and I couldn't have been happier to see him that day in the park. It made me understand the importance of running in packs of friends. You never knew when you were going to need backup.

My rebellious behavior at Steinmetz School continued and my grades kept getting worse. One morning, I was sent down to the administrative offices to meet with Mrs. Peterson, the school's guidance counselor. She sat behind her desk with a puzzled expression as she paged through my student transcripts. The lady didn't have a clue what to do with me.

"What do you want to be, Danny?" she asked, peering over her giant glasses.

"I want to be a drummer," I told her. To me, the answer was obvious. It was the only thing I ever aspired to. I may have been playing in lame bands at the time, but I figured something better would come along at some point.

The forced smile on Mrs. Peterson's face disappeared. "I'm not sure that is the best idea, Danny," she said. "You should consider enrolling in beauty school to learn how to be a barber. There may be a real future in that for you."

I couldn't believe she was being serious. As far as Mrs. Peterson was concerned, I had no skills or talent for anything other than being a menace. In her mind, suggesting a trade was a sensible option. But as my parents already were well aware, telling me not to do something is like pouring gasoline on a fire. *A barber?* That lady was out of her mind.

One afternoon after school, I was walking home past a local hangout called Lindy's Coffee Shop when I noticed a brawl on the lawn of a house next door. Five guys had someone down and were putting the boot to him. When I got closer, I saw it was Tom Padula, my friend from the neighborhood. Tom had saved me from getting my ass kicked in the park, so it was only right to return the favor. Without giving it a second thought, I ran into the mix of bodies swinging my fists.

I connected with a couple of good ones, but wasn't on my feet for long. A kick to my ribs and a fist to my head sent me reeling. The next thing I knew, I was down on the ground next to Tom. I rolled and held my arms up in defense, but it was no use. The blows came from every direction and I soon had the bitter taste of blood in my mouth. A couple of the kids picked me up and threw me headfirst against a parked car. I collapsed to the sidewalk and used my last bit of energy to curl up into a ball. I braced for another round of kicks, but they never came. There was a lot of yelling and I looked up to discover an even bigger fight. Some neighborhood guys had come in and saved our asses. One of them jogged over and helped me to my feet.

"You've got some serious balls, kid," he told me.

I was a total mess. The arm on my jacket was torn and my Italian loafers were all scraped up. I was bleeding and my eye started to swell.

I may have looked like hell, but I gained everyone's respect that day. Little did I know that the guys who came to my rescue were part of the notorious gang called the JPs. They had been sitting in Lindy's watching the whole scene go down. When they saw that Tom and I were in trouble, they ran out to get in on the action. The other hoods who jumped us were members of the Bell Park gang, their rivals.

My ballsy performance in the scrap gave me an instant reputation. The notoriety allowed me to start hanging with the JPs. The name didn't do them any justice; they were just as nasty and dangerous as any of the big gangs in the city. The JPs were under the Pizza Palace gang, who were below the Outfit—the full-blown Mafia of Chicago.

I may have started walking the streets with an exaggerated swagger, but behind the front I put up my life was a mess. My father and I were barely speaking to each other. My mother was scrambling to find some way to get me back on course. But it was no use. My only concern was with my new reputation as a member of the JPs. No matter what anyone said, I was a part of something and was going to do whatever I wanted.

2

The JPs

As my sophomore year at the Steinmetz School came to an end, they called me to the principal's office to let me know I was being suspended for the final week of classes. It didn't come as a total shock, but I still couldn't understand why they were booting me. Aside from a scrape here and there, I had been keeping to myself.

"We're not suspending you for anything you have done recently, Daniel," the principal explained. "We are suspending you for what you *might* do."

That's how bad they wanted me out of there.

When I got home, my father was sitting at the kitchen table reading the *Chicago Tribune*. He looked up from his paper and stared at me as I hung up my jacket.

"You're home a little early, aren't you?" he asked.

There was no use lying to him. "They kicked me out of Steinmetz," I confessed.

I saw the deep disappointment register in his eyes. He got up from the chair and stepped into his house slippers. "That's just great, Danny," he told me, shuffling into the living room. "That's just great."

After being kicked out of Steinmetz, I was supposed to go to a facility called Logan Continuation School located in the slums of Chicago on North Oakley Avenue. It was a small step up from a full-blown juvenile detention center. We had heard the horror stories about the place and I shuddered at the thought of having to attend school there. Luckily, my aunt Terry was dating a guy in city government and was able to pull a few strings to save me from having to deal with that nightmare. It was the way things ran back then in the city.

And with that, I was out of school.

I had no intention of ever going back and nothing my family said was going to change my mind. I tried to find better local bands to get involved with, but it wasn't happening. We didn't even stay together long enough to come up with a group name. The more I played out, the more discouraged I became by the lack of ability around. Not to sound conceited, but most of the kids my age were just beginning to learn their instruments and I had already been drumming for more than four years. There was a wide gap in our skill levels.

Without school to keep me busy, I was out in the streets full-time hanging with guys with colorful nicknames like "Gizzi," "the Undertaker," and "Megaton." My best friend, Rick Bracamontes from Shabbona Park, was also inducted into the gang, so we stayed inseparable. The gang had a uniform: a black cabretta leather jacket, an Italian knit shirt, and workmen's jeans we called "the baggy blues." The JPs were like the brothers I never had growing up. Together, we learned about the code of the Chicago streets and the importance of loyalty. When it came down to it, all we had was each other. If somebody messed with one of our guys, we hit them back so hard they never even considered doing it again.

My first full-fledged gang fight happened one night behind the Hi-Spot Bowling Alley in Franklin Park. A short, feisty Greek kid named Steve and I were the last of our crew to get to the parking lot in back of the bowling alley that night. As we waited for the Franklin Park guys to come out and fight, Steve lifted his shirt to show me the handgun he had tucked into the waistband of his jeans.

"Are you crazy?" I asked him. "What are you going to do with that?"

"Don't worry. It's not loaded. I'm gonna pistol-whip one of these assholes," he told me.

I let out a nervous chuckle. I was a little worried, but there was no turning back. The Franklin Park guys were already making their way across the parking lot toward us. I glanced up to see a gang member running at me. I ducked his punch and connected with a jab that stunned him. He careened into a car and I followed after him to finish the job. The rest of the JPs jumped in to help me, but by that time guys had flooded in from every direction and the lot turned into total chaos. It was like a saloon fight from an old western.

At one point, I looked over and saw Steve on top of a small Italian kid, who was even shorter than me. Steve had him pinned down on top of a car hood and was beating the hell out of him. Suddenly, I saw him lift his jacket and reach for the gun.

"No, no, please!" the short kid cried at the sight of the pistol. He held his hands up in defense as he squirmed on the hood. Steve held him by the neck and raised the gun up over his head. He was about a second away from tearing the kid's face apart when I lunged over and grabbed his arm.

"That's enough," I told Steve. "You don't need to do that."

He looked over at me with an incredulous expression. Seeing I was dead serious, he gave the guy a final punch to the ribs and headed off. I pulled the kid off of the hood of the car and pushed him away.

"Now get the hell out of here!" I yelled after him, not wanting to appear too soft.

What I lacked in size I made up for with heart and determination. I was one of the crazier kids in our hundred-strong crew. We spent hours on end drinking beer down at Riis Park and shooting pool at a place called Little English, owned by a well-known Outfit guy named Chuckie English. When we wanted some action, we crashed the local dances held at places like the Hi-Spot and started fights. Every time songs like "Shout!" or "Hot Pastrami With Mashed Potatoes" by Joey Dee and the Starliters came on over the speakers, we ran out onto the dance floor and started pushing guys around. It became part of our routine.

The head promoter of the dances at the Hi-Spot, an Italian guy named Joe De Francisco, was never happy to see us causing trouble in his joint. He was a giant, barrel-chested Italian who didn't take shit from anyone. He'd charge the dance floor and start chucking guys out of the way like they were rag dolls.

"Get the fuck out of here!" he yelled, dragging kids by the back of their jackets toward the rear exit.

I made sure I got the hell out of Joe's way. Whenever he showed up on the scene, everyone knew the party was over.

In the afternoons, we frequented a hot dog stand called Grace's across the street from Riis Park. The place was owned by a big, stocky Italian named Pete Schivarelli. All the corner guys had great respect for Pete because he was well connected within the community. He knew everyone. We were on our best behavior anytime we hung out at his joint.

Despite our age difference, Pete and I became fast friends and he took me under his wing. We went on long drives together around the neighborhood in his brand-new forest green Cadillac convertible after he closed up the hot dog stand. I felt safe riding around the neighborhood wherever we went. Pete took me by places like the Colony House Restaurant on the corner of Grand and Harlem, which was a local hangout for the older neighborhood guys who were part of a crew that was soon to become one of the most powerful arms of the Outfit. Pete introduced me to people like Tony "the Ant" Spilotro and his younger brother, Michael, Jimmy Leonetti, and Joey Lombardo. Although I only had a limited relationship with the older guys, it still felt like an honor to be in their presence. They demanded respect on the city streets and were untouchable wherever they went. Nobody—and I mean *nobody*—fucked with these guys.

"Hey fellas," Pete would tell them. "This is a friend of mine, Danny. He's a drummer."

To them, a friend of Pete's was a friend of theirs, and they welcomed me in. When I was looking for a ring for a cute neighborhood girl named Franny I started going out with, Michael Spilotro, Tony's younger brother, was nice enough to give me the hookup. We met up one afternoon in the parking lot behind the Colony House at the trunk of his Cadillac. Michael crouched down and flipped open a suitcase full of rings, bracelets, and watches. Of course they were all hot items, but I had no problem with it. I picked up a beautiful ruby ring at a bargain price. Talk about the best deal in the city!

I loved spending time around the older neighborhood guys. I even started getting my hair cut at the same place as some of the Outfit. It was a neighborhood barbershop called the House of Igor, run by a one-eyed barber named Igor. On any given day, I saw the Outfit guys in there getting their hands manicured as I got my hair trimmed and slicked up into a pompadour. One afternoon, a passing car backfired just outside the front door of the shop. After the loud bang, every guy in the joint dove down to the floor and reached into their waistbands for their pieces. I couldn't believe how on edge they were. *Is that how life is as a member of the Outfit?* I asked myself. I wasn't sure if I could ever get used to something like that.

Aside from our stops at restaurants and other neighborhood hangouts, Pete and I paid visits to a local whorehouse. It was an old dilapidated motel called the Near Loop in the seediest part of downtown Chicago. We dropped by on Friday nights after Pete closed up the stand. A man with a limp who went by the name of Tennessee ran the place and sat behind the front desk eyeing Pete and me every time we walked in. As soon as we'd arrive, Pete vanished up the stairwell and I continued to my favorite girl's room at the end of the hall to take care of business. Her name was Kim and she was the most beautiful black girl I had ever seen. She took a liking to me from the first time we met because she said I was gentle and treated her better than her other clients. I was the only one of her clients who held her after we had sex. Although Kim charged me twenty-five bucks for the first time around, the second was often on the house. Being a tender lover had its privileges.

• • •

Just because the JPs were one of the most feared gangs in the area didn't mean it wasn't dangerous out there on the streets. We took some brutal beatings along the way. They came with the territory.

One night, a group of us went down to St. Pascal's Annual Church Carnival to see what we could stir up. It was always one our favorite places to cause trouble and get into fights. We typically traveled in large packs, but on this night we got careless. For some reason, only fifteen guys came out that night as opposed to our usual thirty or forty.

As we walked down the center of the street, the carnival started emptying out. People disappeared behind game booths and squeezed in between vendor trailers. I always trusted my gut, and it was telling me this was the calm before the storm. Everything got quiet, *too quiet*. Suddenly, the Madison and Crawford guys, the MCs, appeared at the opposite end of the parking lot. They were armed to the teeth and there must have been at least 150 or 200 of them! Our gang had beaten up one of their guys at a party a few nights earlier and they were back looking for blood.

"Let's go, motherfuckers!" one of the MCs shouted toward us.

The rest of the JPs and I traded worried glances. We didn't stand a chance. I tried to look tough on the outside, but on the inside my stomach churned. In my mind, I was walking toward my death.

And then up the block, a siren cut through the night air.

I looked up to see a dozen police cars racing toward us from every angle. They had set up a full-on dragnet. Typically we made a run for it when they showed up, but not this time. I had never been so happy in my life to see the cops! They rounded us up and we spent the night in a holding cell at Austin Police Station. I figured it was better to be locked up in the local jail rather than lying on a bed in the emergency room down at Cook County with a busted head.

But my luck took a turn for the worse in the coming weeks. One of my cousins and I were involved in an awful car accident that left me in a hospital bed. I suffered a few broken ribs, and at one point the doctors thought I had ruptured my spleen. It was impossible to breathe without feeling pain throughout my body.

Being laid up in the hospital gave my friends and family the perfect opportunity to get their licks in. There was no shortage of suggestions about what to do with my life. Everyone saw that the next step for me was going to be jail . . . or maybe worse.

"Maybe you should join the Marines," my mother told me. It looked as though the music career she envisioned for me had faded into oblivion. She was looking for any way to get me back on track. I rolled away from her in the hospital bed and sighed. I didn't know much, but I had no interest in becoming a soldier. Deep down, however, my mother was right; it was time to do something constructive with my life.

My sense of guilt for not being there for the daughter I had had with Elsie weighed heavily on me. The child support loomed over my head like yet another dark cloud. I was behind in my payments and couldn't put off getting a job any longer. After a short search, I found work at Polk Brothers Appliance Store for $1.25 an hour, but it didn't last. The car accident had left me with a weak back, so it was impossible to move refrigerators and televisions all day. Later I worked on a factory assembly line for another few weeks, but that was also short-lived. My piddly musical income didn't amount to anything at the end of the day either. On average, I was playing out maybe once a month.

It was a scary period in my life and I aimlessly roamed the streets day and night. The one thing I had a talent for, playing drums, I wasn't using. It wasn't going to be long before I tried my hand at robbing and stealing to make ends meet. Whether I liked it or not, the currents were pulling me in that direction. It was part of the natural progression in the life of a corner guy ascending up the ranks into the Outfit. It was an important line to cross, because after that there was no going back. My life was already intense enough. Time with my gang was turning into a whole lot more than hanging out, drinking beer, and fistfights.

One night, five carloads of us went out looking for a rival gang of Puerto Ricans who called themselves the Simon City Gang.

The week before, they had trespassed in our neighborhood and beat up one of our guys. It was now our turn to exact our revenge. Once we made it to their neighborhood, we began combing the streets. Word of our arrival spread, and not long after, the Simon City gang rolled up on us. An all-out brawl ensued until the sound of police sirens could be heard in the distance. We ended up having to scatter into the unfamiliar neighborhood.

Once the police had come and gone, the Simon City guys came back looking to finish us off. I and a few other guys were separated from the pack and started walking home. Suddenly an old black Chevy came screaming by. One of our toughest guys, a crazy Irish kid named Dougie, kicked the side of the car. It sped on for another twenty feet or so before coming to a screeching halt. Suddenly, two shotgun barrels popped out of the passenger-side window.

"Run!" someone shouted.

I took off toward the entrance to a back alley just as a shot rang out. I ducked and heard the buckshot ricochet off of the brick wall above my head. I hit the alley and kept running until I was completely out of breath. Somehow, I managed to make it back to my neighborhood alive that night.

I jogged back to my parents' house and went straight to my room. I spent a sleepless night shivering in bed. It was only a matter of time before someone got killed. The tire irons were being swapped out for knives, the baseball bats for pistols and shotguns. Straight-up fistfights seemed to be a thing of the past. Everywhere we went there was another gang looking to take us down. I had to have my head on a swivel at all times and I couldn't deal with it anymore. I was crazy and tough in many ways, but more and more I began to understand that I didn't have the same ruthlessness as the other JPs. There was no way I would ever carry a gun or a knife. There wasn't that same level of violence and rage within me. The other guys were in a different league.

A few days after Christmas in 1965, I couldn't have felt any worse about my life. Standing alone in my parents' kitchen early one morning, I hit rock bottom. Nothing made sense. What was going to become of me? Was I going to spend the rest of my life grinding it out in mediocre cover bands? Would I die in a street fight . . . or survive long enough to become a member of the Outfit?

The time had come to reconsider everything. Sure, I thought of the JPs as brothers, but I also understood that they ultimately would lead me down the wrong path. It was a place I no longer had an interest in going. I stared down at the linoleum where I once used to sit for hours on end banging on my mother's pots and wondered what had happened. I was a high school dropout, a teenage father with a daughter I never saw, and I spent most of my time drinking and fighting. Above all, my music was going nowhere. I had lost hope, and for the first time a thought crossed my mind . . .

I am going to quit playing the drums.

What was the use anyway?

I was so distant at that moment that the sudden ringing of the telephone rattled me. I stared at the phone. *What if it's one of the JPs?* I thought. Should I answer? I wasn't so sure.

"Yeah," I finally said into the receiver.

"Hey, is this Danny?" a voice boomed on the other end of the line. "This is Tommy Ullo, man. I'm calling because Jimmy Ford and the Executives are looking for a drummer."

"What?" I asked.

"Jimmy Ford and the Executives," Tommy repeated. "Dwight Kalb, the band's drummer, is splitting to spend more time on being an artist. They need somebody right away. Would you be interested in auditioning for them?"

It was like divine intervention. Even though I had been a part of dead-end bands, I still managed to build a reputation around the neighborhood for being a good drummer. It was as if someone flipped on a bright light and everything was clear to me. Tommy's call instantly pulled me from the depths of despair. Jimmy Ford and the Executives were one of the hottest bands in Chicago. I had regularly seen their flashy candy apple red Cadillac hearse driving around the neighborhood. They were Dick Clark's road band for his Cavalcade of Stars national tours that featured all the major acts. Little Richard, Frankie Avalon, Fats Domino—they all did tours for Dick Clark.

"Yeah, that sounds cool, Tommy," I answered, trying to hide my excitement.

"They'd love to have you come over and sit in with the guys at Dwight's. I'll give you the address," he said.

I rummaged through a kitchen drawer for a pen, but couldn't find anything to write on. I didn't want to keep Tommy waiting, so I began scribbling on the palm of my hand. I couldn't write fast enough. For the first time, there was a shift inside of me. It wasn't the type of adrenaline I experienced before a fight; it was something more positive and uplifting. Tommy's phone call let me know there was a glimmer of light at the end of the tunnel. Maybe my musical dreams had a chance after all.

3

Jimmy Ford and the Executives

On the morning of my audition for Jimmy Ford and the Executives, I was more nervous than I had ever been in my life. The situation didn't get any better when I arrived at Dwight's house and didn't know anyone. The guys were at least three or four years older and our personal styles couldn't have been more opposite. They were straight shooters wearing college sweaters and I was a corner kid with greased-back hair and a black leather jacket. The sax player in the band, a tall guy named Walt Parazaider, introduced me to the guys: guitarist Mike Sistack, drummer Dwight Kalb, bassist Terry Kath, and trumpet player Jimmy Ford. Tommy Ullo had recommended me, but Walt had also seen me perform around the neighborhood and liked my drumming.

After we had gone down to Dwight's basement, Mike strapped on his guitar and turned to me. He was running the show.

"Okay, Danny," he said. "We're gonna do James Brown's 'Papa's Got a Brand New Bag.' You know that one?"

I situated myself behind Dwight's cool set of champagne sparkle Rogers drums and adjusted a few of the cymbals. I had heard the James Brown song on the radio, but never played it. Of course, I wasn't going to explain that to the expectant faces eyeing me. It was time to deliver.

My playing was stiff and mechanical starting out, but I threw myself into the song and found my groove in no time. Once my nervousness faded, my confidence grew with each roll of the toms and crack of the snare. The guys exchanged satisfied looks with each other as I let my natural ability shine through. As we used to say around the neighborhood, I played the shit out of it. When we finished, the guys walked into the corner of the room to talk amongst themselves. It seemed like they were back there forever.

"You got the gig, man," Mike finally said.

I let out a long sigh of relief as a smile found its way onto my face.

Mike went on to say I'd be paid fifty bucks per show and would be starting at an upcoming gig the band had in Pittsburgh two weeks from Saturday. It was an all-star concert for Dick Clark with the Four Seasons headlining, and featuring Lou Christie, Chuck Berry, Simon and Garfunkel, and Sam the Sham and the Pharaohs. Mike explained there was also a new band on the bill called the Yardbirds who were from England. And then he hit me with the biggest detail of all . . .

"We should be playing for around ten thousand people," he said.

I tried to muster a response, but it was hard to string the words together. The whole scene was too good to be true. The band was going to be playing in front of *ten thousand people*? The last time I played, there had been *ten*! I couldn't believe I was going to step in as the backbone of a six-piece horn band that backed up big stars like Chuck Berry and Lou Christie.

Somebody come wake me up because I must be dreaming, I thought to myself.

Standing in Dwight's basement that afternoon, I realized this was a crucial turning point in my life. These were the skilled musicians I had been searching for. The fog had lifted and my future could not have been clearer to me. This was what I should have been doing all along!

I connected with the band on a musical level, but overall I was a stranger in a strange land. They were from suburban middle-class backgrounds. They weren't Chicago street guys like me. I found myself surrounded by a professional musician's culture, not a corner guy's culture. Not only did they dress differently, but they also spoke another language.

"Groovy, man!"

"That's outta sight!"

"Far out!"

It couldn't have been farther from the street element I had grown accustomed to hanging out in Riis Park. Fortunately, Walt and I clicked early on and he took a liking to me. He was a good-natured guy from a blue-collar family who, like the rest of the band, kept out of trouble. Walt sometimes came across as academic and proper, but there was also a zany side to his personality. He had a wild spirit and loved to make the guys laugh with his rubber-faced antics. On top of that, he was an incredibly skilled musician. He was playing the clarinet by the time he was nine and also picked up the saxophone along the way. Walt's father had also played in bands at one time as a trumpet player, so music was in the family genes.

I also grew tight with Terry Kath, initially out of necessity. He was the closest thing to a leader in the band in terms of the direction of the music. Together, Terry and I were the rhythm section of Jimmy Ford and the Executives and had to make sure we were in step with each other at all times. If we were misfiring, then the band was misfiring, so we had to stay in the pocket together. Terry was a world-class bassist and guitarist from the western suburbs, who was almost entirely self-taught like myself. He was a happy-go-lucky guy who always seemed to be smiling. That being said, he also came across as a real man's man and I remember thinking he looked just like Robert Mitchum. Terry had a charisma that intrigued me from the beginning. But at times there was also a feeling that something darker lurked beneath the surface. Terry's family, in particular his father, was having some issues with his deciding to become a full-time musician, but I could only speculate at the time. Terry kept that side of his life to himself.

My parents were overjoyed to hear that I had been hired to play in a legitimate group. The future my mother had envisioned for me was back on the radar screen and there was hope. For the first time in my life, I had a direction and a purpose. I couldn't think of anything else except playing drums and returned to the basement in our house to practice for hours on end. Jimmy Ford and the Executives were giving me an amazing opportunity and I didn't want to blow it.

On the morning the band was to leave for our big gig in Pittsburgh, I came down with a 103-degree temperature and could barely pull myself out of bed. I finally managed to make it down the street to Dwight's house to meet up with the rest of the band. Walt and Terry looked hungover as hell. Terry walked up to me and let out a huge burp right in my face. He must have been eating garlic bread for breakfast, because it smelled absolutely awful. It was his weird way of testing the new guy in the group.

After loading our gear into the Cadillac hearse, we piled in and set out on the road. Walt sat up front in the passenger's seat next to Mike as he drove. Jimmy and I squeezed in with our equipment in the way back, while Terry reclined in the backseat with Dwight, whom the guys had decided to bring along just in case for backup. I had no problem with it. In my condition, I wasn't so sure I would even be able to play.

Terry pulled his bass out of its bag and sat back and lazily strummed it as we got on the highway and made our way out of the city. Up in the front seat, Walt took off his shoes and propped both of his feet up on the dashboard.

"Hey, check this out, man," Walt said, lighting a cigarette and sliding it in between his toes. He brought his foot up to his mouth and took a drag. "What do ya think of that, Danny?" he asked, looking back at me from up front. All the guys busted up laughing. I managed a smile at Walt's goofiness, but his behavior was a little unsettling. I didn't know what to expect next.

What planet are these guys from? I asked myself.

An hour into the trip, we ran headfirst into a brutal snowstorm. Mike gripped the Caddy's massive steering wheel with both hands and strained to keep us straight down the highway. About halfway to Pittsburgh, the hearse blew a tire. Mike kept the car on the road long enough for us to get to a service station. The attendant put the car up on the lift and pulled the wheel off.

"It don't look good," he told us, running a grease-caked hand over the wheel. "Ain't got this size in stock, so I'm gonna have to send someone to the next town to pick one up. Could be a while."

The guys scrambled and hatched a new plan. They made a call to Dick Clark's people in Pittsburgh and filled them in on our situation. "All right, Danny," Walt said, walking back from the pay phone. "You hang out here and wait for the guy to get his hands on a new tire for the hearse. The rest of us have to make it in time for the rehearsal, so we're going to call Dick Clark's people and have them charter the next plane to Pittsburgh for us. Once the car's fixed, you drive the gear and we'll see you when you get there."

My fever was getting worse by the second. "But guys," I pleaded, "I have never even been to Pittsburgh before."

"No problem," Terry said. He pulled a road map from the glove box of the hearse and lobbed it to me. "Just follow this. Once you blow into the city ask someone where the Civic Arena is. You'll be fine."

Walt slapped me on the back. "Good luck. We'll see you in Pittsburgh."

Despite my condition, I was the low guy on the totem pole and nothing was going to change their minds. Before I knew it, they were gone.

I walked over and gazed up at the massive hearse on the lift. What a beast! It might as well have been a school bus. How the hell was I going to pull this stunt off with a throbbing head and a fever? All the way to Pittsburgh? The farthest I had ever driven out of Chicago was to Calumet City.

After waiting around the cold station lobby for three hours, I was back out on the interstate with a new tire. The blizzard had intensified and I could barely see the road through the hearse's frozen windshield. What a nightmare! I don't know how I was able to pull it off. By the time I finally exited off the 579 freeway and merged onto Centre Avenue in Pittsburgh, I was spent. I thought my eyes might have been playing tricks on me because the Civic Arena looked surreal. It was a huge dome with a retractable roof. I had never seen a building like it. The guys met me around back and we unloaded our equipment before returning to the hotel they had checked into earlier in the day.

Immediately after getting to the room, I climbed onto one of the beds and passed out. My body completely shut down at once. I woke up to find singer Lou Christie walking around, talking to a couple of the guys. I recognized Lou from seeing him on television. He had just come out with his No. 1 single "Lightnin' Strikes," which was all over the radio. The scene was unbelievable.

I dozed off again, but before long someone was shaking me by the leg. I gave a kick and rolled over onto my side.

"Hey, Danny," a voice said.

"What?" I moaned. Looking up, I saw Terry standing at the foot of the bed. He was already dressed and ready to go.

"We're on in an hour backing up Chuck Berry," he told me.

"What do you mean? Aren't we going though a rehearsal?" I asked. Although I knew most of Chuck's songs by heart, I still wanted a chance to warm up. The rest of the band had already gone through a complete rundown earlier using some other musicians' equipment. I wasn't going to be so lucky.

"There's no time for that. We're leaving in five," Terry told me and walked out of the room.

I staggered out of bed and scrambled to pull myself together. My body felt worse than before I went to sleep. I dragged myself downstairs to join the rest of the guys and we took off in the hearse. Thankfully, they didn't make me drive.

When we arrived at the Civic Arena, the promoter led us to the backstage area through a maze of hallways. When I caught sight of Frankie Valli walking by, my heart jumped a few beats. Sam the Sham and the Pharaohs were also hanging out in the corner, so I couldn't have felt more on edge. This was the big time.

Once we reached the side of the stage, the band huddled up. Off to my left, Chuck Berry almost magically appeared. I couldn't take my eyes off him. The MC of the show announced Chuck's name and the crowd erupted.

"All right, you're on!" someone yelled from behind us.

I trotted out and was immediately blinded by the intensity of the lights overhead. When my eyes adjusted, I was confronted by the insanity of ten thousand screaming fans. The noise was deafening. I stumbled toward the back of the stage and settled in behind my drum kit.

I'm not sure why, but Chuck Berry appeared to be out of it. After he greeted the crowd, he walked back from the microphone and turned toward the band.

"Hey man, what are some of my hits?" he asked nobody in particular.

There was an uneasy silence. "'Johnny B. Goode'?" Jimmy Ford asked.

"Cool." Chuck nodded. He turned and walked back up to the front of the stage.

The band exchanged a nervous glance. Was Chuck being serious? We hoped it was his idea of a tension breaker.

After the initial jitters, Chuck kicked into gear. Even though we didn't have the chance to rehearse, the band quickly built up steam. Terry confidently thumbed his bass lines as Walt wailed on his saxophone. Jimmy cocked his head back and made his trumpet scream—man, he was an unbelievable player. My head still pounding, I fought to keep us together and in time. We tore through "Johnny B. Goode" and then transitioned into "Roll Over Beethoven." It was spontaneous and thrilling. Chuck hopped around the stage like he owned the place. When he dipped into his signature "duckwalk," the audience in the arena went crazy.

During the guitar solo, Chuck turned around and flashed us that famous grin of his. He nodded along to the beat I laid down as his hands danced over the fretboard of his guitar. It was nice to know we had earned his respect.

After Chuck played his two songs, Lou Christie took the stage and our band backed him up on "Lightnin' Strikes." To this day, I have no idea how I made it through the show without a rehearsal. Overall, I was running on pure instinct. It was the only thing guiding me through each number.

As soon as we finished, I jogged offstage and doubled over to catch my breath. Walt came up behind me and gave me a playful push. "How are you feeling, man?" he asked.

I was too overwhelmed to answer. When I looked up, he was still staring at me and smiling. "You got off on the music, didn't you?" Walt asked.

"Yeah," I finally said.

"So, what do you think?"

"Wow," I answered, nodding my head.

"It's great, isn't it?"

"It sure is."

It was the first time I had been high in my young life, and I couldn't get enough of the sensation. I had never come close to trying any drug. They were considered taboo in my neighborhood. But being onstage was something different. It was a release of all the frustration stored up over the past few years of running around the streets with no purpose. I wanted the feeling to last forever.

I sat to the side of the stage for the rest of the show, watching acts like the Yardbirds, Mitch Ryder, Little Anthony and the Imperials, and the Four Seasons perform. The show was a rite of passage. The band had thrown me into the fire and I had made it through to the other side. I had been pulled out of the darkness, and become something I never thought possible—a *working* musician.

After the Pittsburgh gig, Jimmy Ford and the Executives played three or four times a week all around the Chicago area. Needless to say, the lifestyle was very foreign. In the beginning, I found myself walking around with a wide-eyed stare. Fortunately, Walt made sure I was comfortable every step of the way. Wherever we went, he introduced me to the local club owners, promoters, and booking agents. Walt told me how to act and what to expect. Without his guidance, I don't know what I would have done.

We developed such a close bond, in fact, that he came to me one day and confessed that he was having a love affair with Terry's girlfriend, a beautiful young girl named Jackie. She and Terry were on the outs, but not exactly broken up yet, so it was a tough situation. It meant a lot that Walt would look to me for advice. He was deeply distressed because he thought the world of Terry. The two of them had been friends and bandmates for a long time, and Walt knew the news would crush him. In my mind, there was no use in hiding his relationship with Jackie any longer. The situation was only going to worsen over time. I told Walt he had to sit down with Terry as soon as possible and get the secret off his chest. As expected, Terry took the news hard, but eventually he and Walt were able to work through it. They were too close to let a chick come between them. Besides, Jackie wasn't just any girl. She and Walt eventually ended up getting married.

Jimmy Ford and the Executives continued to headline shows and opened for some national acts whenever they came to the area. In many ways, Walt, Terry, and I became like a version of the Three Musketeers within the band. We hung out constantly and they became like older brothers to me. After our gigs, we'd go down to a place called Bella's for a slice of the best thin-crust pizza in the city. Despite the fact that I came from a drastically different background, the three of us found we agreed on almost everything and had similar views about the world. Although I was younger, Walt and Terry recognized I had knowledge and instinct beyond my years. As they guided me along the path of a full-time musician, I made sure nobody messed with our band. After all, Chicago clubs were tough places and I knew how to handle myself.

I loved the new life I was leading and my feelings of despair were gone. My parents didn't have to give me money anymore. I could support myself. While my father was thankful to see me keeping my nose clean, he was still skeptical. He wasn't convinced that I would keep making a living by simply playing in a band. But my mother's prayers to get me off the streets had been answered.

"What did I tell you?" she said. "I knew you were going to be a famous drummer."

I still occasionally hung out with the JPs, but it wasn't the same. They understood that I was doing well with the group and most of them were happy to see me going in a different direction with my life. Not that they would come out and say it, but deep down they were proud of me. Most of the corner guys didn't have many options. It was the streets or nothing. Somehow, I had managed to find another way.

Then, one afternoon at a band meeting, everything changed. Walt, Terry, and I were told we were being fired from Jimmy Ford and the Executives. We couldn't believe it. Mike Sistack said it was a "last in, first out" type of policy. He explained that the band had decided to merge with a popular R&B horn band from Chicago called Little Artie and the Pharaohs, and were renaming their new group the Mob (how fitting for the city of Chicago at that time).

"Don't take it personal, it's just business," Mike told us.

And that might have been the case, but we were still stunned by the band's decision to dump the three of us. Walt, Terry, and I were hurt and slighted, but there was nothing we could do about it. What was done was done. As quick as my music career began, it seemed it might be in jeopardy of ending.

4

The Missing Links

After being let go from Jimmy Ford and the Executives, I had no idea what my next move was going to be. Was that it? A short run as a working musician and then back to running the streets?

Fortunately, I didn't have long to struggle with the thought of being without a job. I was relieved when Walt told me he had come up with a new plan. A guy he had grown up with out in the suburb of Maywood named Chuck Madden was looking for new musicians to join his group. Chuck was the guitarist in a cover band called the Missing Links and saw our being dumped from Jimmy Ford and the Executives as an ideal chance to improve his band. He was all for Walt, Terry, and me joining right away. The three of us were thrilled because we wanted to keep playing together.

Chuck's father, Bob, had a reputation around the city for being a savvy booker. We figured he could get us plenty of gigs, but were still shocked to find out each of us would be making *five hundred dollars* a week playing in the Missing Links. It was nearly impossible to wrap my head around that kind of money. Needless to say, it took the three of us about two seconds to take Chuck up on his offer. Although we would be performing the same old cover tunes and it wasn't going to musically challenge us, it was still a job playing music—a *well-paying* job. That was the only thing that mattered to me. Besides, being in a band sure as hell beat lugging refrigerators around all day at Polk Brothers Appliance.

The money was more than I had ever made before, and I spent every penny of it. I didn't think to set anything aside. The only thing that interested me was that I could buy my own clothes, go out drinking, and didn't have to rely on my parents to support me. I was even able to buy my uncle Sam's Pontiac coupe for $1,500 and put in a top-of-the-line eight-track stereo. I felt like a real big shot in that car.

The band continued playing the club circuit around Chicago and supported a few major acts when they came through town, such as Tommy Roe, Paul Revere and the Raiders, and the Turtles when they played the Arie Crown Theater downtown. The clubs typically booked us Wednesday through Saturday, so we continued to make good money. Typically, we loaded our equipment into a U-Haul trailer and towed it behind Walt's Plymouth. When the band traveled outside the state to play venues like the Holyoke Club in Indianapolis, the Attic in Milwaukee, and Shula's in Niles, Michigan, Bob had an old van he let us use.

We started referring to Bob Madden as Buffalo Bob because he wore a leather Indian jacket with tassels hanging from the back. He was a colorful character and always had plenty of ideas for the band. At one point, Buffalo Bob thought we might be a bigger draw if we used stage names. He didn't have a problem with Terry Kath, but he wanted Walt and me to change our last names because he thought they sounded too ethnic for mainstream audiences. For a few shows, I went by Danny Sera and Walt became Walt Perry, but it seemed too silly to keep it going. It wasn't long before we switched back.

The Missing Links regularly played at a disco club downtown called the Pussycat. The venue had a dinner theater upstairs where a black dance troupe, called Oscar Brown Junior and Friends, performed as well. As I was getting ready for our band's set one night, a tall black dancer from the show named Glen popped into the dressing room.

"Tonight, you are going to become a man," he said in his deep voice. I knew Glen was gay, so I wasn't sure what he was talking about. A shot of fear went through me when he turned and locked the dressing room door behind him. He was huge and muscular. I actually thought Glen might try to force himself on me, until he jutted a hand into his pocket and pulled out a joint. What a relief!

Walt and Terry had started smoking pot, so I figured I would give it a try. Glen lit up the joint, took two drags, and passed it over. I held it out in front of me, hesitated for a moment, and then inhaled.

"There you go," Glen said, urging me on. "Take a big toke."

I fought to keep the smoke in my lungs but coughed it out anyway. The warm sensation that washed over me with each drag left a permanent smile on my face.

When it came time for the Missing Links to go on, I was still high as a kite. I attacked my drum set and couldn't believe how incredible our music sounded. But at the pause in our first song, I stopped playing altogether. I thought it was the end of the tune! A hush came over the audience and Walt and Terry both whipped their heads around to shoot me a look. They could tell by the glazed expression on my face that I was stoned as could be. Walt gave me a knowing nod, and we started the song back up again. It was a remarkable experience, but after that night at the club I didn't make a practice out of getting high before our shows. As the backbone of the band, it was important for me to stay clear-headed and focused when we played.

Even though our band had a busy touring schedule, I still made my way down to drop in on some of the JPs. They were renting an old tavern, which they called "the Club," to use as their private hangout. It was good to shoot the shit with the guys every now and then. They were supportive of the band and often came out to see the Missing Links perform.

Our band played everywhere around the local club circuit, but one of our favorite venues was a place called the Cheetah on West

Lawrence Avenue, formerly the Aragon Ballroom, a cavernous dance hall that had been built back in the 1920s. The new owners had converted it to resemble a New York–style club in order to attract the younger crowd, covering the furniture with multicolored fabric and putting in psychedelic strobe lights over the painted dance floor. The ballroom had a bunch of pedestal stages where each of the bands on the bill could set up. Interestingly enough, the Aragon Ballroom was where my parents had met way back in the day during a Saturday night dance.

I took a stroll into the club's boutique one night to kill some time before our set and caught sight of a striking Asian girl working behind the cash register. She had long, shiny black hair and a vibrant smile. I thought she was the most gorgeous girl I had ever seen in my life. I tried to act casual, but it was no use. I stared at her until she finally looked up from the register and made eye contact with me. It was a brief glance, but all I needed.

After I worked up enough nerve, I walked up to the counter and introduced myself. She told me her name was Rose and we began chatting. I found out she lived with her mother on the North Side of Chicago around the Montrose and Diversey area, which at the time was a rough part of town. I could have stood there all night talking with Rose, but our band was due to go on soon. Before leaving the boutique, I made sure to ask her for her number.

When our band got out onstage, I was happy to see a few of the guys from the JPs in the crowd. It was always nice to see them out there supporting the band. However, they weren't the only gang in attendance that night. Before long, they got into it with some of the Franklin Park guys as I watched from behind my drum kit. The large strobe lights blinking on the ceiling only added to the chaos as a vicious brawl broke out on the dance floor. It was impossible for the club bouncers to break it up. Nobody could see what the hell was going on, just flashes of fists, arms, and faces. The one thing I could make out was that JPs were outnumbered and getting their asses kicked.

Eventually they made a run for it and disappeared out a side entrance. It looked like the Franklin Park guys were about to leave when one of them recognized me up onstage. He got the attention of the others and they stood together in a group, gesturing in my direction. My heart jumped up into my throat and I scanned the room for an escape route. Were they going to wait until the end of our set or rush me right in the middle of the song? Either way, I was in trouble. Not only was I alone, but there was nowhere to run because my drum set had me boxed in.

Just as they were getting ready to make their move, a short kid walked up and joined their group. He began talking with his hands and pointing toward me. After a short discussion, the Franklin Park guys backed into the crowd and exited through the side door of the club. I couldn't believe my luck. Then it dawned on me. It was the same kid I had saved from a pistol-whipping back at the Hi-Spot Bowling Alley. Before he left, he stopped in front of the stage and nodded. I nodded back. Without that guy saving my ass, I would have been a goner!

After all the commotion died down, I looked out from behind my drum set and noticed Rose standing in the front row with a few of her girlfriends nodding along to the music. She returned my smile from the stage and I was hooked right then and there.

We started dating shortly thereafter and I spent any extra money I had taking her out. Aside from her physical beauty, Rose was a very kind and gentle girl. She took care of her mother, a beautiful Japanese woman who had fled Hiroshima after the war and moved to the United States with Rose's father, a burly Irish soldier, from whom she was divorced after Rose was born. Although I was traveling out of state to play with the Missing Links on a regular basis, Rose and I developed a deep emotional bond and fell in love. It was nice to know that she was waiting for me back in Chicago whenever I came home from our gigs.

The Missing Links were not only building up steam as a group, but also growing as individual players. Walt had begun attending music classes at DePaul University, and one night he brought the head of percussion at the school, Bob Tilles, to see us perform at the Club Laurel. Walt was eager for Bob to hear the music our band was playing. After we finished our set, Bob walked up to me holding some written sheets of music.

"Do you realize what you just played?" he asked. I looked it over, but couldn't understand what he had transcribed on paper.

"You have some serious talent," Bob continued. "If you have any interest taking your technique to the next level, I'd be open to having you come down to study with me."

I was flattered by his praise and decided to take Bob up on his offer. It turned out to be a wise decision, because he opened my eyes to a whole new world of the endless possibilities of percussion. Once we connected, he taught me the finer points of "woodshedding"—shutting yourself off from everything and honing your technique for hours on end. It was the only method that was going to get me to the next level. Our weekly lessons about the inner workings of jazz, along with my endless hours of performing and practicing, transformed me from a good rock and funk drummer into a highly skilled musician. The newfound musical knowledge brought with it a powerful sense of inspiration.

Flawless technique is what separates the great drummers from the rest of the pack. Proper mechanics and a solid sense of timing are essential, but taste is what lets you develop a signature sound. So many influences helped me come up with my style. I listened to everyone from Tony Williams, Elvin Jones, and Grady Tate to rock greats like Ringo Starr, Mitch Mitchell, and Hal Blaine. I recognized what they were doing and then set out in my own direction. Bob also turned me on to the wonders of legendary drummer Buddy Rich and the sheer excitement that came through in his playing. After hearing Buddy, half of me almost felt like giving up because I never envisioned myself reaching such a high level, but the other half was deeply inspired to do whatever it took to elevate my own playing.

As my skills improved, my confidence grew and allowed me to make more daring choices in my drumming. The excitement washing over me while studying with Bob stood in stark contrast to the dread I began to feel playing the same cover tunes with the Missing Links night after night. It was tough to stomach the old standards like "Moonlight in Vermont" and "Misty."

Although most of my days were spent practicing or performing, I still found time to drop in to the hot dog stand to hang out with Pete Schivarelli. He had been away at Notre Dame playing football, so it was good to see him again. One afternoon while we were hanging out, I mentioned I had to split for my drum lesson down at DePaul University.

"Why don't you take my Cadillac?" Pete offered.

"Are you sure?" I told him.

"Yeah," he said. "Leave your car here and come back for it later."

Pete tossed me the keys to his forest green Cadillac convertible and I was on my way. I felt like such a big shot cruising through the downtown streets of Chicago with the top down. I hung a slack arm out the window and drove as slow as possible to make sure everyone on the sidewalk got a good look at me behind the wheel. I was invincible driving the luxurious Caddy . . . for a while, anyway. Turning off of Wabash Avenue, I cut the corner too close and sideswiped a support beam for the el train track. I jerked the car to a stop and stared wide-eyed at the steering wheel. I was already sweating as I leapt out to inspect the damage. It wasn't pretty. The entire left side of the Cadillac was scraped to hell. Pete was going to kill me!

At a pay phone, I dialed his number with a shaky finger. As expected, Pete was irate.

"What the hell did you do, Danny?" he shouted over the phone.

"There was a bit of an accident," I answered.

"An accident? Oh Christ! I'll be right down there. Don't move," he told me before hanging up.

When Pete arrived, he was angrier than I had ever seen him. He was doing everything he could to keep himself from strangling me to death.

"Get in. I'll drive you back to your car," he said through gritted teeth.

We drove in total silence for a few blocks until we reached the first stoplight. When the light turned green, a man was still walking in front of our car. Already on edge, Pete beeped the horn at him, and the guy spun around and flipped us both off. That was all Pete needed to send him into the red. He flew out of the car and took off after the guy. I yelled after them, but it was no use. Better for Pete to take out his anger on some random man than fume at me over what I had done to his prized possession. Pete was one of the meanest guys I had ever seen and if he'd caught up to the guy it would have been ugly. I don't think that man knew how lucky he was.

I tried to console Pete by offering him the stereo out of my car, but its value couldn't come close to covering the body damage to his Cadillac. Eventually, he found some way to forgive me and let it go. Pete knew I didn't have anywhere near the kind of cash to pay for the damage. I may have been pulling in great money at one time, but that had changed.

Although my curiosity for drumming was peaking, the Missing Links started losing momentum in the local club circuit and our audiences were drying up. Each paycheck was smaller than the last. The low point came when we played a club called the Money Tree in a tough section of the West Side. The manager of the place treated the bands he booked like they were his dogs. There was no respect at all. The guy demanded that the band back him up while he sang Frank Sinatra songs. He was completely off pitch and out of time. He had no sense of melody, but none of us could say anything. If we did, we would be fired on the spot and thrown out of the club (or maybe even worse, judging by the look of the customers and workers in the place).

Midway through the manager's first Sinatra number, "Strangers in the Night," a drunk at the bar yelled, "You sing like a monkey fucking a football!"

I'd heard a lot of cursing in my time on the streets, but had never come across that one before. I did everything to stop from bursting out in hysterical laughter behind my drum kit. The other guys in the band turned away from the stage lights to hide their snickering.

The joyful expression dropped from the manager's face as he glared out in the direction of the bar area. He narrowed his eyes and pointed at the drunk. "Geno," he said into the house microphone. "Get this fucking guy outta here!"

Geno, the huge bouncer of the club, closed in on the bar and kicked the man right off of his stool. He picked the guy up by an arm and dragged him through the place, knocking over chairs and tables. When they reached the rear wall, Geno used the man's head to open the back door to the alley.

Our horrible gig at the Money Tree felt like rock bottom for us. Not long after at another show at Club Laurel, the bathrooms in the venue overflowed and the rancid odor of sewage hung in the air for the entire night. The place was wall-to-wall stink and nearly impossible to stomach. In a way, it was almost as if we were the ones stinking up the place. Overall, the gigs marked the beginning of the end for the Missing Links. There was no over-looking that I was in desperate need of something new.

My interaction with the skilled musicians at DePaul was deeply inspiring and I came up with a bold idea. I thought about putting together a band of only the most talented players in the city—a supergroup with a mind-blowing horn section that could play an inventive mix of rock and jazz. Since any band is only as strong as its weakest member, everyone would first and foremost have to be a gifted musician. This new group would be about the music and not about spectacle. There would be no egotistical frontman trotting around the stage. In my mind, there was no place for that. It was time to take everything we were doing to the next level.

Although Walt and Terry may have wanted to get involved with a project that was more advanced, they were working on different plans. Walt and Jackie had gotten married and Walt was still pursuing a music degree at DePaul. He had become the protégé of a guy named Jerome Stowell and was being groomed for the second clarinet chair in the Chicago Symphony. A guy named Jimmy Guercio, a friend of Walt's who had also attended DePaul and was making a name producing hits for national acts like the Buckinghams and Chad and Jeremy, had approached Terry to join a new project he was working on. Guercio had recently signed a band out of Chicago called the Illinois Speed Press, formerly the Rovin' Kind, to his production company, Poseidon Productions. The Rovin' Kind were one of the top bands in the city, with a lineup including the likes of famous blues guitarist Kal David, Paul Cotton (who later went on to join the band Poco and write the hit song "Heart of the Night"), keyboardist Michael Anthony, and Freddy Page on drums. Guercio was looking for a bassist to join the group before he moved them out to Los Angeles to take advantage of the hippie scene that was developing. He was convinced Terry fit the bill.

I wasn't going to sit by and watch Walt and Terry find new projects. We had been connected for the last three years in two bands. I had no interest in playing in other groups without them. I didn't have much time, so I got in touch with Walt and pitched him the supergroup idea.

"Let's at least give it one last shot and get serious," I urged. "Delay your symphony gig for a while and we'll put together an all-star band." The more I talked, the closer Walt listened. "We both love horns," I continued. "Let's bring the horns back to our music." He was into the idea, but told me he needed to discuss the situation with his wife before making a final decision.

I let out a giant sigh of relief when Walt came back a day later and said he was in. One down, one to go.

Terry was considering Guercio's offer to go out west and play bass for the Illinois Speed Press, but hadn't yet figured out what he wanted to do. He had gotten into pot and psychedelics and was starting to get high on more of a regular basis. He was basically going along wherever the current took him. With Walt already on board, I was more confident approaching Terry. What many people didn't know was that although he started off in bands strictly playing bass, Terry was a gifted guitar player with a distinctive Ray Charles type of vocal range. It would be the perfect idea to have him switch over from bass to guitar for the new project Walt and I were planning. The six-string had always been his first love. Being the carefree, easygoing guy that he was, Terry didn't take long to come to a decision. When he let us know he was in, it was just what Walt and I wanted to hear.

Once we had established the core of the group, everything fell into place. Another friend of Walt's from DePaul named Lee Loughnane also expressed interest in joining our new group.

I was already familiar with Lee's trumpet playing because he had sat in with the Missing Links from time to time. He had been performing with a band called Ross and the Majestics around Chicago, but was looking for something new. In the meantime, he and Terry had moved into an apartment together and had become almost inseparable. It was like Lee was Terry's shadow—whatever Terry did, Lee did. When Terry and Walt brought up the idea of Lee joining, I wasn't immediately for it. My standards for a trumpet player had been set ridiculously high from my time playing with Jimmy Ford. Jimmy was an absolute monster, and I wasn't so sure Lee could measure up. He seemed too timid in his soloing ability, but he was also very determined to join our new band. Ultimately, I figured we had to at least give him a legitimate shot.

Walt had another friend of his from DePaul in mind to add to the lineup, a guy named Jimmy Pankow who played trombone and was also a talented arranger. It sounded good to the rest of us. And just like that, we had our horn section.

Lastly, we were on the prowl for an organ player who could sing and also play the pedals. Organ players playing bass pedals were in vogue at the time, so we decided there was no need for a bass guitarist. Luckily, a friend was able to turn us on to a talented musician from the South Side of Chicago. His name was Robert Lamm, but being such a big fan of Ray Charles, he performed under the stage name of Bobby Charles in his group Bobby Charles and the Wanderers. I tracked down his number and called him right away. In our minds, Bobby had the right qualifications: he had an incredible voice and played a Hammond B-3 organ.

"I don't know how to play bass pedals that well, but I can try," Bobby explained over the phone.

Once he agreed, we had our bases covered—a stellar horn section, a great guitarist, and a multitalented keyboard player. Bobby would be able to provide the middle-register voice, while Terry took care of the low-end vocals. I couldn't wait to see what we could do musically as a group. With the amount of talent in the band, the possibilities were endless.

5

The Big Thing

By March 1967, no more than six weeks after seeing the Missing Links dissolve, we had a new project in the works. We scheduled a first rehearsal and everyone met at Walt's mother's house in the suburb of Maywood. Once we had set our equipment up in the basement, we headed back upstairs to the kitchen and introduced ourselves over beers. Not only was I the youngest, but also the shortest. It was like walking through a forest up in the kitchen; most of the guys were six feet tall or more.

I was excited to meet the new guys in person. Jimmy Pankow was good-natured and likable from the start. He came from an upper-middle-class family out in the white-collar community of Park Ridge and had gone to Notre Dame High School before continuing on to study music at Quincy College and DePaul University. To be honest, I had never hung out with anyone like Jimmy before. He was a regular Joe College—good-looking, clean-cut, with his hair perfectly combed to one side. There was almost a nerdy quality to him. As with Walt and Lee, music ran in Jimmy's family and his father had also been a musician.

51

Bobby Lamm was tall and good-looking, but surprisingly quiet and almost introverted. He had grown up in Brooklyn, New York, and later moved to Chicago, where he had gone on to study music at Roosevelt University. Bobby was the intellectual in the room, and having grown up partly in New York City, he was very hip and well-read—a real cool character. He was also five years older than me, which was a wide gap at that age. In contrast to Walt and Jimmy, Bobby had more of a serious personality.

From the moment the six of us started jamming in the basement, everyone knew we really had something. Bobby might have come across as rather unassuming in person, but behind the microphone he absolutely wailed. I couldn't believe how soulful his voice was, and I mean Righteous Brothers blue-eyed soulful! Talk about a major score! And any lingering doubts about Lee's ability quickly disappeared. His intense dedication to his instrument was paying off and he sounded better than ever.

At the same time, the "in the pocket" musical relationship Terry and I had developed during his days of playing bass carried over into his guitar work. Having functioned together as a rhythm section for so long, we had a unique type of groove and swing you didn't hear in most bands.

Walt had told us Jimmy Pankow was a great trombone player, and he was right on the money. Jimmy's talent for writing out horn charts and arrangements was also obvious. He sat down in between numbers and feverishly wrote out horn voicings in his notebook. At one point I looked over at Walt as if to say, *Can you believe this?* I'm sure he was thinking the exact same thing.

After we finished jamming, we went upstairs and found seats around the dining room table. Walt and I had discussed what we intended to accomplish with this new group. It was important to start off by bringing everything out into the open.

"Listen," I told the guys. "Everyone has been involved in bands that have gone nowhere and had to deal with being treated like shit by other members on a regular basis. We've seen big egos take over and ruin groups. Well, this band isn't about any of that; it's about the music. Everything will be done by a democratic vote. I say we make a pact right now that no one is ever going to be fired from this group. You either quit or you die."

The guys had no complaints with what I was saying. We needed this band to be every member's first priority. This group wasn't going to be a job; it was going to be a lifestyle. We made a pact and one by one shook hands on it around the table. It was time to *live* the music. It would be the only way if we were intent on getting anywhere and making careers in the business.

"We follow the music wherever it takes us. For as long as it takes us," I added. Walt reinforced everything I said. We were on the same page every step of the way.

We then consummated the deal by smoking a joint in the backyard. When we came back in the house, Walt's mother, Ruth, had a batch of her delicious homemade chili waiting. Food had never tasted so good. I looked around the table and could see that every one of us was full of anticipation.

Our new group wasted no time in hiring the main promoter from the Hi-Spot, Joe De Francisco, to manage our new project. Joe had been managing the Mob and had them earning solid money out in Las Vegas. Overall, he knew what he was doing. Besides, what he lacked in business knowledge he made up for in persuasiveness. Joe wasn't exactly the easiest guy for club owners to say no to. He did things his way no matter what anyone said. From the start, he had some immediate ideas for our group, not all to our liking.

"I got it figured out," he explained to us one day. "You guys ready for this? Your name's going to be Top Banana."

The band traded a few confused glances with each other. "I don't know if that is such a good name for a band," Walt piped up.

Joe D fell silent for a moment and scratched his head. "Okay then, forget about that other one. Your name's gonna be the Big Thing," he said, only with his thick Chicago accent it came out sounding more like "the Big *Ting*."

The band looked at each other once again. "Do we have a choice?" Terry asked.

"No, that's your name," Joe replied.

None of us knew how to answer. It was obvious we hated the name, but nobody had the balls to argue with Joe. He was the one who was going to be getting us work, so he was calling the shots.

"It's settled then," he said proudly. "The Big Ting."

Joe's intention was to try to mold us into the same type of act that the Mob had become—a Vegas show band. That was where success lay at that time, so we went along with the plan. Back then, it wasn't about writing original music and recording albums; it was about fine-tuning an "act" and performing shows. Joe took the band down to the legendary men's shop Smokey Joe's on Maxwell Street and bought us suits to wear during our shows. Although they were cheaper knockoff versions of the expensive brand-name suits on the market, they still looked sharp.

With our new name and image in place, the six of us practiced constantly in Walt's mother's basement and developed a solid sense of chemistry. We tore through tunes like "Hold On, I'm Coming" by Sam and Dave and "(You're My) Soul and Inspiration" by the Righteous Brothers with relative ease. Bobby's and Terry's vocals perfectly complemented each other. Our horn section was working hard to become as tight as possible and Jimmy continued to show his skills with charting and arranging.

Once we were confident enough, we played our first show out at the Pussycat on a crowded Saturday night. Our sound was massive in the room. We were so tight and controlled that even the band couldn't believe what we were hearing onstage. Up until that point, we had been limited to the acoustics in Walt's mother's basement, and now here we were blowing the doors off of a legitimate nightclub. For the most part, the audience was impressed and couldn't believe what a big sound we had (maybe Joe D wasn't *all* wrong with the name). It was like nothing I had experienced performing in Jimmy Ford and the Executives or the Missing Links. There was a much more interesting and unique type of chemistry between us.

Being a little on the stiff side and having grown up in a different type of community, Jimmy took a lot of ribbing from the rest of us. One of our main sources of ridicule was his relationship with his girlfriend at the time. Everyone thought she had him completely pussy-whipped, and we never let him forget it. Once we caught him in a lie when he made up an excuse for not being able to play a gig. Turned out he was busy taking her to her high school prom. The guys and I started calling her "Chickey Sweets."

"How's Chickey Sweets, Jimmy?" we'd ask him. "Will she let you out of the house tonight?"

We were relentless, but to his credit Jimmy was always a good sport.

Not that I didn't have my own Chickey Sweets to answer to. I had asked Rose to marry me, and in the summer of 1967 she and I tied the knot at the beautiful St. Michael's Church. After the ceremony, my mother cooked up a batch of her famous lasagna and we had a wonderful reception back at my parents' house on Normandy Avenue. The following night, we had a smaller get-together where Rose's mother put together a traditional Japanese-style dinner for everyone. Unfortunately, my schedule with the Big Thing didn't let us have a proper honeymoon. The very next night the band was scheduled to play a gig in Peoria, Illinois, so I brought Rose along for the trip. We spent the night in a run-down hotel that we later found out was a brothel, of all things. It wasn't exactly the best introduction to married life for either of us, but we made the best of it.

When we went back to Chicago, my parents were nice enough to let us live in my bedroom to allow us time to save money for a place of our own. Rose spent her time between my parents' house and her mother's. Her mother's health had taken a turn for the worse. We came to find out that years earlier she had been exposed to radiation from the A-bomb dropped on Hiroshima, and now she had been diagnosed with cancer and was in tremendous pain. It got to the point where she needed around-the-clock attention. It wore heavily on Rose and I did all I could to support her.

My dad had moved on from his job driving the bread truck and opened a convenience store in Arlington Heights. My grandmother thought I should be working in the family business and not running around playing music. "You should be helping your father, Danootz," she told me.

I understood what she meant. Our family had always supported one another, but there was no way I could see myself working in the store. I would never be able to stand behind a cash register day after day. It would have driven me mad.

Besides, the Big Thing was still trying to build a positive word of mouth around the city. The band had to remain my primary focus at all times, even though we still weren't getting the amount of gigs we thought we should have been. One day, I was explaining the band's situation to a guy from the neighborhood named Denny Colucci. Denny was a real man's man whom everyone respected. I told him about the troubles we were experiencing in booking gigs.

"Hell, Danny," he said. "I'll manage you guys. I've got plenty of connections around town."

It didn't sound like a bad idea. Besides, Joe D wasn't making things happen for us. He wasn't able to duplicate the type of success he had with the Mob.

"That would be great, but what about Joe D?" I asked. "He's been handling things for us."

Denny gave me a smile and put his hand on the back of my neck. "I'll take care of Joey. Don't you worry," he said.

In the natural pecking order of the neighborhood, Joe D may have been well respected, but Denny was a level above him. His taking over as manager wouldn't even be an issue. That was the way things went. After they talked, Joe graciously stepped aside.

Denny had the best of intentions, but it wasn't like he was banging down doors trying to get the band to the next level. Even with his connections in Chicago, our shows didn't get any better. When we played a club called Barnaby's in the middle of the brutal Chicago winter, we couldn't draw flies. Even the waitresses stood motionless, staring blankly at us performing up onstage. When we finished our set, two people sitting at the bar offered a couple of claps without even turning to face us. While we were packing up our equipment, the manager came out of the back office. He was a hip young guy named Phil Rapp, who was very supportive of the bands that came through his club.

"You know what, guys? You sound fantastic," he enthused. "But it's all about marketing. I am going to put on a promotion for you."

Phil hatched a plan on the spot to offer free fried chicken with the price of admission to our show on Sunday afternoons to draw the younger college crowd. It sounded a bit zany at first, but I figured *any* promotion was good promotion. None of the band had a clue how it would go over until the following Sunday, when we arrived to see a long line of college kids out in front of Barnaby's waiting to get in. Who knew how popular fried chicken was?

As crazy as it may sound, Phil's Sunday fried chicken promotion played a major role in launching the Big Thing in the city. He also had the bright idea of booking us to open up for another group called the Exceptions, who were the number one act in the Chicago at the time. Phil knew that people would catch on to us if they had a chance to see us play. The draw we needed came with the Exceptions, a highly skilled band that showcased the talents of a young bassist and vocalist named Peter Cetera. Peter was tough to miss up onstage with his free-flowing blond hair. He had the looks and the skill. It was incredible what his band could pull off. They performed flawless cover versions of the Beach Boys' "Good Vibrations" and the Beatles' "Paperback Writer" that sounded identical to the album cuts.

At the same time, the Big Thing started integrating more challenging material into our sets, such as extended songs by Frank Zappa and Beatles tunes like "Got to Get You into My Life" and "Magical Mystery Tour." Above all, the audiences were impressed with Jimmy's arrangements. Not many bands were doing what our horn section was at the time. Barnaby's was packed up to the rafters, and judging by the audience response, the Big Thing was beginning to overshadow the headliner. It wasn't long before we began blowing the Exceptions off the stage.

A few weeks later, Jimmy Guercio came back into town. He had been hired by CBS Records as a staff producer and was working with the Buckinghams. The group had four top ten singles that year, including the number one song "Kind of a Drag." Guercio never understood why Terry hadn't taken him up on his offer to join the Illinois Speed Press and move out to California. He was curious to know the reason why Terry had stayed back in Chicago, so we arranged for him to come out to one of the Big Thing's shows at Shula's Club in Niles, Michigan.

At the end of the night, Guercio came backstage and began pacing the dressing room. Something had really gotten into him. "You guys are the best band I have heard in a long time," he said. "I want to sign you to my production company right away."

Guercio's positive feedback meant a lot to us. I had a tremendous amount of respect for his opinion. We had a legitimate mover and shaker in the music industry telling us we had blown his mind! What more could we hope for?

We had a meeting and decided Jimmy's offer would be good for the future of the band. Denny wasn't going to try and compete with Jimmy. He understood the kind of pull Guercio had in the music industry. Being the skeptical corner guy, I brought the contract Guercio offered us down to a local attorney in the city.

"One thing's for sure," the lawyer said, sliding the papers back across his desk. "Be aware that this guy your band is signing with is going to own you lock, stock, and barrel."

Despite the attorney's feedback, the Big Thing went ahead and signed the contract. There was no negotiating with Jimmy Guercio. Maybe we should have done more to secure a better arrangement, but it was the infancy of the music industry as we know it today and that was just how things operated. Artists were often taken advantage of. Besides, Guercio said he intended to bring us out to California to record an album within the near future. We didn't want to let anything stand in the way of a chance to hit it big.

After signing with Guercio, I found out the Exceptions were having some trouble. There were rumblings that Peter Cetera was leaving the band. Anyone who was a fan of the music scene in Chicago knew Peter was an immense talent, and once the rumor spread, every group wanted him. I seized the opportunity and pulled him aside after a gig one night.

"Listen, why don't you think about joining our band?" I asked. "We've already got Terry handling the low vocal and Bobby doing the middle. You'd be perfect for the high range," I explained.

Peter had a bunch of offers he was considering, but being a fast-talker, there was no way I was letting him off the hook. I was determined to land the best singer in the city for our band. The Big Thing was developing into a finely tuned machine—an absolute steamroller. Peter's talents would make the band stronger, more versatile, and round out our sound.

"We both know that you could join any band in the city. But none of them come close to what we are doing right now," I confidently told Peter. "The Big Thing is going places."

All of us believed it was only a matter of time before we found the right opportunity to break through. I pressed Peter at every opportunity and finally my constant nagging paid off. He agreed to join. Part of me wasn't sure if it was because he truly wanted to or was just sick and tired of me pressing him about it night after night. It was probably a little of both.

Unfortunately, Guercio wasn't initially in favor of the addition, since Peter had gotten a reputation in some music circles in Chicago for being a prima donna. In some ways it was true—Peter's confidence in his playing and singing often came across as arrogance. The bottom line was that Peter knew what an asset he was to our band and wasn't interested in kissing anybody's ass. This mind-set initially rubbed Guercio the wrong way, but I was adamant about including Peter. The group was starting to move into more rock-oriented material similar to bands like the Rolling Stones and the Beatles. If we were to continue in the same direction, Bobby would not be able to carry the load by relying on his pedals. Having a bass player wasn't an option any longer; it was a necessity.

Peter's transition into the Big Thing wasn't as smooth as we would have liked. He was tremendously skilled, but also a complicated individual. Peter came from a strong Catholic blue-collar family from the South Side of Chicago. Earlier in his life he had studied in the seminary to become a priest and had a clearly defined sense of morals. Terry certainly didn't take to him right away. He may have been easygoing most of the time, but Terry also had a strong personality and wasn't ready for Peter's level of self-confidence. Walt, Lee, Jimmy, and Bobby didn't have as much of a problem with him because they tended to go with the flow more often than the rest of us. I acted as referee and peacemaker.

Overall, the band went through a feeling-out process and had to learn to adapt to the newest member of our family. Fortunately, everyone was able to warm up to each other over time.

The band met with Guercio and put a new plan together. We decided to continue performing our original arrangements of cover songs, but also gradually introduce original material into our sets. There was no future in covers unless we were going to move to Las Vegas or Atlantic City and become a show band. To break through, the band had to concentrate on writing music in order to develop our own identity. But our new direction proved to be a problem. Initially, we struggled to find an audience. It was difficult to understand, because our sound was better than ever. If we couldn't break through with a band of this caliber, it wasn't ever going to happen.

The year 1967 was a crucial period in music, and major bands were blowing onto the national scene. The psychedelic era was in full swing and things were starting to explode. There was no shortage of groundbreaking groups releasing albums: Jefferson Airplane with *Takes Off* and *Surrealistic Pillow*, the Beatles' *Sgt. Pepper's Lonely Hearts Club Band*, the Rolling Stones' *Their Satanic Majesties Request*, the Jimi Hendrix Experience's *Are You Experienced?* and *Axis: Bold As Love*, and the Doors' self-titled debut LP. Everyone in our band felt like we also had something to say and contribute.

The political climate was changing too. There was a new consciousness coming up among young people everywhere brought on by frustration over the Vietnam War. The civil rights movement was reaching a fever pitch. There were weekly protests on the streets of Chicago and National Guard troops patrolling the city. If you were young and weren't outraged, then you weren't paying attention.

Before returning to California to manage his other projects, Guercio suggested we listen closely to the new music being released, especially the songs of a band called Vanilla Fudge, who had just hit it big with their hit single "You Keep Me Hangin' On," a slowed-down psychedelic rock cover of the Supremes' original. Overall, their music was similar to the direction the Big Thing had already been going in. And what do you know? They also had a great drummer who was Italian, Carmine Appice.

Our band kept rehearsing and playing four or five days a week. As it turned out, Bobby had a folder full of songs he'd been working on for years. None of us had fully realized what a proficient composer he was until he began breaking out all the original material he had written. Still, the audiences in the Chicago clubs had a hard time accepting the new path our band was on. Club owners were used to us performing our unique arrangements of cover tunes and wanted nothing to do with the original songs we started including in our nightly set. Our new course proved to be a major financial strain. The Big Thing had made a decent living as a cover band, and now we were turned away from clubs for not drawing an audience. It wasn't long before we started getting outright fired from gigs.

Walt, Peter, and I were all married and the drastic cut in weekly income wasn't helping any of us. I was seriously feeling the effects because it wasn't only Rose and me anymore. My daughter Krissy was born on January 11, 1968, one of the happiest days of my life. Not only was I blessed with a beautiful baby girl, but I was also being given an opportunity to make amends as a parent. The guilt of being an absent father for my daughter Maria had stayed with me and I wanted to get it right this time around. I got a second chance at fatherhood and I didn't want to make the same mistakes. But with my income dwindling and the gigs drying up, it wasn't going to be easy.

Everything continued taking a turn for the worse. In the past, whenever we played the Club Laurel on a Saturday night, the place was filled to capacity, but all of a sudden we couldn't attract more than twenty people into the bar area. It was like performing in an abandoned building. At the end of the night, the manager called us over to his office and told us not to come back.

"You're nice guys and everything, but you need a *show*. Right now, you got no *show*," he explained.

When we returned to Club Gigi in the suburbs, we had to stick with a couple of Four Seasons numbers to get any kind of reaction from the crowd. The club owner, Nate Pisaro, met us out in back of the building as we were packing up our equipment. Nate might have run the joint, but it was really owned by Sam Giancana, one of the biggest mobsters in the country at the time. All the Outfit guys regularly hung out there. Nate was another manager who liked to come up and sing with the band. They called him "the singing hypnotist" because he invited people up onstage as part of his act and put them into a trance. He always had plenty of suggestions for our band.

"What you should do is develop some kind of a *show*," Nate told us.

It sounded familiar. We started hearing similar feedback from other club owners. "You got no show," they told us. The Mob had a "show" with an energetic frontman prancing around the stage. We didn't do routines or tell interesting stories or jokes in between numbers; we simply played what we considered good music. I didn't twirl my drumsticks in the air and our horn section didn't really have choreographed dance routines. Although over time, Jimmy Pankow did manage to perfect what we called his "South Dakota flip," a spastic dance move he did onstage with his trombone that always made everyone in the band smile. He was developing into the real ham of the group. But overall, what we were providing wasn't considered entertaining enough for the venues.

The Big Thing was close to a household name at the Attic in Milwaukee. We packed the venue every time we performed. But on a cold March night our original songs confused the crowd. The club owner, a big Greek guy named Zoey, didn't like the direction of our performance. When we played a trippy Frank Zappa ballad called "How Could I Be Such a Fool?," Zoey stormed the stage.

"What the fuck do you think you guys are doing?" he screamed. "You call that music? You're a real asshole, Walt."

Since Walt was our go-between with most of the managers of the clubs we played, he routinely had to deal with the fallout.

On this night, he didn't know what to tell Zoey. But Bobby certainly had something he wanted to say. He suddenly lunged from the stage, swinging his piano stool over his head. "Get the fuck out of our faces, Zoey!" he shouted.

"Don't tell me what to do! You're all fired!" Zoey yelled back.

The audience was shocked by Bobby's outburst, but the band had reached our breaking point. We were running out of venues to play and the pressure was wearing on us. The audiences we had always relied on to support us stopped coming to our shows.

It was official: the Big Thing was stiffing. The end looked like it was in sight.

6

Hollywood or Bust

It was no secret that everyone in the band was losing the desire to continue grinding it out in the regional club circuit. We had hit the proverbial wall. The group may have been running on all cylinders creatively, but we were barely making enough money to survive. The time had come to put a call in to Jimmy Guercio to check on his offer. We had to let him know if he wanted to bring the Big Thing out to California, he'd better do it soon. We had run out of options in Chicago.

After a string of calls back and forth to the West Coast, Jimmy finally gave us the green light to make plans to move out to Hollywood. He said he just needed a few weeks to get everything in place. I couldn't have been happier to hear the news. Guercio had come through in the nick of time. I went back to my parents' house and started packing that same night. The move was going to be hard on Rose, and I promised to send for her and Krissy as soon as I was able. To her credit, Rose knew how passionate I was about making it as a musician and understood that the band had no other options. It was the end of the line—Hollywood or bust.

My family was sad to see me go, but they understood this was a once-in-a-lifetime opportunity to pursue my dreams. My parents were still relieved that I had tangled with the gang lifestyle in Chicago and made it out the other side. Those days were a distant memory. Surprisingly, my sister Rosemary broke out crying after hearing about my impending relocation to the West Coast. Because of our four-year age difference and all my wild behavior growing up, our relationship had always been strained.

"You're never coming back here again," she said through her tears. "You're leaving forever, Danny."

A part of me knew Rosemary was right. Once I left town, I had no intention of moving back to Chicago. I wanted to follow the path as far as it would take me until I achieved my musical goals. In that moment of saying farewell to my family, I understood there was no going back. It was time to turn the page and start a new chapter in my life.

Walt and I decided to make the drive west together in his four-door Plymouth towing a U-Haul trailer full of our luggage and equipment. Peter set out in his Volkswagen Beetle convertible, and Jimmy Pankow drove with a couple of our buddies from the city, Mellow Mel and Mickey Sax. Terry, Lee, and Bobby skipped the road trip altogether and spent their money on plane tickets. Before we left Chicago, Guercio gave us the number of a guy named Larry Fitzgerald, who would be managing the band when we got out west.

Jimmy, Mellow Mel, and Mickey Sax weren't playing around. They packed their car with plenty of drugs for the ride. Walt and I weren't as aggressive. We expected it was going to be a grueling trip, so we scored a bunch of benzedrine uppers, or "bennies," as they were called. We popped a few pills each to get a running start and set out on the road. Walt and I caravanned with Peter and Jimmy for the first few hours of the drive across Illinois, but halfway through Iowa we lost sight of Peter's Volkswagen and got separated from the rest of the group. Neither Walt nor I wanted to spend the money to stay in hotels along the way, so we were determined, with the assistance of our stash of speed pills, to drive straight through until we reached the Sunset Strip in Hollywood.

Starting out, neither of us understood the reality of the distance we were traveling in Walt's old Plymouth. With the aid of the bennies, we even found the drive through the endless fields of Nebraska exciting, probably because we were high out of our minds. I balanced my practice pad on my lap and feverishly worked on my drum rudiments while Walt nodded along to music on the radio. We spent hours talking excitedly about what the scene would be like in Los Angeles. Neither of us could wait to finally get out west.

And then we hit the desert in the middle of the night and ran out of the bennies.

"Damn, what are we going to do?" I asked, turning the pill bottle upside down and giving it a shake. "I'm already starting to come down."

"Me too," Walt said.

As the next hour passed, it was tough to keep my eyes open. I was beginning to crash. To make matters worse, I started to hallucinate.

"What the hell was that?!" I suddenly yelled.

"What?" Walt asked, flinching behind the wheel. My outburst scared the hell out of him.

I could have sworn there was an animal on the side of the road, but at second glance it was gone. "I don't know," I told Walt. "It must have been a coyote or something." The lines of the road looked like they were shifting in place. My vision was blurry.

"We have to get off this road," Walt told me, regripping the car's steering wheel with both hands.

I agreed. The morning sun was just coming up above the desert sands when he pulled the car into a hotel just off of Route 15 in Barstow, California. Unfortunately, the place didn't have any available rooms. We slinked out of the office hanging our heads. Walt absentmindedly left the driver's side door open when he started to back out of the parking spot and it got caught on a concrete pillar. The door hinge bent back with a high-pitched squeal, sending Walt into a frenzy. He sprang out of the car and stormed off across the parking lot.

"I can't take this shit anymore!" he yelled out into the desert. "I want to go home!" He was losing it in dramatic fashion. I followed after him, trying my best to calm him down.

"It's all right, man," I told him. "Everything's going to be okay. We're both burnt out from the drive. We just need some sleep."

And then the desert wind kicked up and both of us fell silent. Almost instinctively, Walt and I glanced back toward the car just in time to see the piece of notebook paper with Larry Fitzgerald's phone number shoot out of the front seat and skip across the asphalt. We took off in a full panic, chasing after it onto the street, but another gust pulled the paper out into the brush. In an instant, it disappeared.

"Oh God," Walt screamed. "What the hell do we do now?!"

We made our way back to the car and drove in silence to another hotel down the street. Walt had to hold the driver's door closed shut the whole way. Luckily, this hotel had a room for us. There was no way we were going to make it another mile on the road. I lay in bed that morning, uncertain of what we would find in Hollywood. We had set out from Chicago full of expectation and now we found ourselves crashed out in a hotel in the middle of the desert.

After we managed a few hours of sleep, Walt and I duct-taped the car door shut and set back out on the road. The three-hour drive to Hollywood felt more like six. In our delirious state earlier, we had put so much importance in losing Larry's contact information that we had forgotten we also had the phone number of a girl named Kiki, who some of the other guys in the band were staying with in Los Angeles. All was not lost! Walt and I had a good laugh as we drove about our freakout scene in the parking lot.

Turning off of Laurel Canyon onto Sunset Boulevard in Hollywood for the first time was like passing through a portal into a new world. The Hollywood sidewalks served as catwalks for the wildest fashion I had ever been exposed to. Girls passed by in next-to-nothing skirts with fluffy boas around their necks and colorful flowers woven into their hair. The guys strutted around in flamboyant paisley shirts, pin-striped pants, and leather moccasins. Everyone wore cool dark wraparound shades or circular frames with colored lenses. It was an emerging scene that I knew little about, but couldn't wait to explore—a culture of hippies, artists, and musicians who shared a revolutionary way of thinking. Needless to say, performing in our tailored band suits from Smokey Joe's was a thing of the past. There was no shortage of creative fashions I couldn't wait to check out.

Once Walt and I reached Kiki, we were able to get in touch with Larry Fitzgerald and the other guys in the band. For the next couple of nights, I crashed at Larry's apartment and slept on his couch. Walt stayed with another one of Jimmy Guercio's business associates, a guy named Mike Curb. I had never met Larry or his wife before, but they were nice enough to welcome me in. Larry was a musician and new to the business side of the industry. He talked a little fast for my liking at first, but his friendly and outgoing personality made him very appealing. I was confident our group was in good hands.

Unfortunately, Larry had a large Alaskan malamute dog that constantly gnawed on the furniture. An upright bass Larry had standing in the corner became a chew toy. I woke up in the middle of the night to the sound of the thing biting the legs of the couch. It was nearly impossible to get a wink of sleep.

Guercio eventually agreed to pay the band forty-five dollars a week each and moved us in to a small two-bedroom house on Holly Drive in Hollywood. *Anything to get away from Larry's dog,* I thought to myself. The living room of the house was designated for the band to set up our equipment in, so the six of us were left to fend for our personal crash space in the rest of the house. Walt, Peter, and I set up air mattresses on the floor of one of the bedrooms. These "mattresses" were supposed to be for floating in backyard pools and not for sleeping. We blew them up every night before bed, only to find them completely deflated in the morning. Waking up on a hard floor took some getting used to. Bobby was the smart one. He hooked into a foxy young girl very quickly and moved into her apartment. Jimmy Pankow put together a makeshift bed on top of the dining room table of all places. It was decided that Walt's brother-in-law, Jack Goudie, was going to be our road manager/roadie, so he came out a few weeks later and joined us in the house as well. Jack was really dedicated and agreed to work for next to nothing. He and Lee took the back bedroom while Terry slept in a small alcove off the living room no bigger than a walk-in closet.

Our neighbors on Holly Drive were Guercio's other protégés, the Illinois Speed Press. They were riding a wave of recent success opening up for premier bands like Steppenwolf and Led Zeppelin. While our band rehearsed day and night, the guys in the Speed Press partied like rock stars with the most gorgeous groupies I had ever seen. They blasted music all night and did drugs until the early hours of the morning. There was a never-ending flow of women in and out of their pad. We attended more than a few of the Press's bashes, but only after our band felt satisfied that our work was done for the day. As excited as we were to experience the wonders of the Hollywood scene, we weren't going to do it at the expense of the dreams we had for our band.

Freddy Page, the drummer for the Speed Press, and I sat together for hours trading stories of playing drums and comparing our techniques. I sensed that Freddy didn't have a great deal of confidence in his playing, but I still considered him a solid, straightforward rock drummer. Being so far from home, it was comforting to have yet another friend from Chicago to talk with. From that point on, we became very close.

It didn't take long for the bright lights of Sunset Boulevard to seduce our band. We were in awe of the free-spirited characters running around the scene—especially by the uninhibited groupies offering their *free* love. I tried to focus solely on the music, but as time wore on I got tired of saying no to girls. With Rose fifteen hundred miles away in Chicago, I got caught up in the scene and couldn't help myself.

We frequented clubs up and down the Strip like the Experience, the Aquarius Theater, the Starwood, the Troubadour, Gazarri's, and the Whisky a Go Go. It was thrilling because in place of the Top 40 covers of the time, most bands were performing their own original music. An overwhelming feeling of expectation was in the air. Something special was taking place all around us— a genuine cultural awakening. We became friends with some of the other bands that were also trying to make a name for themselves out in California, like Three Dog Night, Blues Image, and a band called Black Pearl from Boston. Everyone had moved from their hometowns to pursue our dreams of sex, drugs, and rock and roll. And suddenly we were living it.

The late sixties was a turbulent time for the country. We huddled around the television in horror to watch the news footage of the Vietnam War protestors clashing with Chicago police at the 1968 Democratic National Convention. We had already witnessed the assassinations of Martin Luther King Jr. and Robert F. Kennedy. The violence was yet another indication that the country was in turmoil. Young people everywhere had reached their breaking point. As the protesters and police clashed back in Chicago, I was ashamed of my city and Mayor Daley. The chaotic images from the convention had a lasting effect on the band, especially Jimmy and Bobby. The events deeply influenced the music they were writing, and political themes were finding their way into our songs. Bobby began writing originals like "It Better End Soon" and "Does Anybody Really Know What Time It Is?" in support of the new consciousness among our generation. In many ways, the move to California gave every member of the band a fresh political awareness.

At the same time, the guys and I ate, drank, and slept our music. We practiced day and night, much to the dislike of the neighborhood. There were regular visits from the cops telling us to turn it down. But aside from the unwelcome police visits, Guercio made sure there were no distractions: no day jobs for any of us to worry about and no rent or bills to pay. The arrangement allowed every one of us to make our playing a first priority. Being confined to the house on Holly Drive gave the band the freedom to concentrate on writing compelling original material. It was a non-stop jam session where everyone built upon each other's ideas. We were pushing our art to a new level. The group was tighter than ever and the new originals sounded mind-blowing.

With all of the material he had already written, Bobby single-handedly carried the band on his back. To his credit, he maintained an open-book approach to songwriting and arranging. Bobby was interested in how the rest of us interpreted his compositions. He trusted us as skilled players to help improve on the music.

Jimmy continued to write groundbreaking horn arrangements, which were a signature of the band. Walt and Lee were diligently refining their own styles, while Terry was evolving into one of the greatest guitar players of all time. Peter, although he wasn't being featured, stepped up as a bass player and showcased his incredible vocal ability. He was the unsung hero of the rhythm section. Because Peter sang so well, his playing was often overlooked.

I was woodshedding and studying with the great jazz drummer Chuck Flores. Relying on influences like Gene Krupa, Buddy Rich, Mitch Mitchell, and Hal Blaine, I worked to stretch the limits of what I considered rock drumming and developed my jazz-rock style.

Of course, there couldn't always be a relaxed atmosphere in the house. Egos clashed and arguments broke out. Living with the same people twenty-four hours a day is a surefire way to develop mutual respect. We had to become family because we were practically living on top of each other. Petty squabbles broke out here and there, but if you weren't getting along with one of the guys at the end of the day, there was always someone else who wasn't pissed at you. That's one of the hidden benefits of being in a band of seven musicians.

It wasn't long before Guercio made the decision to change the band's name from the Big Thing to the Chicago Transit Authority in reference to the buses he used to ride to school every day. Thank God. No disrespect to Joe D, but I always hated the name he gave us. We were worlds away from gigging as the Big Thing back in Chicago, so the new moniker felt fresh and appropriate.

A few weeks after we had arrived in Hollywood, Larry was able to book the band our first legitimate gig—a free show opening up for Frank Zappa and the Mothers of Invention on Venice Beach. Our friends Black Pearl were also on the bill. The band made the drive in two station wagons as Jack Goudie followed behind with our equipment in a yellow van we called "the Yellow Banana," and we performed on a gorgeous California beach day in front of sixty thousand strong out by the Venice Pier. The whole event was set up as a "love-in" type of concert and packed with hippies in free-flowing clothing. Everywhere I looked, there were topless women smiling back at me. The strong smell of marijuana cascaded through the air. It looked like a fog had rolled in over the boardwalk, and you didn't even have to smoke a joint to get high.

Overall, we got a positive response from the crowd, but you could tell the audience was only biding their time, waiting for the main man to blow onto the scene.

"Zappa," I suddenly heard one of the stage crew guys say behind me.

I turned around and watched in stoned awe as two sparkling white limousines pulled up the Venice boardwalk. There was murmuring throughout the crowd as word of his arrival spread.

That's Zappa!

Hey man, Zappa's here!

Look, it's Zappa!

Everyone wanted to catch a glimpse of him. A hush came over the crowd as the limousine driver walked to the rear door. He opened it slowly and, lo and behold, Frank Zappa stepped out dressed in white from head to toe. His gorgeous groupies, who were called the GTOs (for Girls Together Outrageously), soon joined him. Talk about being the hippest dude around. What a surreal scene!

Zappa and his band took the stage and absolutely killed. The audience was out of its mind. After the show, I struck up a conversation with Zappa's drummer, Jimmy Carl Black, and sax player, Motorhead Sherwood. It was hard to believe I was standing there talking with the guys from Zappa's band. Terry was also particularly thrilled since he was the one who had really turned our band on to Zappa. Aside from the fact that Zappa was also a guitarist, Terry related to the abstract arrangements and experimental playing. In time we all did, and spent hours listening to his groundbreaking record *Freak Out!* Zappa proved to be one of our biggest influences.

The dead-end clubs of Chicago felt as if they were a million miles away. I walked around the beach in the bright California sunshine smiling from ear to ear.

Welcome to Los Angeles.

7

Making a Name

The next gig booked for Chicago Transit Authority (or CTA, as we started calling ourselves) was at a venue called the Factory in Beverly Hills. The club was an exclusive hot spot for the movers and shakers in town and especially popular among the Hollywood elite. We went in with high expectations, but found the gig to be very restricting. The band knew we were in trouble before our first performance when the management of the club urged us to play as quietly as possible. *Quietly? Didn't they see our three-piece horn section walk in?* They must have intended CTA to serve as a lounge act to provide background music for the dinner crowd. They didn't even want us to tune up our instruments in between songs. When we weren't onstage performing, we were instructed to stand in the corner and keep to ourselves. Although nobody wanted us mingling with the A-list clientele, we still found a way.

One night after we finished our set, I walked off the stage and found myself face-to-face with none other than legendary comedian Bill Cosby. I had to do a double take to make sure it was actually him standing in front of me.

"Hey man," Bill told me. "I really like your band."

I was caught off guard, because up until that point not one of the guests had ever spoken to us in the club. Bill was gracious enough to invite the band over to his table and bought us drinks. We spent time discussing jazz and R&B greats like James Brown, Otis Redding, Gene Krupa, Buddy Rich, and Max Roach. Bill was a true music lover and told me about Uni, the record company he owned. Later, Natalie Wood and Robert Wagner ended up joining us for a drink. Needless to say, I was starstruck by the celebrity activity.

CTA found it increasingly difficult to tone our sound down night after night at the Factory. We went through the motions for four or five nights until the routine was too much to take. All the guys knew it was only a matter of time before our frustration boiled over. After all, the primary reason our band came out to Hollywood was to get people's attention. What were we doing playing the part of a lounge band?

One night, not long before we were about to take the stage, I looked out into the crowd and saw the faces of stars like Johnny Carson, Diana Ross, Doc Severinsen and Dean Martin. *Dean Martin*, I thought to myself. I reflected back on listening to his albums with my mother when I was just a kid. If only she could see me now.

"Screw it," I said to the rest of the guys. "Let's turn it loose and show these people what we've got."

It didn't take much convincing from me. The guys couldn't wait. We went out and tore through our set with full intensity. The volume of our performance was loud, but we were tight and controlled. At the end of the night, we received a standing ovation from the crowd.

But our excitement didn't last. As soon as the band got off the stage, the manager walked up to Walt and told him we were fired. They had no interest in having us return to perform another night. In my mind, it didn't matter. We had made our point. Nobody in the audience was going to mistake us for another lounge cover band. That was for sure. Showing off our full potential was more important than playing more dates in some pretentious club in Beverly Hills.

Our next show was opening for the bands Love and the Chambers Brothers at the Earl Warren Showgrounds in Santa Barbara. Fronted by the dynamic singer and guitarist Albert Lee, Love was one of the first racially diverse bands on the psychedelic scene and performed an interesting mix of acid rock and folk. The soul act the Chambers Brothers were promoting their hit single "Time Has Come Today," which was all over the pop charts. We hoped the show would give us some much-needed exposure.

When we arrived at the showgrounds, we realized that more than fifty thousand people had shown up. Full of adrenaline, CTA took the stage and blazed through our first number, a new song called "Introduction." When we finished, there was some scattered applause, but mostly awkward silence. The crowd had no idea what to make of us. Then we exploded into an energetic cover of the Spencer Davis Group's "I'm a Man" and hurried off-stage. Almost immediately, there were rumblings throughout the dressing room area that CTA was "just another horn band from the Midwest."

The mixed reaction from the crowd was disheartening, because our newly assembled management team was in the audience. Besides Larry and Jack, Guercio had brought in up-and-coming Beverly Hills talent agent Dan Winer and Jimmy's personal accountant, a tough businessman named Howard Kaufman, to manage the band's finances. Maybe we had let them down by laying an egg in front of such a large crowd, but the band had no control over the situation. Some crowds got us and some didn't. Still, Larry was upbeat and philosophical about the show. He told us to chalk it up as nothing more than an off performance.

We were making some progress, but landing regular gigs at the Whisky a Go Go on Sunset Boulevard proved to be a crucial turning point. The owners, Elmer Valentine and Mario Maglieri, were Italian ex-cops from Chicago who took our band under their wing. They gave us the incredible opportunity to play one of the prime venues on the Strip. We couldn't have dreamed for better exposure. A powerful buzz began building throughout the local scene about us. As word spread, CTA started pulling in huge crowds. The lines outside the Whisky snaked around the block.

Guercio had signed a production deal with CBS that allowed him three opportunities to arrange artist showcases. He wasted no time in booking a CTA show at the Whisky for the A&R people in the West Coast division. Unfortunately, the executives at CBS failed to show up for the gig. When Guercio arranged another showcase, the company brass pulled another disappearing act.

Someone did manage to make an appearance, though. One night, the band walked backstage after the show to find none other than Jimi Hendrix and his drummer Mitch Mitchell standing in our dressing room. We had been listening to Jimi's records *Are You Experienced?*, *Axis: Bold As Love*, and *Electric Ladyland* even before we had moved out to California. Jimi had on one of his signature hats, a vibrant crimson frilled shirt, and multicolored pants.

"You guys are great, man," he said with that cool voice of his, lighting up a cigarette. "I love you cats."

Terry was especially in awe of Jimi's presence. "I've been listening to your records for years," he told Jimi. "You're my biggest influence, man."

Overall, it was an all-out lovefest between our bands. I'm not sure what I was expecting, but Jimi was exceedingly modest and respectful. After that night, he came back regularly with his entourage to check us out from his private booth at the Whisky. He also began mentioning CTA in every magazine and radio interview he did, urging people to come out to the shows. As if that wasn't enough, Jimi never forgot to mention what a mind-blowing guitarist he considered Terry to be.

Our group was picking up momentum and things were beginning to happen. A major shift was taking place, and it would only get better.

When Larry broke the news that we would be opening up for Janis Joplin and her band Big Brother and the Holding Company at the Fillmore West in San Francisco, we were ecstatic. Janis was one of the biggest stars on the scene, with a larger-than-life reputation as a hard-drinking, tough-talking rock goddess.

We were also looking forward to checking out San Francisco, because it had become the center of the counterculture movement in the country. Hippies were everywhere. The city fostered a melting pot of progressive politics, creative expression, psychedelic drugs, and free love. The neighborhood of Haight-Ashbury overflowed with young people who had a new mind-set and were searching for a different way of life. Kids everywhere connected through the new music. CTA couldn't wait to experience Northern California and become a part of the scene.

On the evening of the Fillmore West show, the opener was a little-known group called the Santana Blues Band. Not long before they were due to go on, the wild guitarist and frontman, Carlos Santana, came flying backstage in a panic.

"Danny, Danny, Danny," I could hear him yelling as he made his way across the room. I had heard of Carlos but we had never met before, so I didn't know what to think.

"Hey Danny! Listen man, can you play the blues?" Carlos asked, fighting to catch his breath.

"I think so," I told him. "After all, I'm from Chicago." I was trying to disguise my anxiety with bravado.

Carlos's face lit up. "Cool, man! My drummer's not showing up and I need to find someone to sit in. Can you come out and play the set with us?"

Minutes later, I was onstage behind a drum kit with Carlos and his group. Luckily, their material was traditional blues-based jams, so there wasn't much trouble keeping up on the fly. Carlos signaled me for any specific cues in the songs and we ended up pulling off a solid performance. The crowd was locked into the music and never knew the difference.

At the end of the Santana Blues Band's forty-five minutes, CTA took the stage and I stayed behind the drum kit for our set. The audience ate it up. As soon as we ended our last song, the crowd erupted. The room was electric.

Once we exited the stage, Janis and her band kicked into their set. From the start, I was in awe of her enormous stage presence and vocal range. Up until that point I had only heard her music on the radio. Although the studio material was intriguing, it paled in comparison to the passion Janis brought to her live performance. Her talent knocked me out.

When her set was over, I began making my way back down the hallway toward the backstage area. Janis and her band rolled up behind me, still pumped from their breathtaking show. Before I had the chance to turn around, a familiar voice growled from over my shoulder.

"Get the fuck out of the way, man!" Janis yelled. "We need to get to our dressing room!"

I whipped around to face them and my blood began to boil. It was as if I was right back on the streets of Chicago and ready to throw down with anyone who stepped to me.

"Fuck you!" I yelled back. "Who do you think you're talking to?"

Janis paused for a beat and returned my glare. It was obvious she wasn't used to being spoken to that way, but I wasn't backing down. The look on my face was sending out a pretty clear signal to the guys in her band not to mess with me. I was truly insulted and ready to fight. A couple of them initially tried to appear tough, but thought better of it. After a few tense moments, Janis and her group continued on, disappearing into the shadows at the far end of the hallway.

"Bitch!" I hissed after her. I stood alone for a few moments still fuming from our exchange, then made my way to CTA's dressing room in the back of the club.

There was a knock on the door a few minutes later. Everyone was too preoccupied smoking joints or taking swigs off a wine bottle to notice. The door opened, and to my surprise, Janis entered the room. She tiptoed between and around the bodies splayed all over the floor and made her way to where I was standing. I had mellowed by then, but was ready to go at it for another round if she was. I wasn't going to let some egomaniac singer disrespect me in front of my band.

Janis huddled up next to me and gently touched my arm. "Listen, man," she said. "I'm really sorry about that scene backstage earlier. I don't usually talk to people like that."

Her words were kind and soft, in contrast to the shouting earlier. I paused for a moment to process what she was saying, because

I wanted to be sure she was being sincere. Janis flashed me a friendly smile, and with that any tension between us fell away.

"No problem, Janis," I told her. "I understand. I'm sorry too."

Janis went on to explain how impressed she was with the high level of musicianship of our band, especially by our horn section. When the rest of the guys weren't around, I even heard her telling her manager, "I want a band like these cats, man." I witnessed a different side of Janis's personality that night. Sure, she could be abrasive, but underneath that hardened rock-star exterior was a sweet and vulnerable little girl. She even talked like a young girl sometimes in conversations.

Later on, the guys in Janis's band passed around a bottle of orange juice for everyone to drink. Jimmy Pankow and I each had a swig and were then told it was dosed with LSD. Not that I was surprised. I suspected something was up. In a way, part of me *hoped* it was laced with acid. I had heard about the drug, but never tried it.

Before long, the backstage area turned into a loony bin. Everyone was red-faced and almost incoherent. The colors in the room were so vibrant they looked like they were pulsating. My senses were heightened and it was as if I could see and hear everything going on in the dressing room at once. Everything became surreal as I developed a strong awareness of my surroundings. People had a mad gleam in their eyes, especially Jimmy. We kept exchanging sideways glances with one another. The more mentally unstable we felt, the harder we laughed.

After what felt like an eternity of standing in the dressing room, Jimmy and I shared the need to explore. We left the Fillmore West and spilled out onto the streets of San Francisco. The evening breeze coming off the bay felt so refreshing on my face, and we eventually stumbled onto a giant ground-level lighted sign in front of a Holiday Inn. In our abstract state of mind, we both climbed into the giant flashing letter "D" of the sign. Jimmy and I must have lounged in there for hours banging against the metal wall with our hands.

Boooooom. Piiiiiiiiing. Booooom.

We tapped in time to the lights flashing and could hear the ticking of each light going off. The whole letter reverberated around us with each thump. We created a mystical rhythm together—an otherworldly experience.

On our way crawling out of the sign, we were spotted by a San Francisco police squad car. It pulled up alongside of us as we shuffled out of the parking lot.

"You guys all right?" one of the officers asked, poking his head out the passenger-side window.

"Yes, sir," Jimmy answered. "Everything is wonderful." Somehow he managed to keep a straight face.

I thought they might hassle us, but San Francisco cops were used to seeing stoned hippies roaming the streets at all hours. They left us alone and drove back into the night.

Walking the streets of San Francisco that night, there was an air that anything was possible. The LSD had opened my mind to a new perspective. I always felt like we had a bright future ahead of us. Now I was convinced of it.

A few weeks later, we found another opportunity to drop acid when we performed a gig at Eagles Auditorium in Seattle and had the following day off. Everyone, with the exception of Peter, took some LSD and went out to a popular rock club in the downtown area. Peter pounded cocktails to try to keep up with us, but it was no use. The more frantic we became, the slower he got. As soon as we arrived at the club, a hush came over the place. CTA's reputation had preceded us. Word of our live performances had spread through the underground scene and people took notice.

Although we were twisted on LSD, the band made the decision to take the stage to treat the crowd to a blazing CTA jam session. I stared out from behind the drum kit with distorted vision as the rest of the guys picked up their instruments. Terry looked back and flashed me a smile, but it was hard to focus on his face. Suddenly we launched into an ominous musical interlude. Bobby's organ hummed deeply, Terry's guitar wailed, and Peter's bass walked underneath, building in intensity. We were *locked in*—to *what* I have no idea. The music was moody, classical, and extremely bizarre.

I played with my unique manic syncopation and pulled back every so often to allow the other guys room to solo. I didn't pick my head up once during our inspired jam. When I finally did glance up, there wasn't a soul left in the place. What we were hearing and what we were playing were two different things. We had cleared the club out!

We laughed our way back to our hotel and piled into our rooms. Despite our chilly reception at the club, we were still inspired. At the time, John Lennon and Yoko Ono had just posed nude for photos together. Still being high, somebody came up with the bright idea to pose for a naked group photo of our own. We got undressed and mooned the camera. Peter was the smart one; he stayed behind the lens to snap the picture. It was all in good fun.

Later we met up with Janis Joplin and her band again to open for them during a few northwestern gigs. Playing with Janis was a big break for us and helped add to the powerful buzz building around our band. The people who were showing up to see Janis perform every night were coming away fans of CTA as well.

When we all met up at a bar one night after a gig in Vancouver, Janis showed up in a stunning dress and one of her signature scarves. She had a sexy and seductive way about her, and I thought she looked absolutely gorgeous. Our whole band did. It was a magical night and Janis made us all feel special, like she was interested in every one of us. And of course, we *all* wanted to be with her. But one of my bandmates was the only one to get up the nerve to make a move, and they later disappeared together at the end of the night. The next day, when he showed up in the dressing room for our gig, he had long scratches up and down his back. It looked like he had gone at it with a mountain lion! I didn't bother to come right out and ask what had happened, and he didn't offer us anything. None of us could believe it. I have to admit I was jealous, but there wasn't much time to dwell on any lost opportunities.

By then Walt, Peter, and I had brought our wives out to Hollywood. In the six months since the band had left Chicago, Rose had become close friends with Walt's wife, Jackie, and Peter's wife, Janice. We all moved into one-bedroom apartments in a complex right around the corner from our band house on Holly Drive. Our wives were excited to finally make the move west. They had been hearing stories about what was going on in our careers and wanted to see everything firsthand. Of course, we didn't let them in on *everything* that had been going on.

Although things were starting to pop for the band, money was still tight. Rose and I were on a strict budget. Almost every other meal we ate was hot dogs and beans because it was all we could afford. When the holidays rolled around, Peter and I didn't have enough extra money to get Christmas trees for our apartments. So we put our heads together and hatched a devious plan.

Late one night, we drove in Peter's Volkswagen convertible down to the Mayfair, a local supermarket on Franklin Avenue in Hollywood. After cutting down a side street, Peter pulled up at the darkest corner and turned off the car's headlights. The Christmas trees were lined up all the way to the curb. As soon as I was able to get a firm grip on a good-sized trunk, Peter floored it around the corner. It took all my strength to drag the thing alongside of the car until we were out of sight and Peter could pull over. I jumped out and hoisted the tree into the backseat.

"All right," Peter said, checking the rearview mirror to make sure nobody had followed us. "Let's get the hell out of here."

"No way, man," I told him. "I need one for my place too."

Peter rolled his eyes and shifted the car into gear. We made another run by the lot and I leaned out the window and snagged another Christmas tree.

"Go, go, go!" I yelled.

It was a cheap thrill, but neither of us could stop howling with laughter.

To celebrate New Year's Eve, CTA played to a packed house at the Whisky in front of our wives and close friends. During our set, our crew put a light show up on a large movie screen that hung over the stage. Toward the end of the night, the nude photo the band had taken back on our LSD-soaked night in Seattle flashed on the screen. Our asses were larger than life as we mooned the camera. Everyone erupted with laughter and I turned to see our road manager, Jack Goudie, standing up behind the projector with a smirk on his face. We had a little explaining to do to our wives. The joke was on us.

Guercio had been shopping us around town, trying to secure CTA a record deal, but it was proving to be more difficult than he thought. Columbia didn't want to sign CTA initially because they already had the band Blood, Sweat and Tears on their label. When Columbia approached Guercio to produce their album, Guercio made them a proposition: he would do the record if in return the label would sign CTA to a recording contract. It was a delicate situation, because Blood, Sweat and Tears had in some way become our rivals in the same genre of music. We had moved out west first, but they had hit the street before we did because they were out of New York City where Columbia's headquarters were at the time. Before he even brought it up to Columbia, Guercio checked with us to make sure we were okay with the situation. He didn't want us to feel betrayed. We reluctantly agreed that Guercio should produce the album if that was what it was going to take for CTA to get a record contract.

Guercio went ahead with the deal. After he had completed the Blood, Sweat and Tears album, the head of the label, Clive Davis, stepped up to the plate and signed CTA.

"Looks like you're going to New York to record an album, guys," Larry announced at our next band meeting.

I took the first plane ride of my life back to Chicago and stopped in to see my parents. They were curious to learn about everything that was happening with the band. Of course, I left out the details of the rock-and-roll lifestyle I had been leading prior to Rose moving out west. My mother wasn't too thrilled when she found a small jar of pot in my suitcase. It took some convincing to make her believe I wasn't on my way to becoming a full-blown drug addict.

Two days later, I continued on to New York City, where the record company put the band up at the City Squire Hotel in Times Square. Every morning, we made the trip to CBS Studios on 42nd Street to lay down the songs we had road-tested over the previous two years. It was the first time I had ever been in a recording studio, so the experience was overwhelming. The tracking process was unfamiliar to all of us. We were used to performing live and tried to apply the same formula in the studio, but it didn't work. One of us made a mistake on each run-through. It was close to impossible to capture a clean take of all seven members nailing our parts. We made the decision to record drums, bass, keyboard, and guitars first, and then the horns and vocals.

When we wanted to stretch out our version of the Spencer Davis Group's song "I'm a Man," we inserted a drum solo in the middle of the track. The band played the entire section off the cuff in the studio with Jimmy on cowbell, Walt on tambourine, and Lee on claves. The final mix turned out amazing.

While we were recording Bobby's song "Beginnings," Al Kooper, formerly of Blood, Sweat and Tears dropped in to the studio. Al had gotten his hands on one of the early versions of the video camera and walked around with it as we recorded. Guercio stood in the control room playing air drums along with me and nodding, which was his way of letting me know he wanted to stretch out the end of the song and insert as many fills as possible. He wanted the song to end with an extended outro à la the Beatles' "Hey Jude." It was a truly magical moment. Unfortunately, Al later ended up taping over the footage he captured of us. What I wouldn't give to have it back today!

Being an accomplished musician himself, Guercio knew what he was doing. He had been around CTA long enough to know our strengths and weaknesses as a group and as individuals. He pointed us in the right direction and left us to our own abilities. If he wasn't thrilled with something, he wouldn't try to strong-arm anyone. He would say something like, "Are you sure you like what you are doing in that section of the song?"

At the end of each long day in the studio, we headed back to our hotel in Times Square for some much-needed relaxation. We were surprised to find that the famous comedian Redd Foxx was also a guest and got to know him well during our downtime. Redd connected with the jazz element in CTA's music and made it a point to tell me how much he liked our sound. He was hysterically funny and always up for hanging out.

"You guys got any weed?" he always asked us, giving his signature sideways grin. "You're hippies, right? Man, I like the hippies . . . *especially* hippies with weed."

In between recording sessions, the band went to Philly to play a few gigs at a place called the Electric Factory. The crowd went wild for our music. After we had finished our set, they called us up for an encore, and then another, and then *another*. The City of Brotherly Love certainly loved Chicago.

When our band clicked onstage and became one, it was an otherworldly experience. Nothing beat the feeling. It was the thread that kept our brotherhood intact. A lot of times, performing in front of packed houses felt too good to be true. Had we really come this far together? Backstage after our gigs, we routinely asked each other, "Can you believe we get *paid* for doing this?" In fact, we were so amped up from playing live that we sang it like it was the chorus to a funk song: *"We get paid for doin' this, we get paid for doin' this . . ."*

Ten days after arriving in New York City, we put the final touches on our debut effort, *The Chicago Transit Authority*.

Remarkably, the self-titled album Guercio produced for Blood, Sweat and Tears went on to win a Grammy for Album of the Year in 1969. The record ended up featuring three hit singles: David Clayton-Thomas's "Spinning Wheel," Brenda Holloway's "You've Made Me So Very Happy," and a cut of Laura Nyro's "And When I Die." It seemed Guercio could do no wrong and was on a major hot streak. CTA hoped the success would carry over to our new album as well.

Paisano cowboy in the old
neighborhood

With my first set of Slingerlands
at twelve years old

MISSING LINKS
FAN CLUB

Write to:

DIAN SEVERINO, Pres.
1135 HEWITT DR.
DES PLAINES, ILLINOIS
Phone: 827-4226

Personnel Manager:
BOB MADDEN
FI 5-3032
BROADVIEW, ILL.

an
INTRODUCTION
to America's Sensational
NEW GROUP

SEE THEM   HEAR THEM

THE MOST VERSATILE AND TALENTED
GROUP APPEARING ON CHICAGO'S
NITE-LIFE SCENE

Walt and I
take on our
pseudonyms

CHUCK MADDEN
(GUITAR)
Young and Old alike love his vocals
and fine guitar.
A real pleasure to see and hear.

WALT PERRY
(SAX)
The greatest sax to come along
in many, many years.
With a personality to match.

TERRY KATH
(BASS)
Mr. Soul, himself - In every sound
of his voice and bass.
A great performer.

DANNY SERA
(DRUMS)
His technique and style puts him
in a class of his own.
Copied but never equaled.

As a working musician in the Missing Links

The Big Thing: (left to right) Lee Loughnane, Terry Kath, Walt Parazaider, Bobby Lamm, Jimmy Pankow, and me

Early CTA days in Los Angeles after getting a perm— what a mistake

CTA performing at the Isle of Wight Festival in 1970

Peter and I playing in Des Moines, Iowa, in 1970

Recording "Motorboat to Mars" from *Chicago III*

Chicago in full swing in 1971

Coming of age behind my set of Slingerlands

CHICAGO DRUM CENTER

BRINGS TOGETHER

DANNY SERAPHINE & GRADY TATE
with
"CHICAGO"

with
"THE TONIGHT SHOW"

FOR A MOST UNUSUAL DRUM CLINIC

SUNDAY, NOV. 28, 1971
1:30 P.M.

SHERMAN HOUSE
COLLEGE INN
Clark & Randolph Sts.

PHIL UPCHURCH - Guitar
CRAIG RASBAND - Bass

Admission $1.00 ● Tickets Available Now ● Don't Delay

Stop In or Call JOHN at the **Chicago DRUM Center**
159 N. Dearborn St.
ST 2-0855

OOR PRIZES

The flyer for a 1971 drum clinic I did with my mentor, Grady Tate

Terry and me with Walt Parazaider, Jimmy Pankow, and Lee Loughnane (in the back, left to right) and Peter Cetera (on bass) in 1972

Practicing
in the Santa
Monica
mountains
in 1972

Back at the ranch in
1972: Peter, Jimmy,
Robert, and Marty

Tearing through "Feelin'
Stronger Every Day": Chicago
and the Doobie Brothers at
Balboa Stadium, San Diego,
on July 15, 1973

Playing congas at Balboa Stadium

Terry working
his magic

Rebel with a cause

Terry and Peter at my daughter Danielle's
christening party in 1974

Songwriting session in my garage in Encino for "Aire" from *Chicago VII*

The gunslingers at Caribou Ranch: (left to right) Jimmy, me, Peter, Walt, Terry, Lee, and Bobby

Rehearsing a song for the *Chicago in the Rockies* television special

8

CTA

Our first album, *The Chicago Transit Authority*, was released in the late spring of 1969. Although it received some favorable reviews, sales were sluggish and the record had trouble gaining traction. We couldn't break into popular AM radio because our songs were too long for the format of the stations. Still, the newly developed FM format embraced CTA and helped push the record along. Once college audiences hooked into us, our popularity grew nationwide on school campuses.

From a business standpoint, Guercio knew it was going to be more of a gradual climb for our band and understood that he would have to reach out to his connections in the smaller markets to get us airplay. CBS's main marketing focus centered on Blood, Sweat and Tears because they were the fair-haired boys of the company. CTA had to rely on the help of others, especially dedicated promotion guys at the label like Steve Popovich, Terry Powell, Sal Ingemi, and Ron Alexenburg. They went the extra mile to spread the word on a grassroots level about our band.

Knowing we needed to promote ourselves as much as possible, CTA set out on the road in support of our debut album. After warming up with a few gigs in the Hollywood area with the likes of Iron Butterfly, Three Dog Night, and the Animals, we got some mind-boggling news—Jimi Hendrix wanted CTA to open a few shows for him on a southern tour. Of course, we instantly jumped at the chance. Since his groundbreaking performance at the Monterey Pop Festival, Jimi was the talk of the national music scene, and being associated with anything he did was the gold standard. He was one of the biggest draws in the world, so it would be unbelievable exposure for CTA.

We met up with Hendrix and the rest of his band and boarded a Piedmont Airlines flight bound for our first gig at the Coliseum in Charlotte, North Carolina. Not long after we lifted off the ground, turbulence kicked in and our small prop plane started getting tossed around like a little toy. A few minutes into the flight, I leaned forward in my window seat and tried to get ahold of myself. My stomach was doing somersaults. Before I knew it, I vomited into one of the barf bags. I happened to be sitting behind Jimi, who I absolutely idolized, so I couldn't have been more embarrassed. All I wanted to do was find a place to hide. Jimi, an ex–army paratrooper, wasn't the least bit affected by the rocky flight. He stayed relaxed while the rest of us kept white-knuckled grips on our armrests. When Jimi noticed that I was a complete wreck, he came back to comfort me.

"It's okay, kid," he told me, patting me on the back. "You're gonna be all right."

Like Janis, Jimi had a kind and sensitive side the public never got to see. He was supposed to be a larger-than-life drugged-out rock star, but that was just a character he portrayed to the outside world. It was a true privilege to get to know a different side of him that not everyone had access to.

We played amazingly on the tour, but Hendrix blew the doors off the places. His use of loud feedback, overdriven amplifiers, and effects pedals simply amazed me as he confidently grooved across the stage and showed everyone what was possible on electric guitar. It was obvious to everyone that Jimi was a guitar god and an instant rock legend. The dates we opened for Hendrix took the promotion of our first album to a whole new level. Word of our band was spreading.

After the shows opening for Jimi, CTA returned to California for some much-needed rest and relaxation. Everything was happening fast for us and we needed to stop and regain our bearings. Walt, Terry, Peter, and I found out the Chicago Cubs were coming into town to play the Los Angeles Dodgers, so we took our wives out to a game one Saturday afternoon. It was a beautiful summer day at Dodger Stadium and free of distractions. Around the seventh-inning stretch, I went inside to the concessions stand to get a few Dodger Dogs and drinks for everyone. As I got back toward our seats, a group of Marines started hassling Peter. They didn't like that there were "longhairs" in their row, and on top of that, we were all Chicago Cubs fans.

"Fuck you, hippie," one of the guys told Peter. He got up from his seat and pushed Peter down the aisle. When Peter regained his balance and started back up the stairs, another guy from the crowd hauled off with a right hook and hit him square in the face.

Not only did I have my hands full, but the row was too packed with people for me to get any closer. When I finally made my way back to our seats, I wanted a piece of one of the Marines. Nobody messes with part of my group, my gang. It was always an eye for an eye.

"Why would you do that?" I yelled at them. "You're a bunch of assholes!"

I was about to make a move when a guy sitting across the row grabbed my shoulder and stepped in front of me.

"Listen," he said. "You don't want to get into it with those guys. They're only looking for trouble."

He was right. Alone, I had no chance against a group of combat-trained Marines. Besides, we were with our wives. It wasn't the time or place to try to be a tough guy.

Needless to say, our baseball game was cut short and we had to drive Peter to the hospital. His jaw was badly broken in multiple places and he had to stay in the hospital for three days. The doctors even had to wire his mouth closed.

It was an awful situation, but Peter's injury didn't prevent CTA from performing. He showed the band his mettle as a true professional and continued to sing and play live with his jaw clamped shut. (The funny thing is that Peter still sings with his jaw clenched in the same style.)

The band continued promoting our album all over for audiences in Indianapolis; Boston and Framingham, Massachusetts; the Fillmore East in New York City; Asbury Park and Lambertville, New Jersey; Wallingford, Connecticut; San Francisco; and Vancouver, British Columbia. In between the dates of our touring schedule, we somehow found the opportunity to jump into CBS Studios in Los Angeles and record a second album in August 1969. Whereas the first record was a compilation of raw energy, we took a more controlled approach to our new effort.

Following Bobby's lead, Terry and Jimmy started to come into their own as songwriters. During our previous tour, Jimmy had crafted a beautiful thirteen-minute classical-influenced song he called "Ballet for a Girl in Buchannon" (the word was he had written it for his old girlfriend Chickey Sweets). Structured like a classical piece with several movements, each with a different title, it had everyone excited. We could immediately tell how special it was; the music challenged every one of us to our core. The band rehearsed it for hours on end while we were out on the road and came up with our own parts.

We went into the studio in New York and recorded the song in sections. Afterward, Guercio and the studio engineer, Don Puluse, spliced it all together. The last element remaining was the lead vocal. Initially, Jimmy had written it for Bobby's voice. After all, Bobby had sung lead on the singles like "Beginnings" and "Does Anybody Really Know What Time It Is?" When it came time to lay down the lead vocal, Bobby began running down the song. Immediately an eerie silence came over us as we stood watching him from the control room. It was obvious to everyone that Bobby's voice simply did not fit. His track just sat there with no life or magic. Everyone traded a few worried glances. Here Jimmy had written this masterpiece, but Bobby's vocal wasn't cutting it.

Guercio turned to Peter and Terry. "Does either one of you want to take a crack at this?" he asked them.

Peter knew that the two sections called "Make Me Smile" and "Colour My World" were too low for him. So Terry went in the booth and took his best shot. From the moment he sang the first line, everyone's faces lit up, especially both Jimmys (Pankow and Guercio). You would have thought they had discovered gold, and you could say they did. Terry hit it out of the park.

During recording, Bobby also brought in a wonderfully catchy song he was calling "25 or 6 to 4." Like everyone else, I asked him what the track's title meant.

"It's a song about the frustration of writing a song. And me wondering whether it is twenty-five minutes or twenty-six minutes until four o'clock in the morning," Bobby explained.

The overwhelming excitement of our new material didn't erase the fact that the band as a whole was run-down. We were burning the candle at both ends with our nonstop partying. Walt's behavior in particular on the road had grown more and more bizarre. He stopped making any sense in conversations and I was the only one willing to share a room with him. He had taken to putting his hair in pigtails, wearing an old Chicago Cubs baseball jersey, and carrying a baseball glove around. He also walked around carrying a rubber duck in his briefcase, which he called "Grandpa Duck." The psychedelics had caught up with him and Walt was losing his mind. He buckled under the pressure of becoming a rock star and regressed into acting like a teenager.

We were in the process of recording "25 or 6 to 4" in the studio one afternoon when Walt walked in smacking a ball into his baseball glove. Out on tour was one thing, but in the studio his weird antics were getting to be too much to handle. It was a real distraction and had begun to get in the way of our work.

"Hey, you guys want to play catch?" Walt asked, making his way around the control room.

My frustration finally boiled over. "Walt, what exactly is your deal?" I asked him. "You're freaking everybody out and you need to pull it together. You should go home and cool out."

Without another word, Walt shuffled out of the studio. It was the last we saw of him for the day. Later on that evening, he called to tell me how what I had said hurt his feelings. I apologized, but explained that the band had lost its tolerance for his nonsense. In a way, I held myself responsible for the difficulty Walt was experiencing. I had persuaded him to pass up his opportunity with the Chicago Symphony and set off on this outrageous musical path in the first place. Toward the end of recording, word came back to the band that Walt had been admitted to a mental hospital. His wife, Jackie, had reached her breaking point and could no longer deal with his mood swings and wild behavior.

At one point, we held a band meeting to discuss how to handle the situation. The other guys had the nerve to bring up the possibility of *firing* him. I couldn't believe it. Fire Walt? Had the rest of the band already forgotten about the pact we made?

"If Walt goes, then I go," I emphatically told the rest of the band.

My firm position put an abrupt end to the discussions and the topic was never brought up again.

We kept in close contact with Jackie and she kept us updated on Walt's condition. Because he wasn't able to go out on tour, we were forced to hire a substitute horn player named Bobby Roberts for a few shows. When fans and media asked about Walt, we explained that he was sick with the flu and would be back soon.

It was scary because none of us knew whether we'd see the old Walt again. We hoped he would be able to get the well-deserved rest he needed and rejoin the band when he felt healthy enough. It was hard to set out on the road knowing the trouble he was having back in Los Angeles. I wanted to be there to support him as much as possible, but Chicago had performances to honor.

Fortunately, when we returned to Los Angeles from our gigs, we found that Walt had completely regained his health. Whatever he had been dealing with was long gone and he was back to his old self. His recovery was nothing short of a miracle. Once Walt rejoined us, our band was once again intact and ready to pick up where we had left off.

From the afternoon when we held our first rehearsal in Walt's mother's basement, I had had supreme confidence in our talents as a group. However, I was still shocked at how far we'd come since then. After just a few short years, we were routinely sharing stages with the best bands in the world and playing to larger audiences than I could ever have imagined. CTA performed at the Atlantic City Pop Festival in the middle of the summer in front of a crowd of more than one hundred thousand! When I looked out from behind my drum kit over the sea of fans, I thought I must be dreaming. Only a couple of years earlier, the band had struggled to draw crowds in small Chicago nightclubs.

When we heard the initial rumblings about the promoters putting on Woodstock, the band wanted desperately to perform at the festival. Word was that it was going to be the most sensational event of the era. But there was a problem. CTA was under contract with Bill Graham to perform at the Fillmore West during the same span of dates and Graham wouldn't let us out of it. I had a suspicion the reason was because he also managed Santana and may have thought of CTA as a threat. He didn't want us to overshadow his top act—the less competition for Santana at Woodstock, the better. We pleaded with Larry Fitzgerald, but he insisted that his hands were tied and there was nothing he could do. CTA's only option was to honor the contract and do the Fillmore West dates.

"Besides," Larry told us, "this Woodstock gig's going to be a logistical nightmare and a total mess. You don't even want to be anywhere near that place." (I still razz him about that statement to this day.)

Shortly after we had finished recording our second album, CTA played the Texas International Pop Festival at the Dallas International Motor Speedway on Labor Day weekend. As at the Atlantic City festival, there were amazing performers on the bill: Led Zeppelin, Canned Heat, Janis Joplin, Grand Funk Railroad, Santana, and Sly and the Family Stone. Zeppelin drummer John Bonham and I acted almost like rival gunslingers backstage. For some reason, we kept a distance from one another and neither of us wanted to make the first move. In retrospect, I should have taken the time to get to know him. We both came from similar backgrounds, and we probably would have become fast friends. I consider it a real missed opportunity. There was no reason for either of us to act aloof. After all, one of the elements I enjoyed most about touring was the opportunity our group had to mingle and bond with other talented artists.

After performing at the festival in Dallas, CTA's tour continued across the country. Even though there were a few previous offers, up until that point we had purposely chosen not to return home to play Chicago. The band had agreed to go back only once we had made something of ourselves. Well, everyone agreed that the time had finally come. We returned to the Windy City around Thanksgiving of 1969 to perform in front of a sold-out crowd at the Auditorium Theater. As we expected, the town was alive and buzzing. All of the band's family and friends came to see us play and partied backstage after the show. My parents, my sister Rosemary, and even my old buddy Rick Bracamontes from the neighborhood made it out. It was a glorious evening and a rewarding return to our old stomping grounds. The future of the band was brighter than ever.

In the wake of our group's newfound notoriety, the local government back home also took notice of us. Our namesake, the actual Chicago Transit Authority in Illinois, threatened legal action against us unless we agreed to change our band name. So we did; from that point on, we were simply known as Chicago. I always liked the name CTA and was sorry to see it go, but there was nothing we could do about it.

Not only was our name evolving, but our career was changing as well. We carried our momentum overseas, where the band's popularity was at an all-time high. On our first European tour stop, we played to a capacity crowd at London's Albert Hall. We were doing well in the States, but it was surprising to see how big we were overseas. Each of us was introduced individually in Albert Hall under a spotlight and got raucous applause from the audience. We were suddenly the darlings of the English press, who gave glowing reviews of our albums and live shows.

From the outset, I noticed that audiences reacted much differently to our music in Europe. At the Palais D'Hiver in Lyon, France, the audience sang along to every word of our songs. We never saw that in the United States. The international crowd showed us a certain amount of intellectual respect we hadn't seen with American audiences. We felt like we were true artists and not just another pop music commodity. It was during that time in Europe that I began to understand that our musical achievement was substantial.

We were on a very tight schedule during that particular tour, so we didn't have much time for ourselves. The exhausting pace turned out to be a real grind. I got up early in the morning, ate breakfast, went to the venue for soundcheck with the band, came back for a nap at the hotel, and then went back to play the show. After the gig, the European promoters took us out for a ridiculously late dinner around ten or eleven at night. It wasn't the easiest routine to settle into.

Luckily, our tour manager, Jack Goudie, was a hard-ass and kept us in line. He was like our personal drill instructor and made sure we always made it to where we needed to be every step of the way—meet-and-greets, photo shoots, soundcheck, you name it. It was a tough job and he put up with a lot of nonsense, but Jack had the strong personality for it. After our shows, getting backstage to meet us was like trying to get back to meet the Beatles. Jack always ran a tight ship and we were fortunate to have him on tour.

Out on the road was like living in a fantasy world. Sex with groupies became a constant. Girls were everywhere and more than willing to do anyone or everyone to get to our band. The rock-star party lifestyle was a free-for-all. Excess, excess, and more excess. I didn't think about whether something was good for me before I did it. I was carefree and reckless. The entire band felt invincible.

Being on tour overseas really opened my eyes to the thriving European groupie subculture. The girls loved American bands.

In Switzerland, I awoke to find a gorgeous blond Scandinavian girl standing at my bedside. She had come home with one of our roadies, who had let her into my hotel room.

"Are you the drummer?" she asked, taking off her sweater.

I couldn't do anything but blankly stare up at her. At first I wasn't sure if I was in the middle of a dream or not. Overall, I was somewhere in between.

"Yes, I'm the drummer," I answered, still a bit hazy.

At that moment, I would have been anyone she wanted me to be. She could have asked me if I was the bassist, keyboardist, manager, whatever . . . the answer was *yes*.

I was stunned at the things some of the groupies were into doing. Many of them wouldn't think twice about doing our entire road crew in order to gain access to the band. And once they did that, the girls had no problem sleeping with the *whole* band, individually or at once. They were sexually available to us and for the taking. And I certainly took.

When we returned to the United States from our wild tour overseas, the band found that our second record, *Chicago* (also known as *Chicago II*), had gone certified gold—500,000 copies! All of us felt a great sense of achievement in hearing the news. We had moved from our homes, left our families, and dedicated ourselves to a common goal. Our group took the leap into the unknown and came out the other side. All the miles logged on the road in buses and planes and the long hours spent in the recording studio were well worth it. Our intention was never to be famous, but suddenly we were.

Not that the success didn't have a downside. Walt wasn't the only one who experienced the negative effects of nonstop touring. After performing one evening in front of a packed house in New Hope, Pennsylvania, Lee and I got ahold of some LSD and I experienced the worst acid trip of my life. Aside from dealing with the intense paranoia, I began spitting up blood. It scared the hell out of me. Deep down in my gut, I knew something was seriously wrong.

Upon arriving back in Los Angeles, I wasted no time in getting a blood test and chest X-rays done. When the results came back, the doctor stunned me with the news that I had contracted tuberculosis. Luckily, they had detected the disease in its early stages and prescribed me a new experimental drug.

My illness seemed like the direct result of the abuse I had inflicted on myself over the previous few years. My body and mind had been pushed to the absolute limit and now they were pushing back. Rose helped nurse me back to health and I stayed in bed for two weeks at a guesthouse we were now renting in Studio City, California. With the help of rest and medication, I made a full recovery. My bout with tuberculosis served as an important wake-up call for me to improve my lifestyle. I quit smoking (for a while anyway), changed my diet, and started exercising. At the rate our band was going, I was going to have to be in much better shape to make it out there on the road. There was much more to come for Chicago.

9

Chicago

At the end of our grueling year of touring and recording, Walt and I went to a meeting at Howard's office on Sunset Boulevard. The band's popularity had been growing exponentially. We had done something like 250 dates during the year, and I was looking forward to reaping the benefits of our hard work.

"It's been a good year, guys," Howard told Walt and me, pulling his chair in closer to his desk. He flipped through a stack of spreadsheets until he found the one he was looking for. "But as it stands now, with the tremendous production costs being what they are, each of you owes Guercio *seven grand.*"

I nearly lost my mind. "What?" I shot back. "Is this some kind of a joke, Howard?" I leapt out of my seat and began pacing his office.

"What do you want me to tell you, Danny?" Howard answered with upturned palms.

"*We* owe *Guercio* money?" I asked. "How on earth is that possible?"

117

"Now calm down," he told me. "There's no need to overreact." Howard paused and then added, "Don't forget. You and Walt would be the easiest to replace."

Who did this guy think he was? *Replace* us? It took all my self-control not to lunge across the desk and grab him by his collar. Walt was usually easygoing, but he was just as upset. I flew out of the room, slamming the door shut behind me, and marched down the hall to Larry Fitzgerald's office to see what he had to say. Larry managed to calm me down and smoothed everything out between Howard and me that afternoon, but it was the beginning of a long-running good cop/bad cop routine the two of them would perfect in the coming years. One would light the fires and the other would put them out. What I didn't understand was that I was obligated to repay Guercio my share of all the money he had fronted the band early on. Until I was able to do that, I wasn't making a profit.

Even though the band was becoming well-known, there was an underlying sense that it could end at any time. As a musician and an artist, there was always self-doubt lurking in the back of my mind. I was constantly insecure about how long the band would last. None of us had any idea. There was a feeling somebody would step in one day and say, "Okay guys, that's it. You're done." And Chicago's crazy trip would be over.

Executives in the record industry and entertainment business use the artists' sense of insecurity against them from time to time to get their way. They don't think twice about leveraging fear to control the decision-making process. Even if I wasn't worried about something, there were always other people there from the record company or Chicago's own management to plant the seeds of doubt in order to keep us on edge. They'd use anything and start making off-the-cuff remarks.

"Well, you never know if you're going to be around that long."

"Maybe the next record won't sell, guys."

"What if we don't get a good fan turnout to the show?"

I understood the game, but it didn't change the fact that the continuous doubting deeply affected me. The band worked at a breakneck pace and a tight schedule. There were always new gigs to play, promotions to do, songs to record in the studio, and magazine interviews to sit down for. It was never-ending. We thought we needed to stay in constant motion or we would suddenly lose momentum and give up everything we had worked so hard to achieve.

Most of the guys in the band didn't understand the anger and frustration I was experiencing over our business arrangement with Guercio. Bobby, Jimmy, and Terry had no reason to bitch, because they were earning big songwriting royalties. Howard and Guercio were not going to hear any complaints from them. Having grown up a corner guy, I was sensitive to people trying to screw me over. The rest of us didn't have any piece of the publishing and were making our living off of touring. It was a hard pill to swallow. I was driving around in an old Volkswagen Bug that had just turned over 150,000 miles while the other guys were buying brand-new cars. I should have been more understanding, because Bobby, Terry, and Jimmy were Guercio's go-to guys at the time. The focus was on Bobby's songwriting, Terry's skilled guitar playing, and Jimmy's groundbreaking horn arrangements. Peter may have been the most talented singer in the band, but he found himself third in line behind Bobby and Terry. He started understanding that he was going to have to write his own material in order for his vocals to be featured.

The money issues ate away at me. The band had been recording, selling albums, and touring tirelessly for more than an entire year straight and it wasn't making any difference. Forget *making* money; I owed money. I was *paying* to be a part of the group.

The bottom line was Jimmy Guercio controlled it all. The publishing, album sales, ticket sales . . . you name it. He had a stranglehold on every facet of Chicago's business. We had made the decision as a band to sign his five-year agreement and now I was feeling the sting of its consequences. The way it was structured, the band paid for everything. I was appreciative of everything Guercio did for our group, and I never forgot that without him we wouldn't have had a record deal in the first place, but I didn't completely understand general overhead, production, and recording costs. I couldn't process how much of his own money Guercio was investing in the band in order to launch our career. Fortunately, there wasn't much time to dwell on the inner workings of the business arrangement. I had to force myself to put up with it in order to focus on the music. After all, that is what mattered most.

Our second album, *Chicago*, was released in January 1970 and featured the band's new striking and distinctive logo on its cover. Guercio had very definite ideas on how he wanted our image presented to the public and insisted that the logo remain dominant in all of our artwork from that time forward. We had always let the music do the talking and now we had a trademark logo to complement our distinct sound.

Not long after the record came out, I was driving along the 405 freeway in Los Angeles when a familiar piece of music came over the AM radio. For the first ten or fifteen seconds, I didn't recognize it as ours. Something was wrong with the arrangement. It had been cut down from Jimmy's thirteen-minute "Ballet for a Girl in Buchannon" and spliced together into a radio-friendly three-minute tune. Enraged, I nearly swerved off of the highway and crashed my car into a guardrail. After regaining control, I found a pay phone at a gas station and called Larry to find out what the hell was going on. Nobody had told us the song was going to be chopped up and released as a single.

"I thought you knew," Larry explained. "Jimmy finally gave in to Clive Davis. He's the head of the company and can pretty much do what he wants. But it's been doing great and climbing the charts. It's looking like a big hit, man."

And Larry was right. "Make Me Smile" broke it wide open for the band and launched us big. Our popularity skyrocketed and our second album pushed into the mainstream. "Make Me Smile" and "Colour My World," both sung by Terry, became Top 10 hits. Bobby's "25 or 6 to 4," sung by Peter, got constant airplay. The band continued touring and exceeded everyone's expectations.

The unbelievable success of "Make Me Smile" changed everything. It opened up a whole new world of luxury and excess.

The band went from underground scene artists to bona fide rock stars. We stayed in the most luxurious hotels, dined in exclusive restaurants, and chartered a private plane instead of flying commercial. Our first plane, a weathered Martin propeller model, was flown by a World War II veteran pilot we called Captain Bob. He reminded me of John Wayne's hard-nosed character in the movie *The High and the Mighty*. Every once in a while, Captain Bob got on our case for being too rowdy while we were in flight.

"Hey, some of you guys need to sit down. You're throwing off the balance of the plane!" he'd shout back to us from the cockpit.

Any time spent aboard the plane was party central. The drugs and the booze flowed freely and we stocked the cabin with the most stunning groupies imaginable. The more the band toured the country, the more I indulged in affairs. Women were everywhere—backstage after the show, on the tour bus, and at the hotel. Being out on the road for me was like giving a kid the keys to the candy store. Women had become a destructive vice and I could not overcome the temptation. I tried to justify my behavior in my mind, but I was only lying to myself.

Despite Guercio's sizable commission, every member of the band began to see big earnings, even the nonwriters like Walt, Lee, Peter, and me. Because of the new spike in income, Rose, Krissy and I moved from our tiny guesthouse in Studio City to a modest place in Encino. Instead of moving to upscale locations such as Malibu like Jimmy and Peter or inland to Beverly Hills like Bobby, I followed Walt into the San Fernando Valley, which was a little more sensible to me. Cash may have been plentiful for the first time, but I was always practical when it came to finances. Coming from the streets, I'm more interested in getting proper value for my money. That being said, the days of living on hot dogs and beans were behind us forever.

The band was entering yet another phase in our brotherhood. In the beginning, we struggled through the early days together in Chicago and then made it through the time of living on top of each other in the same house in Hollywood. Now each of us was moving out on his own to concentrate on family. Times were changing. We could now focus on giving back to those who had supported us over the years.

When my dad called me up one night and told me the convenience store was having problems making ends meet, I didn't hesitate in lending him $14,000 to help ease the strain. Nothing made me happier than being able to do that for my mom and dad. Over the years, they had done everything they could to help me through the rough times. I got a great sense of satisfaction out of being able to repay them.

After the early friction between us, Howard and I smoothed things over. Not only did he help me negotiate the purchase of the Encino house, but he even offered to help me buy my first new car down at the Mercedes dealership in Sherman Oaks. Howard had always been partial to driving around in big Cadillacs and couldn't understand why I would want to buy a foreign car. But nothing he said was going to change my mind. I wanted a Benz.

In the end, bringing Howard down to the dealership paid off. I got a great deal and couldn't have been happier to drive that vintage Mercedes coupe off of the lot. The new air suspension was a welcome change from the hard ride of my old Volkswagen beater.

Although the quality of my life was steadily improving as money started rolling in, I remained a fly in the ointment about our business arrangement. My anger flared up once in a while, but there was always someone there from our management team to placate me. There is an old adage among managers and talent agents in the entertainment industry: pay your acts just enough money so they don't start asking questions. And that is precisely what our management did. They kept us content and we continued to work without skipping a beat. There was always another tour to set out on and another album to put out.

In late 1970, the band went into the studio in New York City fatigued and road-weary. We had hit a point where we had used our excess material on the previous two albums and the guys had to work nonstop to write new songs. We took the opportunity to experiment with instrumentals and showcase our skills as musicians. I contributed "Motorboat to Mars," a drum arrangement, and also collaborated with Peter on a tune he had come up with called "Lowdown." Peter was incredibly supportive during the writing process and knew how much it meant to finally notch my first cowriting credit on one of Chicago's songs.

During the recording of *Chicago III*, I was introduced to cocaine for the first time. A few of the other guys in the band had begun experimenting with it, so I figured I would give it a try. After the initial high wore off, I came down with one of the worst cases of the flu I've ever had in my life—the Hong Kong flu, they called it. The band was forced to cancel an important promotional photo shoot the next day because I was incapacitated in my hotel room. While the rest of the band set off for Los Angeles, I spent the entire following week sprawled out in a New York City hotel room. Guercio lived in the city and stopped by to check up on me. He and his wife, Lucy, even invited me to stay at their apartment with them, but I didn't want to impose because of my condition. The entire experience turned out to be a blessing in disguise because it cemented my attitude toward cocaine. I had no interest in trying it again anytime soon.

At this point in our career, the band was operating at a breakneck pace. Although it felt like we were rushing the recording process, it didn't come through in the finished product when *Chicago III* was released two months later. With our first *three* double albums in as many years, the band had secured itself among the premier acts in the world. Because of the momentum we had built up, Columbia Records was able to rerelease the singles "Beginnings," "Questions 67 and 68," and "Does Anybody Really Know What Time It Is?" from our first album. They all went on to become hits.

We continued to tour, but the road was starting to wear on us. Exhausted, we made another pass through England and found that the British press had changed their opinion of our band. They were particularly harsh in their reviews of *Chicago III*, maybe because we had become successful and were no longer the darlings of the underground music scene.

Not long after our arrival in London, we held a press conference and were confronted by a group of hostile journalists. When Terry had had enough of their attitude, he decided to vent his frustration. During the post-interview photo shoot, he had something he wanted to share with the British press.

"Fuck all of you. Eric Clapton sucks," he told them as the cameras flashed.

Oh Christ, I thought to myself. *That will go over smashingly with these British journalists.* They were already looking for reasons to bash the band, and Terry had given them a juicy sound bite. As expected, his Clapton quote was all over the papers the following morning. Terry didn't mean what he said, but it was his way of lashing out and venting his frustration for the way the band was treated during the press conference. He certainly knew how to make headlines.

In April 1971, Chicago played an entire week of shows at Carnegie Hall and recorded them for a live box set. Although it was a remarkable venue, we had serious sound difficulties. The acoustics in Carnegie Hall weren't what we expected, and despite the best efforts of our engineers, nothing sounded right. The horns came across thin and tinny like kazoos. As soon as we got the proper levels on the stage, someone from the production truck came in and started adjusting them again.

The beginning of the record never sounded right to my ears, but in the middle of "South California Purples," Terry kicked out an amazing guitar jam and everything almost magically fell into place. The band connected in that moment and the rest of the set took off from there. In all, the shows turned out great. I was at the top of my game.

Our Carnegie Hall shows marked a historic event in our career and were later released as a gigantic live four-LP collection. Not only were we the first rock group to sell the place out for an entire week, but the albums also went on to break records as the top-selling rock-and-roll box set. Chicago had set sales marks that would stand for years.

We graduated from playing two-thousand-seat clubs such as the Fillmore East and West to packing giant twenty-thousand-seat venues like the Boston Garden, Chicago Stadium, and the Great Western Forum in Los Angeles. Those buildings were built for major sporting events, not music concerts. I felt like the luckiest corner guy on the planet.

Just when I thought my life couldn't get any better, Rose got pregnant again and we had a beautiful baby daughter we named Danielle. I almost missed the birth altogether and had to rush back from a gig the band was about to play in New Orleans. I arrived just in the nick of time to see my new baby girl come into the world. Even though my family was growing, I didn't break stride. Chicago was an unrelenting force that could not be stopped. We were already in the middle of preproduction for *Chicago V*. So, a day after Danielle's birth, I went back to work while Rose stayed at home with our young ones.

During our production meetings for the album, our band made a conscious decision to shy away from writing long pieces of music that would be edited down for radio airplay. The new focus was going to be on singles. Bobby wrote new three- and four-minute songs as opposed to the extended pieces the band had been doing for most of our career. We also decided to put out our first *single* full-length release instead of our typical double album.

Our new direction marked a critical turning point, because we started to gravitate away from what we were all about. In changing our format, we lost some of our die-hard fans, but the move also opened our music to a mainstream audience that was previously untapped. It felt like we weren't being true to ourselves and were allowing record sales and revenues to influence our decisions, but we felt the obligation to feed the big machine we had created to satisfy the needs of the radio stations and our millions of fans across the globe. Although *Chicago V* turned out amazing, the new direction of the band alarmed me because we were altering the DNA of our music. After we made the choice to write more commercial songs, like "Just You 'N' Me" and "Old Days," I continually tried to crowbar in my jazz licks. My role had altered within the band and it took me a while to adjust. Eventually, I gave in to what the songwriters *wanted* me to play in place of what I *thought* should be played.

In support on the new album, Chicago set out on our first full-fledged world tour, playing in sixteen countries in twenty days. We were already larger than life in the States, and our sold-out performances cemented our status as international stars. Like on our earlier European tour, the audiences sang along with every lyric. It was a rewarding experience, but also very grueling. The trip didn't go without incident. Bobby and Terry had gotten married and decided our tour across the globe would be the perfect opportunity to bring their wives out with the band.

Bad idea.

Halfway through our trip, Bobby's wife, Karen, and Terry's wife, Pam, were at each other's throats. Everything came to a head while we waited in the airport terminal in Stockholm, Sweden, for a departing flight. One of them called the other a "tramp" and chaos ensued. Before long, Bobby and Terry also jumped into the fray and started going at each other.

"Fuck you, then," Terry shouted at one point. "I quit!"

"No way. *I'm* quitting!" Bobby yelled back.

Larry and Jack attempted to step in and play the role of peacekeepers, but Larry also quickly became unraveled. "You guys are a bunch of goddamned kindergarten schoolchildren!" he yelled, throwing his hands up in frustration. "I'm through taking any more of your bullshit. I'm out of here!"

The band was imploding in front of my eyes. We had reached the point of total exhaustion, and I was next in line to lose it. I took off running through the airport and found Jimmy Pankow at a newsstand.

"Jesus, man," I told him in a panic. "These women are ruining our band! You have to do something quick. Everything is falling apart!" I ripped off the camera hanging around my neck and slammed it against the wall.

Jimmy skillfully calmed me down and sorted everything out. Once we managed to get on our flight, everyone got some much-needed sleep and the ordeal was finally over.

The fatigue of the road overcame us that day. Touring was difficult enough; adding wives and girlfriends to the equation was a recipe for disaster. We were a band of brothers out on the road.

We could tell each other to go to hell once in a while. But you couldn't just tell someone's wife to fuck off if she got on your nerves. It was a different dynamic altogether. From that moment on, we had an unspoken rule that we wouldn't bring our wives out for an entire tour. A few dates here and there were never a problem, but any more than that was too much. None of us ever wanted to see a repeat performance of what went down in Stockholm.

After its release, *Chicago V* climbed the pop charts with the help of Bobby's song "Dialogue (Part I & II)" and the smash single "Saturday in the Park," and went on to become our group's first No. 1 album. I was particularly proud of the drum part in "Saturday in the Park". It was a tribute to Rascals drummer Dino Danelli, whom I listened to when I was younger.

There was no doubt the hit single was an important commercial benchmark for us, but one of the absolute highlights in Chicago's career came later that year. Our management was contacted by famed producer Quincy Jones and invited to play at a CBS television tribute in Los Angeles to jazz great Duke Ellington, called *Duke Ellington . . . We Love You Madly*. When I found out we would be sharing the stage with legends like Count Basie, Sarah Vaughan, Ray Charles, Aretha Franklin, and Peggy Lee, I was thrilled. They were artists I looked up to immensely.

Quincy took some heat from jazz purists who didn't agree with Chicago's spot in the lineup, but he didn't let anything interfere with his decision. He was a big fan of our band. Being a skilled musician and composer himself, he had a tremendous respect for Jimmy's horn arrangements. Above all, Quincy understood that having Chicago on the bill would open the tribute up to a larger white television audience. At the same time, our band would get some much-needed exposure to a wider black audience. It was a win-win for everybody.

At rehearsal, I wandered around starstruck. The room was a who's who of jazz greats and Hollywood stars. It wasn't easy fitting in among so many accomplished entertainers. Not only was Chicago musically different from the rest of the big band talent on the bill, but our image was also in stark contrast. We walked around in our full '70s hippie garb. Some artists might have felt out of place, but I was too young to let it affect me. I was just a twenty-four-year-old kid who was happy to be there.

After Chicago tore through our version of Ellington's "Jump for Joy," I made my way down an aisle in front of the stage to my seat. A moment passed before I realized Count Basie was in the seat next to me. It was the ideal opportunity to make conversation.

"I really love your song 'Satin Doll,'" I finally piped up. It was true. The tune had been a mainstay in the Big Thing's set list back in our early club days.

"No, man," he answered, shaking his head. "That's the Duke's. He wrote that number."

Talk about putting your foot in your mouth.

"But thanks anyway," the Count added with a smile.

Count Basie was gracious about my mistake, but I still couldn't have been more embarrassed. *Looks like I should have done my homework*, I thought to myself. I got up from my seat and slinked down the aisle, feeling almost like I was crawling away. Overall, though, it was just a hiccup in an otherwise mind-blowing experience. All the acts on the bill embraced our band and welcomed Chicago's contribution to the tribute. We had connected with an audience that might have otherwise remained closed off to our music. The end result didn't surprise me, because we were incredibly ambitious and persistent. If an audience didn't gravitate toward our music, we brought it directly to their doorstep. Chicago wasn't going to be overlooked.

We traveled nonstop and toured across the country and overseas. We lived show to show and recording session to recording session. It was a constant routine: limos, airports, baggage claims, shows, hotels, and *repeat*. The days blurred into weeks, then faded into months. Aside from occasional visits home to California to spend time with Rose and the girls, my life seemed like one long, never-ending tour. Each morning I woke up in the same nondescript hotel room in a host of different cities. The repetition of the road lifestyle kept me locked into a semi–dream state. I was rarely home for those few years, and when I was it was for maybe a week or so at a time. Our band did not know when to stop.

The road took its toll on my family life most of all. I was a caring father to my two little girls, Krissy and Danielle, but that side of me was in direct conflict with the side that was cheating while out on tour. There was more than enough free time out on the road. When it came down to it, I was obligated to be onstage for maybe a few hours a day. Being so far away from family and friends, some guys did drugs to pass the time and some drank. I chose to chase women. The guilt over my infidelity was a weight I carried around at all times. Instead of confronting the awkwardness and taking steps to repair my relationship with Rose, I pushed her further away and shut her out. I acted increasingly cold to her, but felt powerless over the situation. Temptation lurked around every corner. Although the constant touring was a necessity for the promotion of the band, I left part of my soul out on the road. And I had nobody to blame but myself.

I thought back to the road trip Walt and I took out to California and remembered the dreams and expectations I had for our band. I desperately hoped we would be able to achieve some level of success. Well, only a few years later Chicago was everywhere and I was spread thinner than ever.

Be careful what you wish for.

10

Caribou Ranch

The band decided to record our sixth album in Colorado, where Jimmy Guercio had finished construction on a full recording studio at his Caribou Ranch high up in the Rocky Mountains. The property sat on over three thousand acres of land and had a main house with a series of guest cabins and a state-of-the-art recording studio in a converted back barn. It was one of the first "destination studios" of its kind and it let the band take a different approach to writing and recording.

Chicago owed our sensational success to Guercio's financial backing. He was the guy who made everything happen. Together with the top-notch management team of Howard and Larry, he had done remarkable things for the band—performed miracles even. But seeing firsthand the wealth Guercio had amassed up in the middle of the Colorado mountains didn't sit well. I couldn't stop thinking about how my family and I were living in a place that was basically the size of the living room of the main house at Caribou Ranch. *What's wrong with this picture?*

The experience of recording in Colorado was radically different from working at an established studio in New York or Los Angeles. Those facilities were expensive and restrictive. When the band booked studio space, we were there for a certain amount of time at a set hourly rate. As soon as we walked into the building, the meter started running. Up at Caribou Ranch, there were no scheduling conflicts. There was no other band booked behind us waiting to come in. Chicago had total freedom to work for as long as we wanted at our own pace, and being so far removed from the hustle and bustle of New York or Los Angeles, the band stayed focused and concentrated on writing and recording.

The converted back barn had three massive floors: the first was a tech room, the second was the main recording studio, and the third floor was a lounge area with a bar and a pool table. Guercio had spared no expense in developing the property. He knew what he was doing.

For our new record, I brought in a brilliant Brazilian percussionist named Laudir de Oliveira to add dimension to the signature Chicago sound. We had previously jammed together while he was a part of Sergio Mendes's group and immediately hit it off. Our styles fit together perfectly, creating a layered and full sound that reinforced the strong Latin influence that had been building in our music. The rest of the band welcomed Laudir, so it made for a smooth transition.

Guercio was way ahead of his time as a music producer. Back in those days, it took forever to get a good sound quality and levels, but Jimmy had a great ear for getting full-bodied drum sounds and creating a signature horn sound. He knew what he wanted but also allowed us the freedom to follow our instincts. He often rolled tape during our practice sessions when he felt our playing was more relaxed and fluid, a smart choice because we never knew when that magical first take was going to occur. When it did, he wanted to be sure we captured it. Some of the rehearsal recordings, like the tracks for "Searchin' So Long" and "Just You 'N' Me," were so good that we could never top them. In the end, with mistakes and all, they were solid enough to be included on the album.

During the sessions at the Ranch, Dick Clark Productions came up to film for a CBS television special called *Chicago in the Rockies*. They joined us in the studio and recorded footage of the band hashing out the arrangements for songs such as "Feelin' Stronger Every Day" and "What's This World Coming To?" Also visiting the ranch was another group from Chicago that Guercio had been producing called Madura, formerly known as Bangor Flying Circus. They also lived up on the ranch recording an album, so we hung out in between sessions. Their drummer, Ross Salomone, and guitarist, Al DeCarlo, were from my neighborhood back home. The band's songwriter and keyboardist was a guy named David "Hawk" Wolinski. Hawk buzzed around like he was always on speed and was pretty avant-garde, but we ended up hitting it off.

It was an ideal atmosphere, but being up at Caribou was also a double-edged sword. The isolation cultivated many existing bad habits we had picked up over time. With our wives and children back in California, there were no rules. Chicago fell into a routine of recording in the afternoon and evening, then partying late into the night. The band broke up the boredom by flying in Playboy bunnies from Los Angeles and getting whatever drugs we wanted. Drug dealers, whom I considered to be hangers-on, frequented the ranch more than I would have liked. There was plenty of cocaine to go around and its use had become a regular activity. I hated the drug because it turned people ugly. Their personalities changed and they became selfish, irritable, and paranoid. It also had a negative effect on people's work. Guys became sloppy about rehearsing. Because of my awful experience with coke back in New York City, I would excuse myself from the party and retreat back to my cabin. Typically, I was the lightweight of the group and couldn't make it past midnight or one in the morning. I enjoyed the occasional joint or few cocktails, but I couldn't function under the influence all the time. It wasn't in my nature. Besides, women were my drug of choice. When I wasn't flying a girl in for the weekend, I focused my attention on one of the Caribou Ranch maids. Over time, my ego inflated to the point where I didn't even attempt to hide my cheating anymore. My habit was proving to be as destructive as any drug.

That said, Terry's hard partying disturbed me most of all. There was a side of him that was never at ease with the high level of success we had achieved. The whole idea of fame confused him on many levels, and he had trouble finding his comfort zone. As a result, he turned to substances and routinely stumbled around the ranch in a daze on pills and booze. To make matters worse, he had picked up a new hobby: guns. He took to wearing his pistols in holsters at his hips and fired at aluminum cans out in the field. I wasn't a big fan of firearms and tried to convince Terry to leave them in his cabin when he was high, but he didn't always want to listen. However, Terry never let his partying affect his playing. His unbelievable tolerance for substances was a blessing as well as a curse—in fact, *much* more of a curse. Unless he was completely out there, it was hard for any of the band to tell if he was using. Although he was able to perform at a high level on coke, it still took its toll on his body and mind. He was beginning to physically break down.

The band and our management went to great lengths to keep our partying under wraps. Chicago was never identified with the outrageous sex, drugs, and rock and roll lifestyles of bands like Led Zeppelin or the Rolling Stones. We were widely known as the "Mercedes of Rock," as one newspaper referred to us, and wanted to maintain our squeaky-clean image. We did most of our partying behind closed doors or out in the middle of nowhere at Caribou Ranch. None of us wanted anything to disrupt the hugely successful machine we had created together.

As many members of the band drifted off into drugs and excess, I became kind of a designated driver in our group and the captain of what had become a ship of fools. I had always been the most vocal member, so it was only natural to eventually step into a leadership role. It wasn't a position I exactly pursued, but I had no problem assuming it. Anybody who wanted to contact the band with a business matter knew to approach me first. I had a type A personality and admittedly had always been a natural control freak. Not many of the guys were interested in the business side of things anyway. They understood that I was on the prowl and left me to network my way though the industry. Whenever I had an idea for the band, I lobbied the rest of the guys like a politician to make sure I could count on their vote. Peter was typically the first member I consulted because he was the toughest nut to crack. It was wise to keep him in the know about all upcoming business issues first, then continue on to the rest of the guys.

My position in the band might have been more stable than ever, but my personal life was a different story. After being away for long stretches of time, I struggled to find a comfort level around Rose and my girls. Whenever I went back home to Los Angeles, I was overcome by the same sense of guilt. Typically it took a few days for my anxiety to subside before I was able to settle back into home life. One evening, Rose and I went out to the theater to see a new movie called *A Touch of Class*, starring George Segal and Glenda Jackson. At one point in the film, one of the characters said, "I've been married for ten years and I've never cheated on my wife in the same town." Without thinking, I guffawed in the theater. Luckily, I regained my composure before Rose shot me a look. I always figured I was fooling her, but now I got the feeling she saw right through me. As I have learned over time, women have a sixth sense about detecting cheating . . . or should I say a *sick* sense. But it seemed as long as we didn't talk about it, it wasn't happening.

A month before *Chicago VI* was to be released, the band went back out on the road for a twelve-date tour and hired an up-and-coming musician named Bruce Springsteen as our opening act. Bruce had released his debut album, *Greetings from Asbury Park N.J.*, to critical acclaim and we had heard great things about his live performances. Unfortunately, our audience did not respond well to Bruce's music. It was difficult to watch him go out onstage night after night and get almost no crowd reaction in the packed venues. The audience seemed to be biding their time waiting for him to finish his forty-minute set so Chicago could take the stage. Bruce misfired with our audiences, and I'm sure he found the twelve-show tour to be a very frustrating experience. But, of course, the tour didn't have a lasting effect on his career. The next time I saw him perform, he was a completely new force onstage. He had become the Boss.

When *Chicago VI* came out at the beginning of the summer of 1973, it proved to be yet another success. The album went gold in under a month and then platinum. Overall, it stayed at No. 1 on the *Billboard* pop charts for five weeks and the singles "Just You 'N' Me" and "Feelin' Stronger Every Day" made it into the Top 10.

The band swapped our old prop plane with Captain Bob at the helm for a more luxurious private jet called a Falcon. Our new pilots were Vietnam veterans who were almost as crazy as our band, and the party raged on. To pass the travel time, we had the pilots do parabolic turns at high rates of speed and negative Gs, where they flew the jet straight up and then dove straight down. The result was around ten seconds of complete weightlessness in the passenger cabin, during which we all yelled and screamed. It was a little difficult to keep ahold of your cocktail. Talk about a wild party ten thousand feet up!

Out on tour, Peter and I tended to keep similar hours and regularly got up to play tennis together in the morning. Bobby also joined us every so often. We tried to maintain this routine whenever we were out on the road to stay in shape. Typically, I found myself hanging out with Peter and Bobby during the day. Later in the evenings after shows, I'd switch gears and head out to the clubs with Walt and Jimmy Pankow. Terry and Lee joined us once in a while, but not often. They were mostly off doing their own thing.

As the five-year term on Chicago's contract with Guercio came to a close, management approached the band about renewing the agreement. Everyone knew I was going to be the most difficult to persuade out of the group, so they handled me carefully during that time. I asked for a copy of the new contract and had Jay Cooper, a renowned entertainment attorney, scrutinize every line and clause of it. As expected, he said it would not be in the band's best interest to sign the deal. Not that it was a surprise. We had heard basically the same thing five years earlier.

There was far too much conflict of interest in the management. It didn't seem wise to have a business manager, a band manager, and a production company under the same umbrella. There was nobody to answer to because outside counsel wasn't involved in any of our business transactions. The band was left unprotected. If we weren't skeptical of the business deals and arrangements, who would be?

In a way, I was a man without a country, because I had no backing from the rest of the group. Everybody was satisfied musically and financially and didn't feel there was any reason to disrupt the balance of the business. I, on the other hand, wore my heart on my sleeve. In questioning the fine print of the new contract, I was like a general going into battle without any troops. As everyone knows, you can't win a war without an army. I was torn because Chicago was riding a massive wave of success. How far was I prepared to push it? The band was more popular than ever and I didn't mind the checks coming in. What was the alternative? Ultimately, I backed down and once again Chicago signed a five-year contract with Guercio under similar terms. None of us at that point, myself included, was strong enough to challenge anything.

When the band went back to Caribou Ranch to record our next album, I decided to invite my old friend Pete Schivarelli out to Colorado for a few days. I needed to shake things up a bit and keep the management off balance. Pete and I had reconnected and every now and then spent time out at my house in California. Over the years, he had become an important figure back home in Chicago and had been appointed commissioner of streets and sanitation. He was also still friendly with the likes of Michael and Tony Spilotro and some of the other Colony House crew.

Whenever I walked into a room with Pete at my side, I felt more confident. The band all knew him from back in Chicago, but I got a kick out of watching the expressions on our management's faces when they met him. My intention was to stir the pot, and it worked—maybe too well. Howard pulled me aside one afternoon up at Caribou. I was surprised to see he had a genuinely fearful expression.

"What's the deal with this guy, Danny?" Howard asked. "We thought you were just kidding around with that talk about the Outfit and the mob. Is this guy for real?"

"Oh come on, Howard," I told him.

To be honest, I knew little about Pete's situation. I didn't ask and he didn't say. So I didn't have answers to anyone's questions. All I understood was that nobody ever messed with me when I was with Pete. *Nobody*. It worked for me when I was a fiery young kid and I figured it might work now. Having him up at Caribou gave me a newfound sense of confidence, and I regained my swagger. The band may have re-signed, but that didn't mean we needed to feel intimidated in any way and let everything happen around us without giving our input.

Not only was the band reestablishing our boundaries with management, but we were also reclaiming some of our musical integrity as well. The new album we recorded at Caribou, *Chicago VII*, turned out to be a welcome return to Chicago's jazz and R&B roots. The pendulum now swung back after we had concentrated on writing shorter and more focused singles on *Chicago V* and *VI*, and we used the opportunity to let our music breathe and stretch out. In the process, I incorporated some of the brush playing I had been studying with legendary jazz drummer Jo Jones, especially on the track "Devil's Sweet." Jo had a great influence on my playing over the years; he taught me how to swing. I learned so much about discipline and technique from Jo—for example, to look at the audience and sit up straight when I played. I tried to layer his teachings into our music wherever possible.

At the same time, Laudir and I created a unique blend of jazz-rock and Brazilian rhythm. It laid a perfect foundation for songs like "Call on Me," "Mongonucleosis," and "Happy Man." Laudir was also the perfect foil for me to solo off of in our live performances. We fit together like hand and glove. With my help, he had become a full-fledged member of the band.

Peter channeled his inner Beach Boy and contributed his song "Wishing You Were Here" to the record. Guercio had taken over management of the Beach Boys and even arranged to have Al Jardine and Carl and Dennis Wilson sing backup harmonies on the tune.

The engineer who mixed the album was a talented guy named Phil Ramone, whom the band had previously worked with on recording our CBS television special at Caribou Ranch. The first thing that struck me about Phil was his talent for achieving natural drum sounds. I was setting up my kit early in the recording sessions when he came into the studio.

"What do you want me to do with my drums?" I asked him. Typically, we would tape napkins to the heads of each drum to deaden the sound.

"Leave them the way they are," Phil told me without a second's pause. "They sound great."

It was refreshing to hear, because engineers always had specific ideas about dampening my drums. Phil went for the natural tone.

Once again, Dick Clark Productions came to Caribou over the course of recording to shoot a CBS television special called *Meanwhile Back at the Ranch*. As the band tore through hits like "25 or 6 to 4" and "Just You 'N' Me," the TV crew edited in cutaway footage of us hanging out at the ranch: Terry speeding across a field on a motorcycle, Laudir and his son fishing by a stream, and Lee standing next to a horse eating a *whole* watermelon, for some reason. We definitely hammed it up for the camera. There was even a long sequence of me riding a horse in slow motion across the property (to get that over-the-top dramatic effect). What they never showed on television was me falling off my horse at breakneck speed. He got spooked because of the production crew's lighting reflector, and he bucked me right off. Everybody held their breath to see if I would get up, and Guercio's father, Jim Sr., came running up and helped me to my feet. Even though every bone in my body hurt, I still reshot the scene. After that nasty spill, Jim Sr. gave me the nickname of "Paisano cowboy." That was our riff together every time we saw each other.

After our stint at the ranch, Chicago set out on a national tour with the Beach Boys, who were reviving their career in a major way with Guercio's help. In the summer of 1974, the guys released a double album of all their early hits. The record, *Endless Summer*, ended up going to No. 1 on the *Billboard* chart. It was the Beach Boys' first gold record since *Good Vibrations*.

I spent a good amount of time hanging out with Beach Boys drummer Dennis Wilson on the road. The ladies absolutely loved him. He behaved like a teenager trapped in a forty-year-old body—crazy and unpredictable. I couldn't believe the circus atmosphere that surrounded the Beach Boys. They made Chicago look like the Brady Bunch.

Just when we thought it couldn't get any bigger, we started playing baseball parks and football stadiums. The Beach Boys killed onstage every night. They did all their hits—"Good Vibrations," "California Girls," "Surfin' USA"—and every now and then I even joined them onstage to play on "Darlin'" and "Sail On, Sailor."

After our show at Chicago Stadium, I invited my sister Rosemary backstage and introduced her to the Beach Boys. In the years since I had left Chicago, Rosemary had gotten married and moved to the beautiful suburb of North Barrington, Illinois. She had always been a huge fan of their music, so her face was absolutely beaming when she met the band. As I watched my sister talking with the Beach Boys, I felt so blessed that I had the ability to give her such a great gift.

11

New B.Ginnings

As the money continued to pour in for Chicago, Howard tried to keep a watch over the band to ensure that we didn't fall into making poor business decisions. We worked hard for our money, and he didn't want to see us piss it all away. Bobby had opened a high-end boutique with his wife off of Melrose Avenue called Zazou. It was directly across the street from Chicago's management office, so it became a regular hangout for everyone. Terry had started a company called Pignose Amplifiers, which he got the rest of us to invest in as well.

Even with Howard's supervision, we still managed to make a few mistakes. The band invested in an oil well that turned out to be nothing more than a dry hole in the middle of a field. I loaned money to people who I never saw again. At one point, I invested in my childhood friend Rick Bracamontes's retail clothing store, Peabody's Rock & Roll Boutique, which carried wild and flashy clothing. Unfortunately, once the fashion trends started to change the store struggled to adjust and went under.

That being said, not all of my ventures were busts. In late 1974, Rick put me in touch with his brother, John, who had an idea to open a nightclub called B.Ginnings in the suburbs of Chicago. John came up with the name, which was a throwback to Bobby's song "Beginnings" off the first CTA album. I was interested in the concept from the start and couldn't wait to invest in the twelve-hundred-seat nightclub out in Schaumburg, Illinois. Howard wasn't thrilled with my $150,000 contribution, but I wasn't going to let any doubts he had change my mind. I was dead set on opening a musical showcase nightclub where bands would be excited to play. If we were going to do the project, we were going to make sure it was done right. It was important to separate B.Ginnings from the dive bars and dead-end clubs the Missing Links and the Big Thing played while coming up on the Chicago music scene. I wanted it to be seen as the gold standard of rock clubs in the area.

John and I had specific ideas on the interior design of the place and thought it should resemble the Chicago streets we spent so much of my youth hanging out on. We hired set builders who brought in actual street signs, stoplights, and even train tracks to create a three-dimensional mural along the wall of the dance floor. The decor gave the main ballroom an authentic feel and a unique identity. We installed an oversized stage with state-of-the-art monitors and lights and also outfitted the place with the best sound system money could buy.

I was grateful for the success Chicago had achieved and wanted to return the favor. It was only right to give something back to the new generation of musicians paying their dues. As I thought back on my years gigging in run-down bars, one thing that stood out in my mind was how much I hated the tiny backstage areas and dingy dressing rooms. Most of the time, bands were forced to change in dirty men's bathrooms and musty coat closets. I wasn't going to let that be the case in my club. I designed an enormous backstage area and deluxe dressing rooms with all the amenities a band could want, like showers and vanity mirrors. Hell, there was even cold beer on tap.

Two weeks before the club was set to open, I flew back to Chicago from Los Angeles to check on the status of the construction. From the second I laid eyes on the place, I was in awe of what the builders had managed to pull off. The scenic artists we brought in to work on the Chicago-themed skyline wall had gone above and beyond what we envisioned. I couldn't wait for people to see it. But it was a different story when I went backstage to check out the dressing rooms. They were half the size the builder and I had agreed upon. This was the one element of the club that had to be exactly the way I wanted. When I asked what had happened, John told me they had decided to make the other half of the dressing room area into a space for more liquor storage. Well, there was no way I was going along with that. I had them immediately change it back to the original plans. There was going to be nothing less than complete comfort for the musicians in my club. There were plenty of other places to store booze.

Without giving it a second thought, my bandmates agreed to perform on back-to-back nights for the grand opening of B.Ginnings. For business reasons, the band got paid a dollar a night. It was the lowest-paying gig we ever had, but nobody cared about that. The guys playing at the club was the definition of what our brotherhood was all about. I don't think they knew how much the gesture deeply touched me. Where I come from, loyalty ran deeper than anything—when somebody did something good for you, you never forgot it. Conversely, when someone did something bad to you, you never forgot it either. The Italians called it a debt of honor, and it was serious stuff. If you didn't have loyalty, you didn't have anything. The guys understood how much effort I had invested in the club and they came through big time. From that point on, there was no question that their friends became my friends and their enemies became my enemies.

The club went above and beyond my expectations on so many different levels, but there was one thing working against it: location. The suburb of Schaumburg was nearly an hour's drive out of downtown Chicago and there wasn't access to any public transportation. From the start, the club relied on the draw of the nightly talent to bring in a crowd. We turned the booking duties over to a company called Jam Productions, run by a couple of guys named Arny Granite and Jerry Mickelson. They did a wonderful job bringing in up-and-coming acts like AC/DC, Tom Petty and the Heartbreakers, and Billy Joel. Besides the headliners, other regional bands were also booked in support. In all, the plan seemed to be working, because people were showing up.

The club quickly became popular, but it didn't turn out to be an immediate financial success. Despite the packed house night after night, I wasn't seeing any return on my investment. I couldn't wrap my head around it. I decided to bring in Pete to check out the club on a busy Friday night. If anyone was familiar with Chicago nightlife and running a cash business, it was Pete. He would give me an honest opinion of the place. As I gave him a full tour of the offices, backstage, and bar areas, he nodded in appreciation of the work that had been done. It felt reassuring to see he was pleased with how B.Ginnings had turned out. At the end of the night, we walked into the back parking lot to get some fresh air.

"So, what do you think?" I asked him, smiling. "Pretty nice joint, huh?"

"Yeah, you've done good, Danny," Pete told me. "But guess what? You got about fifty partners in there."

"What do you mean?" I asked. I wasn't sure where his train of thought was going.

"Every bartender and waitress in the place is stealing from you," he said, gesturing back toward the building. "The whole joint."

I didn't want to believe it, but Pete was giving it to me straight. As a street guy, he knew the ins and outs of every scam in the book. If he thought he spotted something going on, I was in no position to doubt him. Pete made it sound so obvious that I was embarrassed I hadn't picked up on it myself. My other partners had been either too incompetent to see what had been going on since the opening of the club or were somehow in on it.

It might have been a little drastic, but I forced every one of the club's employees to take a lie detector test. Man, were they pissed! In the end, only two people out of the entire staff passed and we had to bring in a new crew of bartenders and waitresses. But I made my point. Everyone knew the free-for-all was over.

I bought my partners out of their shares of the club and took over complete control of B.Ginnings. Although the move put an enormous strain on my longtime friendship with Rick, it was also an essential business decision that had to be made in order for the club to survive. I brought Pete in to manage the club, and lo and behold, we immediately started turning a profit. With Pete on-site, the days of employees skimming cash from the registers were a thing of the past. He kept me updated on the status of the club and also hired a friend of ours from the old neighborhood named Dino Coletis to manage the place on a daily basis. (Ironically, Dino was from the rival Bell Park gang that beat up Tom Padula and me back on that front lawn by Lindy's Coffee Shop.) Within the next year, there was a full return on my initial investment. I couldn't have been more thrilled, and even Howard, who was skeptical from the beginning, was impressed with the success of the club.

Although they did a great job running the place, I gave Pete and the promoters from Jam Productions a lot of flack because I wasn't into many of the rock acts they booked. I had always been more of a jazz-fusion guy and Jam Productions brought in up-and-coming performers I had never heard of. When I caught wind that they had booked a group named Cheap Trick to be B.Ginnings's house band, I wasn't thrilled.

"Who the hell is this Cheap Trick band?" I asked Pete. I was constantly breaking his balls. "We should be booking Buddy Rich in the place, not Cheap Trick," I told him. Since I had the final say, everyone humored me, but my tastes weren't exactly in tune with what the audiences wanted to see. It was a good thing Jam Productions worked with us, because if I had had my way with booking, the joint would have gone under in six months!

After Pete and I reconnected out at Caribou Ranch and he started running the nightclub for me, there was a dramatic change in my life. I felt a newfound respect and sense of power. Back in Hollywood, word spread fast about the guys we had grown up with in the old neighborhood like the Spilotro brothers, Jimmy Leonetti, and Joey Lombardo. All of my business contacts knew where I came from and the people I had connections with. Just the suggestion of underworld pull did the trick.

Power attracts power. Entertainment executives want to be gangsters and gangsters want to be entertainment executives. It was nothing new. Show business has operated like that since the beginning. The Italian Mafia and the Outfit had another name— the Cosa Nostra. Well, the guys and I thought the mostly Jewish entertainment executives in Hollywood had their own type of crime syndicate behind the scenes—we called it the *Kosher* Nostra.

Because of Pete, almost overnight I became popular with the upper echelon of the record industry. I had been called up to the big leagues. The power brokers, record company presidents, managers, and top producers all wanted to be my friend. I got to be on a first-name basis with them. I'm not going to lie; it felt great to be pursued.

Talk about respect—I was on the A-list for all industry events, fund-raisers, and parties. The red carpet rolled out wherever I went. Whether it was true or not, it was believed that through Pete I was connected to one of the most feared factions of the Outfit in the country. I never confirmed people's suspicions or denied them. I was already one of the most respected rock drummers in the world and part of a band who was talked about in the same sentences as the Beatles, Rolling Stones, and the Who. Now there was even more influence at my fingertips.

Pete kept me insulated from the rest of the Outfit and never let me know too much. He understood that if they got to me it would be all over. As much as we liked each other, they would like nothing better than to sink their hooks into me. There is no doubt their influence corrupted me. I didn't realize it at the time, but it was beginning to happen.

Pete and I talked on the phone every day. I hardly made a move without checking with him first, and vice versa. We watched each other's backs. When my father started having health issues and decided that running the store was too much stress and strain, Pete pulled a few strings back home and got him another job. My dad would get up early in the morning and open a hot dog stand Pete owned, called Demon Dogs. It was a landmark location, right below the el tracks on Fullerton near DePaul University. My dad sat at the counter and served people their morning coffee and doughnuts. Around midday, he went to another job Pete had hooked him up with answering phones at his ward's office for a few hours.

From an early age, my father had prostate problems. He was always in a great deal of pain and discomfort. Being a truck driver for the Tip Top Bread Company didn't do his health any favors. All of the constant bouncing in the seat left him with kidney problems as well. Because of his health, my dad had trouble getting around. The new low-stress jobs were perfect for him. I was very thankful to Pete for helping him out in a time of need.

Once Pete and I got everything running the way it should, B.Ginnings became wildly popular. At one point, I even entertained the thought of opening a chain of them across the country. But I soon reconsidered. My schedule was already hectic enough without having to deal with that headache.

In many respects, life was good. I owned a successful nightclub outside Chicago and my band could do no wrong. Everything we touched seemed to turn to gold—or better yet, platinum. Through Jack, our road manager, the band even got word that back in Chicago they wanted to give us the keys to the city! Jack said a buddy of his had helped arrange a meeting with Mayor Daley for the band. I couldn't believe it. But when I told Pete about it, he was a little skeptical. He made a few calls and said he heard we would only be meeting with the deputy mayor for the ceremony. I truly didn't mean to undermine what Jack had done for us, but I went ahead and had Pete check into the whole situation. In the end, he was able to get Mayor Daley to agree to a meeting.

Needless to say, Jack was pissed.

"I had it all set up and you had to go and make me look bad, didn't you?" he asked me.

Nothing I said made the situation any better, and from that day forward there was a negative undercurrent between us. But hey, Jack pulled his strings and I pulled mine. In the end, the band still got the keys to the city from the mayor, didn't we? It might have been a power play on my part, but I was intent on getting what I wanted.

• • •

With the fruits of the constant touring and chart-topping success, I bought a gorgeous Tudor home for Rose and my girls in Westlake Village, California. It was a wonderful piece of property with a detached guesthouse I decided to make into a home recording studio. A professional designer from Westlake Audio came in and put it together with state-of-the-art sound equipment. There was even a drop-down Murphy bed in case anyone wanted to crash for the night. Since the studio was completely soundproof, it was the ideal sleep chamber. It quickly became the perfect place for Chicago to rehearse. And the location was ideal because I never had to worry about showing up late for band practice!

The stunning home and studio may have been a newfound luxury, but there was also an unfortunate downside to the success and good fortune. Rose and I both knew we were at a crossroads in our relationship, and the move to Westlake was a last-ditch effort to save our marriage. I figured that if we bought our dream home somehow everything would be miraculously repaired between us. It turned out we were both fooling ourselves.

Our location might have changed, but our marital problems stayed the same. The excitement of our new home didn't change the fact that our marriage had been imploding for years. We weren't going to be starting over with a clean slate. There was no overlooking my cheating and how I had disrespected Rose. Not long after relocating, she and I decided it was best for the two of us to separate.

Rose and my daughters deserved much better treatment from me. I had failed miserably as a husband to her and as a father to my two little girls. I was devastated at the thought that they would have to grow up without a full-time father in their lives. But I only had myself to blame. Nobody had forced me to do the things I had done. I repeatedly gave in to the temptations of the rock-star lifestyle and I alone was responsible for my awful behavior.

When it came time to sit our daughters down and explain the situation, I was heartbroken. After hearing the news, my oldest daughter Krissy ran up and wrapped her tiny arms around my neck. The tears streamed down her face as she cried.

"Who's gonna take care of you, Daddy?" she sobbed.

I couldn't have felt lower. Instead of showing anger at the situation, she was worried about what was going to happen to me. It was a moment I will never forget.

Rose and I may have been separated, but she and the girls were never that far out of my life. I bought another house in Westlake only a few blocks away for her and my daughters to live in. I wanted to keep them as close to me as possible. If I couldn't be around on a daily basis, having them live in the same neighborhood was the next best thing. I was determined to keep a great relationship with my daughters. Whenever possible, I took them on day trips to Disneyland and had them stay the night at my house. I also bought Krissy a pony and together we went out riding on the weekends at the Equestrian Center. On a few occasions, I even took her on the road with me during short promotional trips for the band. The separation was difficult on my girls and I was determined to do everything within my power to make it easier. Spending time with them was more rewarding than anything.

Needless to say, I was overcome with guilt and regret after seeing my marriage crumble. I threw myself into recording, touring, and running B.Ginnings. Back home in California, I hit the Hollywood nightlife and filled my time with women and partying. Whenever Chicago wasn't working, we tried to take a break and spend time away from one another. It was important that each of us developed our own pockets of friends and were able to take a break from one another. Together with my buddies Hawk Wolinski, Marty Derek, and Tom Jans, I did the town and spent my nights on the Sunset Strip or in Beverly Hills. We put together our own version of the Rat Pack. When we weren't sitting in to jam with the house bands at the jazz clubs, we trolled the bar scene and played the field. After last call, which can be pretty early in Hollywood, we kept the party going back at my house in Westlake or headed up Beverly Glen Boulevard to Hawk's place in the Valley.

Whenever there was a long enough break in Chicago's schedule, Hawk and I jumped out to Hawaii to vacation. We rented a big house and spent our days relaxing on the beach and swimming in the crystal-clear waters. I loved the area so much, I ended up purchasing a half acre of land in Haena, in the northwest corner of Kauai. It was a glorious time in a lot of respects, but in the back of my mind I knew something was still missing. There was an underlying emptiness about everything and it was nearly impossible to shake the feeling.

I got more and more into spending time in my home studio. I wanted to learn everything there was to know about the recording process and begin work on my own ideas. I had spent top dollar to put the equipment in, so I might as well put it to use. Hawk and I had also been throwing around the idea of starting to produce bands on our own. Eventually I reconnected with an old friend of mine named Bobby Colomby, who offered to help us. Years back, Bobby had been the drummer and leader of Blood, Sweat and Tears, and in a lot of ways he and I were rivals early our careers. Although Blood, Sweat and Tears were an important part of Chicago's scoring our record deal, there was also always a healthy competition between our groups. For the type of music we were performing at the time, Bobby and I were considered the top drummers in our genre. Even the late great drummer Buddy Rich, who rarely complimented anyone, said we were two of the best young drummers he had heard. After Bobby left Blood, Sweat and Tears, he had gone on to head the West Coast office of Epic Records, a subsidiary of our label, Columbia. Bobby's transition made sense because he was a gregarious guy who had a strong sense for the business side of things. He was no fool. He even owned the name Blood, Sweat and Tears. He had recently started working with acts like Boston and Dan Fogelberg.

Bobby was the perfect person to talk to about getting into other facets of the business, because he was an ex-drummer who had successfully made the transition. There weren't many musicians at that time who managed to pull off something like that. I wanted to start putting the producing knowledge I had gained over the course of recording to good use.

I passed on a couple of demos Hawk and I had been working on at my home studio and Bobby loved them. At the time, he was working under my old friend Ron Alexenburg at Epic, whom I knew well because he had started out in promotions at Columbia. Soon after hearing our demos, Bobby came through and signed Hawk and me to a production deal at Epic Records. Our newly created Street Sense Productions would deliver two acts a year, which Epic had the option to release. The company gave us some decent production money to finance the development and studio costs for any projects we developed. It was basically a budget to record demos. Although it wasn't the most lucrative contract, Hawk and I were thrilled to have the opportunity to branch out into something new.

When Chicago's soundman, Mike Stahl, caught wind that I was on the prowl for new talent, he passed on a demo tape a few of his friends had made, a group called the Jerry-Kelly Band. I immediately liked what I heard. The guys sounded like a more refined version of the Eagles. Hawk and I flew into Scranton, Pennsylvania, and signed them to a small deal with our Street Sense Productions on the spot. Unfortunately, we never had much success taking them to the next level, but the whole experience gave me the confidence to continue to pursue my interest in producing. I wasn't going to let the fact that we didn't hit a home run out of the gate get me down. There were more than enough talented bands out there waiting to be discovered. It was only a matter of time before Hawk and I found the right one.

The days of Chicago being the darlings of the underground scene were a thing of the past. We had always been antiestablishment, but once the band started becoming successful that changed. There were still political groups approaching the band to lend our support to their causes, but it was a slippery slope to navigate. On one hand, the band wanted to stay true to its roots; on the other, we had obligations to record companies and corporations. Chicago was an essential part of the machine now.

We were against the hypocrisy of capitalism, but we found ourselves making huge amounts of money. As reluctant as we were to admit it, we had become capitalists and full-fledged members of the Hollywood elite. I had no problem booking reservations to the best restaurants and getting into the most exclusive nightclubs. Lou Adler, one of the early music business moguls, who had worked with the Mamas and the Papas, Carole King, and Cheech and Chong, gave every member of Chicago a membership to his VIP club upstairs from the Roxy called On the Rocks. On any given night, I found myself sitting at the bar next to celebrities like Warren Beatty, Ringo Starr, Dustin Hoffman, and Michelle Phillips. It was a surreal experience, and I never felt comfortable around that type of elite circle. I didn't know whether to try to hang out with the celebrities or ask them for their autographs.

More and more, Pete started coming out to California to visit me and spend time with the band. With my new power and influence, I introduced him around town and showed him everything the city had to offer. We'd have an incredible dinner at one of the most exclusive restaurants or drive down to a club in Hollywood. I had gotten season tickets for the Los Angeles Lakers, so one night I drove Pete down to Inglewood and we took in a game.

The Forum was always quite the scene. The crowd consisted of a who's who of the entertainment industry. During halftime, I spotted Lou Adler at his courtside seats, where he was sitting with Jack Nicholson. The two were a mainstay at every Lakers home game (and still are). It seemed like the perfect opportunity to have Pete meet them, so we made our way down to where Lou and Jack were sitting. As I began making the introductions, an usher came up behind me and put a hand on my shoulder.

"Excuse me, sir," she said. "I'm going to have to ask you to leave. You can't be here."

Lou raised a hand and stepped forward. "It's okay," he told her. "These are friends of mine."

His explanation didn't make any difference to the woman and she kept eyeing Pete and me. I gave her a smile, but she wasn't going for it.

"Don't worry," I said. "We'll only be a minute."

Thinking everything was cool, I leaned back against the railing and continued talking to Lou and Jack. A minute later, the woman came up from behind me again and grabbed my wrist.

"I told you you're not supposed to be here," she said.

I reached my breaking point. "Keep your fucking hands off of me!" I yelled, pushing her out of the way. Within seconds, a group of burly ushers advanced toward us.

Despite Lou's pleading, a huge usher put me in a bear hug and lifted me up off the floor. He was about to carry me up the stairs when he suddenly stopped dead in his tracks.

"Put him down right now," I heard Pete say from somewhere behind me. "Now!" he shouted.

The usher released me from his hold and I turned around to find Pete standing next to him with a hand around his throat. The usher could barely breathe. I looked around and noticed that ushers and security had surrounded us. It was a full-blown standoff on the floor of the Forum. Luckily, Lou stepped in and explained the whole situation to the head supervisor and everyone eventually wandered off. Pete and I went back to our seats, hysterically laughing over the spectacle we had made. Lou and Nicholson came and found us after the game.

"Good God, man," Nicholson howled, "that whole scene was something right out of a movie! I loved it!"

Going out on the town was always a good time. I would never complain about mixing with A-list celebrities and being given the royal treatment all over Hollywood. But the silence of my empty house was always deafening when I came home at the end of the night. My partying only covered up the fact that I was as lonely as ever.

12

Lyrics and the Blonde

Chicago X, released in June 1976, ended up being a major achievement in the band's career. During the course of recording out at Caribou Ranch, Guercio wasn't convinced there was a solid single on the album until Peter's ballad "If You Leave Me Now" came along. To tell the truth, it was a throwaway track when we recorded it—a pretty little number with some string arrangements and French horns. I wanted to keep the band jazz and there was nothing jazz about the song. We felt that other songs like Terry's "Once or Twice" or Bobby's "Another Rainy Day in New York City" were strong enough to be released as singles, but Guercio didn't want to hear it. He had already made up his mind.

In the end, I have to admit he was right on the money. "If You Leave Me Now" went on to become a smash and became Chicago's first number one single in both the United States and Britain. The band couldn't believe it. We took home Grammy awards in early 1977 for Best Arrangement and Best Pop Vocal Performance. We had previously been nominated for Best New

Group in 1970, but lost to Crosby, Stills and Nash, and Album of the Year in 1971 for our second album, but lost to Simon and Garfunkel. Third time is the charm, I guess. *Chicago X* also went on to be nominated for Album of the Year in 1977, but Stevie Wonder's *Songs in the Key of Life* landed the Grammy.

"If You Leave Me Now" changed the public's perception of what we were capable of as a group. Peter's hit song suddenly pushed him to the forefront, a place where he would remain for many years to come. He became the voice of Chicago. The single set off a growing demand for down-tempo ballads on future records. We had whetted people's appetites and now they wanted more. Even after all the success it brought, I found myself still bitching and moaning about the song. It hadn't come out of our true identity as a group. We might have notched a number one single, but in my mind we had veered way off course.

I was riding high professionally, but personally I was about to be dealt a painful blow. Late one evening, I received a call from an old friend named Marty Grebb, whom I had known from the early days back in Chicago when he was a member of Peter's old band the Exceptions, and who later played keyboards in the Buckinghams and enjoyed a successful music career. At first, I was happy to hear from him, but unfortunately he wasn't calling to reminisce. Marty had some bad news to pass on. Our old friend Freddy Page from the Illinois Speed Press had been admitted to a hospital in Southern California with an unknown illness. Marty wanted me to come down to the hospital and pay Freddy a visit.

I sensed the seriousness in Marty's voice, but Chicago was supposed to leave on tour in the next few days. I wasn't sure if I was going to be able to fit a trip to the hospital into my schedule before we set out on the road. I offered to see Freddy the second we returned to town.

"I don't think that will work, Danny," Marty said. "You better come and see him now because the doctors don't know how much time he has left."

It was difficult to process what Marty was saying. The last time I had seen Freddy, he was healthy and in good spirits. I jumped in my car and drove down to the hospital.

The heartbreaking sight of Freddy lying withered and frail in his hospital bed proved almost too much for me. The doctors weren't sure what was wrong, but they concluded he had some sort of rare blood disease. Sores all over his body had made him barely recognizable. I held it together as best I could and sat down in a chair beside the bed. Freddy reached his hand out and laid it on top of mine.

"Man, I don't think I am going to make it," he told me weakly. "But I wanted to tell you what a great friend you have been to me, Danny."

I patted Freddy's arm tenderly and smiled.

Freddy managed a smile in return. "I love you, man," he said.

"I love you too Freddy," I answered. "We sure had some good times, didn't we?"

"We sure did, Danny."

When the nurse came in to give him his medicine, Freddy let out a long sigh. "Listen," he told me, "I want you to remember me for the way I used to be and not the way I am right now lying in this hospital bed."

"Of course, Freddy," I assured him.

I said goodbye and left. The encounter weighed heavily on my mind as I set out on a northwestern tour with the band. It reminded me of the fragility of life. It doesn't matter who you are or how successful your band is. You could be here today and gone tomorrow. Money and fame have nothing to do with it.

A few days later on the Seattle stop of the tour, I had a vivid dream about Freddy. He came to me, not as the sick and feeble man I had last seen, but as the young aspiring musician who used to invite me over to the Speed Press's house to practice drums on Holly Drive back in the early days. In my dream, Freddy looked me straight in the eye and smiled. "Take me back to Chicago," he told me. And with that he disappeared.

I woke from my sleep and restlessly paced back and forth in my hotel room. I couldn't get the image of Freddy out of my head. Eventually, I grabbed a pen and paper and sat back down on the corner of the bed. I wrote the words Freddy had spoken in my dream down on the paper, "Take Me Back to Chicago."

And then more thoughts came together in my mind. They began to flow in a steady stream of consciousness. I wrote the words down as fast as they came:

> And lay my soul to rest
> Where my life was free and easy
> Remember me at my best
> Take me back to Chicago
> 'Cause hustlin's not my style
> L.A. was just a bit too hard
> I wish I could be a child
> Livin' back in Chicago

The next morning, Marty called to say Freddy had passed away during the night. I was sorry to see him go, but at least he said his final goodbye in my dream. In writing the song, I was being guided by some kind of higher power to express my inner feelings. The experience brought with it a new type of awareness. It led me to open myself up through my writing.

My creative awakening still had a strong hold on me when I took my daughter Krissy to Paris on a promotional tour a month later. One morning, I sat in silence staring at her as she slept in her bed. A ray of sunlight was shining through the window and falling across her face. She looked like an angel. I sat down and came up with the lyrics for a song I titled "Little One." I wanted to express the emotions I was never able to convey to her as I wrestled with the guilt for not being there for her and Danielle as a full-time father. My girls loved me, but we spent a great deal of time apart from each other. I poured my heart and soul into the lyrics as I wrote them down in my notebook:

> Little one, it's so nice to have you near me
> To feel once again the love you bring here
> Ooh, my little one, I am sorry for the pain you've felt
> Say the word and Daddy will make it disappear
> Oh, my little one
> Bring your love here

Little one
I need you near
Little one
Don't live in fear of the future
'Cause I will always be there
Oh, my little one
Music is my life, I hope you understand
Traveling on the road with me you can see the way
  we live
Oh, my little one
I will always cherish these days with you
As time goes by I hope you see the love I tried to
  give
Oh, my little one
Let your love flow
My little one
Like a flower you'll grow
Someday you'll have your own little one
And you will always be there

Upon returning to California, I gave my lyrics to Hawk. We got together in my studio and hashed out the music to the two new tracks. The guys in the band were very supportive and Bobby in particular told me how much he liked "Take Me Back to Chicago." It was nice to hear, because I had written it with his voice in mind. The rest of the band recognized that my material stood up to what everyone else was doing. I may have been a newcomer to writing lyrics, but I was quickly becoming another voice we could draw from.

While Chicago was on tour in Europe in 1977, I met a stunning pop singer from Germany named Ingrid Peters and fell for her on the spot. I jumped in with both feet, and almost immediately Ingrid and I were enmeshed in a passionate relationship. I had been in love before, but my feelings for Ingrid were far more intense than anything I had ever experienced. I could not stop thinking about her night and day. Luckily, Chicago was touring Europe, so I was able to fly her in regularly so we could spend time together.

When the time came for the band to return to the United States, I became very depressed. It was terrible that I had to return home without Ingrid. I called her daily from California to tell her how much I missed her and wanted us to be together. On more than a few occasions, I jumped on a plane to Europe with only a moment's notice. I visited her at her home in Saarbrücken, Germany, and we often drove down to the south of France together for the weekend. It was like something I'd seen in a movie, but I was living it.

My heart jumped when she told me she wanted to try to get signed with CBS America and move to California. I assured her I would do everything I could to help. I even talked to Guercio about having him secure a recording contract for her. But when Ingrid visited the United States and stayed with me at my house in Westlake, it was a complete culture shock. She wasn't used to the wheeling and dealing associated with the fast-paced Hollywood music business. She saw it as a big turnoff and couldn't wait to get back home to Germany. It broke my heart.

It was never going to work between Ingrid and me, but the intensity of my emotions was overpowering. I was lovesick—desperate to be with her. My daily calls to Germany from Los Angeles weren't cheap, either. Over the course of the year, my telephone bill added up to somewhere around $20,000!

A few weeks after she returned home to Germany, Ingrid called to tell me she was getting back together with an old boyfriend. The news didn't come as a surprise, but that didn't lessen the sting. Although it was over, I still couldn't let her go. Somehow, I convinced her to see me one last time in Stockholm. I needed to hear the words from her in person. Our relationship wasn't going to end over the phone.

When we met in the town square, I begged her not to break it off.

"I can't do it, Danny," she explained. "I'm sorry, but I can't move to America. This is the way it has to be."

The walls caved in all around me. Even though I had seen the end coming, there was no choice but to follow my heart. The affair had taken off like a speeding train and I couldn't get off the tracks in time to avoid being run over.

As always, the band served as a comforting escape from my increasingly disappointing personal life. Our career was still in high gear and we were already getting ready to go into the studio to record our next album, *Chicago XI*. Again, I got together with Hawk and we crafted my lyrics for "Take Me Back to Chicago" and "Little One" into full arrangements. The recorded demos came out better than I'd hoped. Thankfully, the rest of the guys in the band felt the same way and both songs made it onto the record.

But after *Chicago XI* was released in late 1977, tensions between the group and Jimmy Guercio finally came to a head. We hired a high-powered attorney by the name of Ken Kleinberg to spearhead an audit of Chicago's business arrangements, and the process turned up some unbalanced numbers that finally piqued the band's interest. It wasn't only a case of Danny being paranoid anymore; the proof was in the black-and-white digits on the spreadsheets. The profit margins and gaps in the royalty splits between the band and management were shocking. At one meeting, Bobby got so angry that he tossed a chair across the conference room and shattered it to pieces.

Are you listening now? I wanted to ask the guys. *Do I have your attention?*

A few of the lawyers suggested that the band sue Guercio for millions, but we had no intention of taking legal action. We didn't want anything to disrupt our unbelievably successful band. We initiated the renegotiation process with Guercio, but our relationship was permanently damaged.

It wasn't long before Howard and Larry had a falling-out with Guercio and were both let go. Everyone in the band knew how important those guys were to the success of Chicago, and we weren't too happy with the decision. In Howard and Larry's place, he brought in a guy named Dick Duryea to manage us. Dick had talent as a tour manager, but as far as managing our band on the whole was concerned, he wasn't the right guy for the job.

Guercio's choice to book Chicago to play a bunch of festivals throughout Europe in the fall left me scratching my head. Suddenly, we were playing outdoor venues in thirty-five-degree weather to less than capacity crowds. The shows weren't successful and most of the concert promoters lost money. On top of that, life on the road with our new manager Dick Duryea wasn't getting any better.

Needless to say, CBS Records panicked because they didn't want anyone to kill their golden goose. They were terrified Chicago might implode. The infighting between the band and management drove the suits at the label crazy. They wanted us to settle with Guercio as soon as possible and be done with the entire ordeal. But it wasn't going to be that easy. The time had come for the band to part ways with Guercio once and for all. We never wanted things to reach the point of no return, but there we were. Our confidence in our management was at an all-time low and in the end, there was no way we could re-sign.

The band had to act fast and brought in a renowned manager named Jeff Wald, who was best known for being married to Helen Reddy and masterminding her career. He was also notoriously difficult in dealing with record companies, so CBS clearly wasn't thrilled with our choice. They tried to persuade us to go with Earth, Wind and Fire's management team of Ruffalo and Cavallo, but we had no interest.

It should have been the perfect launching point for a new direction in our career. But everything was going to get a hell of a lot worse before it got any better.

13

Losing Terry

More than ever, cocaine had gained a powerful hold on the band. The drug was everywhere in the 1970s and nobody knew exactly how destructive it was. There were many times when I considered coke a ninth member of our group. The guys thought they would be able to control its effects, but it often ended up controlling them. Over time, they became slaves to it. As we played on, relationships within Chicago soured. Guys were stoned and erratic or burnt out and irritable. There was no middle ground. "Tune out, turn on" was a motto of the past. The beauty of the hippie movement had long since turned ugly. The drug culture had cast a shadow over everything. People like Jimi Hendrix and Janis Joplin had already succumbed to their addictions. Nobody simply experimented anymore. Drugs were being used for daily maintenance, not recreation and exploration.

Occasionally, I saw kids come up for autographs and watch Bobby and Terry snap back at them. It bothered me to watch any of the guys disrespect our fans, and I regularly got into it with them over the way they treated people. That wasn't who they were. Both of them were good-hearted guys, but more and more the drugs were turning them into strangers to me.

Coke had its hooks deep into Terry and his behavior spiraled out of control. Drugs turned him from a fun-loving guy into a nasty, short-tempered mess. To make matters worse, he had taken to carrying his guns around with him whether we were out at Caribou Ranch, in the recording studio, or out on the road. Each band member was his own man, but when that behavior started disrupting the group as a whole, it had to be dealt with. There was no alternative but to address what was going on. It wasn't going to be easy. Everyone did their fair share of the stuff, so it was difficult to stand in judgment. How aggressive could any of us be without sounding like complete hypocrites? We all had our short-comings and were getting high in one way or another, but Terry took it too far. Don't get me wrong. I wasn't a holy roller by any standards—maybe a little grass here and there, but nowhere near what Terry was doing. In my mind, I could be more vocal because I was fairly clean at that point.

"I am worried something bad is going to happen to you, man," I told Terry at our band meeting. "You have to be careful of the drugs. Besides, you're carrying guns around everywhere you go."

Terry smiled and ran a hand through his hair. No matter what was going through my head at the time, he had the type of genuine smile that always made me think everything was going to be fine. And I hoped it would be.

"Don't worry, I'm okay, Danny," he told me.

When he showed up to a barbecue at my house a few weeks later, Terry was a complete wreck. He was strung out like I hadn't seen him before and I had to pull him aside at one point.

I looked him in the eye and put my hand on his shoulder. "Man, you don't look too good," I told him.

Terry let out a long sigh and stared down at the ground. "I know," he said, shaking his head. "This shit is killing me. I've got to stop."

Not only was Terry the most talented guitar player I had ever played with, but he was also an incredible person with a wonderful heart. It hurt me to watch the coke eat away at his soul.

Because of his ridiculously high tolerance, an aura of invincibility had set in over time. I desperately wanted him to regain control of his life and make his health a top priority, but I couldn't force him to do anything. Nobody could. Although Terry understood he needed to make some major changes, it was difficult for him. He couldn't manage to pull himself away from the party crowd he had fallen in with. The hangers-on he had picked up along the way tightly clung to him like leeches. I supported him unconditionally in whatever he did and encouraged him to take the steps to get help. But my urging alone was never enough.

On the night of January 23, 1978, I was driving home from a Lakers game at the Forum when I received a call on my car phone from our new manager, Jeff Wald. It was one of the earliest models of mobile telephone, and I wasn't used to being contacted on it.

"Did you hear?" he asked.

"Did I hear what, Jeff?"

There was an extended silence on Jeff's end of the line that made me uneasy. And then he spoke:

"Danny . . . Terry's dead. He killed himself."

"What do you mean?" I asked confusedly.

"Terry is dead, Danny," Jeff repeated.

My stomach shot up into my throat and the surging adrenaline in my veins caused me to grip the receiver tighter in my hand. I fought off the urge to smash it into the dashboard.

"What the hell are you talking about, Jeff?" I screamed. "Don't joke around like that!" I jerked the steering wheel of my car and cut across two lanes of the 10 freeway.

"Listen, it's the truth," Jeff said. "But stay away from there, Danny. It won't be long before the police and the press are crawling all over the place."

"Stay away from *where*, Jeff? Where is Terry?"

He fell silent once again.

"Jeff!" I screamed.

"It happened at Don's house in Canoga Park," he finally confessed. "I just got a call from Don and I didn't know if he had talked to you first or not. He was rambling about Terry playing around with a gun and it going off."

Donny was a keyboard technician and roadie for the band who partied with Terry on a regular basis. No matter what, I had to get to his house. I needed to see Terry. I pushed my Mercedes as fast as it could go. Jeff's words continued to reverberate in my head.

Terry's dead. He killed himself.

In my mind, I desperately hoped it wasn't true, but in my heart I knew it probably was.

I needed air. I rolled all of the windows down in the car and the front seat was suddenly a churning windstorm. The sound of the air whistling into my ears was deafening, but I didn't mind. Maybe the noise would drown out my racing thoughts.

When I finally arrived at Donny's house in Canoga Park, everything was eerily silent. I burst through the front door to find Donny standing in the corner of the living room absolutely hysterical. He hugged me tightly like I was a life preserver.

"It wasn't my fault, man," Donny sobbed. "I tried to warn him but he just kept fucking around with that gun. I'm telling you the truth."

My focus shifted to the center of the living room. Terry's lifeless body sat back on the couch, his head angled up toward the ceiling. When I saw a pistol down on the floor next to his foot, a wave of dread shot through me. Another two steps forward revealed a bullet hole in the side of his head. His eyes were wide open, staring off blankly into the distance.

I let out a pained sigh as all of the air rushed out of my lungs. The tears welled up in my eyes as I looked up at the hazy vision of my brother.

Donny paced back and forth on the other side of the living room and began rambling. "We were partying for the last few days and came back here to hang out. Terry got some of his guns out of his car and brought them in the house. He picked up that damned revolver and started fucking around! I told him to put it away but he wouldn't listen and put it to his head like he was playing Russian roulette. When he pulled the trigger, the gun went 'click' because the chamber was empty."

I glanced over and made eye contact with Donny for the first time. He looked incredibly strung out. His nerves were already fried from all the partying he and Terry had been doing, and now he had to endure a scene like this. I truly felt awful for Donny. He would never be the same. And I guess neither would I.

"Terry wouldn't listen and just kept laughing. After that, he grabbed one of his other guns and put it to his head," Donny continued, stamping out his cigarette in an ashtray and lighting another one. "I pleaded with him, fucking *pleaded* with him, Danny! But he kept laughing and told me not to worry because it wasn't loaded. Before I knew it, he put the gun up to his head" —Donny stopped, then fought to push the words out—"and the thing just fucking went off."

I could barely comprehend the harsh reality of the scene I had walked into. I almost had the urge to leave, go outside, and come back into the house again, hoping to discover some other outcome. Maybe Terry would still be alive and walking around again. Maybe everything would be different.

Donny finally stopped pacing and got very quiet. He put his head in his hands. "Christ, Danny," he whispered. "Christ."

I sat down next to Terry on the couch and placed my hand on his. It was still warm to the touch, but all of the life was drained and gone. The hands I had spent countless performances watching dance up and down the fretboard of his guitar, passionately bending strings and sliding up to notes, were still and finally at rest. They would never play again.

"I know this has been really hard for you," I whispered to him. "I understand dealing with all the success was difficult, but you are going to be able to rest and find peace now, Terry. I'm really going to miss you, my friend."

In that moment, I was somehow convinced Terry was listening to me. I waited a moment for a response I would never get.

The three of us sat in silence together. My thoughts turned to Terry's loved ones he had just left behind—his pretty young girlfriend, Camelia, and his beautiful baby girl, Michelle. I thought back to the last time I had seen Terry at my barbecue in Westlake, back to watching him lay down an amazing vocal on my song "Little One" in the studio not long ago, and back to riding in that old Cadillac hearse during that brutal snowstorm with Jimmy Ford and the Executives. I saw Terry's bright smile beaming at me from the backseat as he strummed his bass.

Then I heard footsteps coming up the walkway of the house. I opened the front door expecting to find police, but instead was confronted by a few of Terry's drug buddies he regularly partied with. I glared at them as they filtered into the living room. If looks could kill, they would have been goners. I wanted to tear them apart with my bare hands.

Moments later, the sound of sirens approached in the distance. Police and paramedics arrived and flooded the house, unpacking equipment and searching every room. As officers questioned Donny and me about what had happened, the coroner came into the living room and strained to fit Terry into a black body bag. When he had given up, I noticed that Terry's boots were left sticking out of one end. They were his signature pair of snakeskins he had been wearing for as long as I could remember. I couldn't stop looking at them.

"Hey buddy," the coroner said, breaking me out of my distant stare. "Do you think you can help me lift the body?"

Without acknowledging him, I walked away toward the front door. I had to remove myself from the awful scene. On my way out, I noticed Terry's black satin tour jacket draped over the back of one of the dining room chairs. I don't know what came over me, but I took it. I guess I needed to keep some part of Terry.

Word of his death quickly spread. There was an official statement released to the press. CBS was notified. When the rest of the band heard about what had happened, they were equally devastated. A public funeral was held at Forest Lawn

Cemetery in Los Angeles, where television news crews and photographers lined the street. There were even some of Terry's fans who came by to give their condolences. I cried my eyes out during the service. I had lost not only a true brother on that dark night, but also a musical soul mate. How would I ever find the strength to recover?

After the ceremony, there was a get-together back at Bobby's gorgeous home in Bel Air. I glared at people making trips to the bathroom over the course of the afternoon. It was no secret what they were doing in there. Who did they think they were fooling? We had just lost one of our dear friends to the darkness of drugs, and here these people were doing blow on the day of Terry's funeral. It made me sick.

I wandered around the house in a daze until Doc Severinsen, leader of the *Tonight Show* band, walked up to me in the hallway.

"Listen to me, Danny," Doc told me. "Don't even think of stopping. You hear me? The world needs musicians like you and bands like Chicago."

I halfheartedly assured Doc I wouldn't and continued into another room.

Terry's death shook the band to its core. None of us were convinced we had the ability go on without him. But the thought of Chicago breaking up terrified me. We had come too far to let it slip away. That's not what Terry would have wanted.

We put our differences aside with Guercio for the time being and had a final band meeting at my house to talk about everything that had happened. It would be the last conversation I had with Guercio for many years. The band settled with him shortly thereafter and went our separate ways. We were emotionally and physically drained and didn't want to fight the fight any longer. It wasn't in our best interest to settle. We could have fought tooth and nail and probably squeezed millions out of Guercio, but we wanted to put everything behind us and continue on with our lives. To Jimmy's credit, he returned 80 percent of our publishing and significantly increased our royalties across the board. Unfortunately, the damage was already done.

14

Picking Up the Pieces

In the wake of Terry's death, each member of the band fell into a personal crisis as we tried to regain our bearings. As much as we hated the idea, we had to start the painful process of auditioning guitarists to take his place. It was heartbreaking. How do you replace someone who is irreplaceable?

I could hardly bring myself to go to the sessions. I sat like a robot behind my drum kit for most of the afternoon, watching guitarist after guitarist file in and out. The more we listened to them come in to play Terry's parts, the more we understood that a piece of the band's soul had been lost forever. There wasn't a musician in the world who had the ability to fill the void.

Recognizing we were struggling, Walter Yetnikoff, the president of CBS Records at the time, recommended a guitar player named Donnie Dacus. Walter believed Donnie would be a perfect fit for Chicago. He had played with Stephen Stills in the early 1970s and also had recently wrapped shooting the movie *Hair*. When the band played a handful of songs with him, including

"25 or 6 to 4" and "Dialogue," Donnie knew every note by heart. It was easy to see he had a positive attitude and was confident in his abilities. He was tremendously skilled, so he had every right to be self-assured. The one thing that stood out to me was that Donnie was one of the few musicians we auditioned who could play and sing "Little One" at the same time. He not only was a talented guitarist, songwriter, and singer who seemed to fit in well with the dynamic of the band, but was also adored by the executives at the record label. They loved that Donnie had a young image. Still, the band alone decided what guitarist fit best with Chicago.

Although Donnie had rock-star good looks, I wasn't sure that was necessarily a good thing. Our band wasn't about appearance and had never made it a priority. Although Donnie had the entire package, a large part of me was hoping to find someone with a deeper artistic side and a little less of a showman. In the end, despite any concerns we might have had, the band hired Donnie.

In many ways, the band understood that we were stepping out into the unknown, but we desperately wanted to make sure we reestablished our presence. Despite losing Terry, we believed we were still a formidable group and couldn't wait to prove it not only to our fans and the music world, but also to ourselves.

Phil Ramone was first on our list to produce for us in the studio. Over the years, the band had established a solid relationship with Phil and we were impressed with the work he did mixing many of our singles and television specials up at Caribou Ranch. Since then he had gone on to achieve success working with artists like Billy Joel and Paul Simon. Personally, I had the highest respect for Phil's talent and thought he was one of the most considerate people Chicago ever worked with in the studio. At that point in our career, Chicago needed someone nurturing and kind like Phil. I often referred to him as "the painless dentist" when we were recording because musically he could pry what he needed out of the band without all of the stress and the strain. In the late spring of 1978, the band went to Criteria Studios in Miami to record a new album together.

I once again collaborated with Hawk and contributed "The Greatest Love on Earth," a song written about my torrid love affair with Ingrid Peters. I had worked on the lyrics over the years and worked out the music with Hawk. I needed an outlet for my overflowing emotions. Peter ended up doing a soulful vocal for it in the studio.

It's a long-distance love affair
Tender are the moments that they rarely share
They hope their time will come someday
When together with the fraulein they'll steal away
It's the greatest love on earth
He's come from so far away to see
When she holds him in her arms he can feel the
    warmth
Of her gentle ways
And when she kissed him it was just like making
    music
That no one else will ever play
It's the greatest love on earth.

Part of the reason Phil suggested that Chicago record in Miami was because the Bee Gees were also in town working on their album *Spirits Having Flown*. We spent a few days hanging out with them and even got the Gibb brothers to lay down background vocals on the track "Little Miss Lovin'." The keyboard player in their band, Blue Weaver, also added synthesizer on "Show Me the Way" and "No Tell Lover." To return the favor, Walt, Jimmy, and Lee played horns on a few tracks on the Bee Gees' album, including the hit single "Too Much Heaven." I got to be good friends with Barry and Maurice and we had plenty of time to hang out in the studio together.

The Miami sessions were a welcome change of pace after years of recording up in the mountains at Caribou Ranch. The band rented mansions and took the time to check out the beauty of the Florida coastline. Phil and I were both divorced, so we became pretty tight. We each understood what the other was going through on a daily basis. When there was a break in recording, he and I even flew our children out for a long weekend and took them on a day trip to Disney World.

Recording in Miami marked the beginning of a new era. We had a new guitarist, a new producer, and new management. The band also decided to change from our traditional style of naming our records by roman numerals and came up with the proper title *Hot Streets*. Instead of simply using our logo as the cover art, we featured a photo of the entire band.

To promote the new record, Jeff Wald devised a unique way to reintroduce Chicago's new lineup to the world. He hired composer Bill Conti (famous for his theme for the movie *Rocky*) to compose an overture of all of Chicago's hits and conduct a full orchestra to play behind us at the Greek Theater in Los Angeles. Ballet dancers were also brought in to perform choreographed routines along to each song. Standing off to the side that night, everything seemed dreamlike. We were preparing to walk out and perform live for the first time without Terry. I was waiting to wake up and find it really wasn't happening. I hadn't been that nervous before a performance since our gigs opening for Janis Joplin and Jimi Hendrix and our extended stint at Carnegie Hall. After the overture finished and the dancers left the stage, everything went dark as we moved in behind our instruments. When we finally broke into Jimmy's song "Alive Again" from our new album, the crowd erupted. The song title said it all. We had risen from the ashes of Terry's tragic death.

It turned out to be an incredible performance. Once I got over the stage fright and settled into a groove, it felt incredible to have that orchestra behind us on songs like "Searchin' So Long," "If You Leave Me Now," and "Old Days." Needless to say, it was a success and a major coming-out party for our new lineup. But there was also an empty feeling in the pit of my stomach having to be up there onstage without Terry.

Even after the tragedy, cocaine was shockingly still a mainstay in the band. The guys had tried to pull back and regain control of their partying after Terry died, but it didn't happen. Drugs were the eight-hundred-pound gorilla in the room nobody wanted to talk about. As long as it wasn't interfering with the

day-to-day operations of what we were doing, there was a sense
we had to keep the Chicago machine rolling by any means necessary. Although the partying might have been excessive, it wasn't
my place to step in and make it an issue. It had become part of
the band's accepted secret lifestyle. Howard Kaufman's brother
Lester, who was still the band's business manager, even hinted that
the band had spent more money on the mansions and the cocaine
down in Miami than we did on the recording of the album. It was
ridiculous.

By the late 1970s, I had achieved wealth, fame, and power
professionally, but my private life had grown dark and depressing.
At one point, Rose and I even discussed the possibility of getting
back together again. I knew it would mean the world to my daughters, but I would only be going through the motions. Too much
time had passed between us. I was too busy leading a bachelor's existence, throwing wild barbecues at my house in Westlake, hitting the
Hollywood club scene, and running around with different women.

To celebrate my thirtieth birthday, Phil Ramone threw me a
big bash at an exclusive nightclub in New York City called Tracks.
The room was filled with supermodels, musicians, and record
industry executives. Booze. Drugs. You name it, it was there.
Although I didn't usually indulge, that night I cut loose and ended
up doing cocaine. A *lot* of cocaine. I had too much to drink and got
caught up in the spirit of the party.

The rest of the night was a blur. I emerged from my stupor at six
in the morning to find myself sitting alone in my hotel room. I could
barely breathe because my nose was caked up from the blow, and I
started getting cold sweats. My mind raced out of control. I should
have been happy with the status of my life, the mind-blowing world-
wide success of Chicago, the beautiful homes in Westlake, the cars
and the money; but I wasn't. Because I was in a popular rock band,
I never knew if women liked me for *who* I was or *what* I was. So I
always kept a side of my personality closed off to everyone around
me. It was nearly impossible to let anyone completely in.

There were some unbelievable highs in my career, but personally the pendulum had swung back hard the other way. As a result,
I tried to concentrate on the positive aspects of my music, like the

fact that our new album *Hot Streets* had gone platinum. The record proved that even without Terry the band was a force to be reckoned with. Many people had counted us out after Terry's death, so the success was validating. Chicago had stumbled along the way, but we were still standing strong. *People* magazine even featured us on its cover with the caption, "Chicago—America's classiest rock group survives a tragic death in the family." It was true. We couldn't wait to get back out on tour and show what our new lineup could do. Besides, being out on the open road would be good for all of us.

During a layover at Chicago's Hyatt Regency at O'Hare Airport, Jimmy and I hung out in the bar and struck up a conversation with two pretty stewardesses. Once I introduced myself, one of the girls shot me an odd look.

"Danny Seraphine?" she asked.

"Yes," I said. "Nice to meet you."

She narrowed her eyes at me. "You're *not* Danny Seraphine," she said.

"Well, I believe I am," I answered, smiling. Her behavior was oddly amusing. What was she talking about?

The stewardess went on to explain that a few months earlier she had met a man named Danny Seraphine while staying at a hotel airport in Cincinnati. The guy told her he was the drummer from the band Chicago and was in town for a few days. They had a few drinks together and everything seemed to be going well until he followed her up to her hotel room at the end of the night and tried to force himself on her.

"He had a beard and mustache just like you," she said. "I would never joke about something like this. I swear," she told me.

I had seen and heard some crazy things over the years on the road, but this was a new one. Was she saying I had an *impostor* running around somewhere? I chalked it up to being another random occurrence and the band left town the following day. I hoped to leave the nonsense behind, but unfortunately it wasn't going to be the last I heard of the *other* Danny Seraphine.

When Chicago played the Summit Arena in Houston, I was told that a week before I came into town a man claiming to be me showed up at a party at a local promoter's house and robbed the place blind. There were a lot of influential people at that party who were steaming mad at me. It even reached the point where Chicago's management started getting death threats on me! Terrified, I was given police escorts from the hotel to the gig and then back to the hotel after the show. Officers stood guard outside my room when I slept. Can you imagine?

A few days later when we reached Austin, a waitress at the hotel bar pulled me aside. By the sideways glare she was giving me, I already knew what was coming next.

"So, you said you're Danny Seraphine?" she asked.

She explained she had gone out on a date with a guy claiming to be me a few months earlier. At the end of the night, he parked his car on a side street and started grabbing at her. Fortunately, she got out and ran away to safety. After hearing about all these crazy sightings, I couldn't get out of Texas fast enough. It was like being trapped in a bad episode of *The Twilight Zone*.

On the Las Vegas stop of our *Hot Streets* tour, I met Tony Spilotro for dinner at one of the premier steakhouses on the Strip. We'd crossed paths on a few occasions over the years as Chicago had become successful. Tony was always hospitable and usually greeted me with outstretched arms.

"Look who we got here . . . Danny boy!" Tony said. "The kid drummer from the old neighborhood doing the big time!"

To say Tony was well connected in Vegas was quite an understatement. He practically ran the town. When I asked if he could help a friend of mine get a job as a blackjack dealer in one of the casinos, he immediately made a call for me. Pete always cautioned me about asking Tony for favors. He told me Tony would eventually want something back in return tenfold. But I didn't see any harm in what I did. It wasn't anything suspicious or illegal. Besides, Tony said it was no problem at all. I left our dinner completely at ease with my decision to reach out to him.

I didn't give it much thought after that until a month later when a phone call came late one afternoon at my home in Westlake.

An associate of Tony's was on the other end of the line. He spoke in clipped sentences and said he wanted to meet me at a coffee shop near Los Angeles International Airport. Before I could ask any questions, he hung up.

I arrived at the diner to find the guy already seated at a booth up at the front window. It was right down to business. He explained that Tony was backing a gubernatorial candidate in Nevada and wanted Chicago to play a political fund-raiser at the Aladdin Casino in the coming month.

"We're gonna put this guy in as governor," he explained.

I didn't like the sound of that. "Um, well, I would have to check with the other guys in the band and see what they think of the idea," I told him.

He shifted his weight in the booth. "Tony wants you to know he's really counting on you to get this done," he told me.

His wording made me uneasy. It sounded like more of a command than a request. There was no way the rest of the guys in the band were going to agree to perform at Tony's fund-raiser. Even though panic surged inside me, I assured Tony's guy I would get back to him as soon as possible. Now all I had to do was find some way to get out of it.

When I told Pete about my meeting with Tony's guy, he didn't have time to say I told you so. There was something more important on his mind. He explained that a reporter from the *Wall Street Journal* had contacted him. Pete said the guy was asking questions about his relationship with Tony and Michael Spilotro and some other guys from back home in Chicago.

"I don't know what the deal is, but he was on a fishing expedition. If he contacts you, I wouldn't say nothing to him," Pete told me. "He was trying to trap me on something. He's looking for anything to write about."

It was unsettling to hear that a reporter was out there asking questions. Pete's call had me worried because I was familiar with how the press twisted the truth. Not only did I have Tony to deal with; now I had this reporter to worry about as well. *What have I gotten myself into now?* I thought. Who knew what kind of story the guy was working on?

15

Making Headlines

The butterflies had been churning in my stomach since Pete told me about the phone call he had with the reporter. The possibility that a news story might be coming along at some point didn't lessen the sting. The oversized headline of the *Wall Street Journal* leapt at me from the newsstand as the band made our way through the Honolulu airport terminal in Hawaii. It was larger than life: "Are Mafia Mobsters Acquiring a Taste for the Sound of Rock? A Band Called Chicago Gets Proposition to Take Role in Night Clubs, Police Say."

My heart began pounding in my chest. The band was already burnt out after a grueling world tour of Europe, Australia, and the Far East. We didn't need any more stress and aggravation, but here it was. Without hesitating, I rushed over to the stack of *Wall Street Journal*s on the floor and grabbed one. The rest of the guys weren't far behind. Each of us flipped to the front-page story and stood in silence. Pete had been right on the money. The reporter had set out on a fishing expedition. And now I was face-to-face with what he had managed to reel in.

It began with random odds and ends, saying that major figures within organized crime, namely Tony Spilotro, had tried to parlay their relationship with Chicago into an ongoing business arrangement. It said there were "reports" I regularly met with mobsters.

It took all my strength just to swallow. The timing of the article couldn't have been worse. In the year since Terry's death, the band had fought so hard to regroup and now I had to deal with questions about being involved with the mob. I was embarrassed to have brought this on the rest of the band. Up until that point, our group was only known for our music. We didn't fall into the wild rock-star stereotype onstage or offstage. Our band didn't have publicized blowouts with each other or lead flamboyant lifestyles. So much for our "Mercedes of Rock" image. I kept hoping the article would end, but it continued for another column.

The next paragraph made note of how successful our band was: selling an average of two and a half million copies of each of the eleven records we had put out; playing sold-out venues all over the world and generating around ten million dollars a year in income. And then it touched on my relationship with Pete. It made our connection sound shady, saying it was "unclear" where we met each other. Pete and I were from the same neighborhood! The article detailed how he ran my nightclub for me. How we both had "underworld acquaintances." It brought up Pete's prior record with the cops back in Chicago. According to the story, police back home considered Pete a "close associate" of many crime bosses in the Outfit. They had taken notice of any interaction Pete had with his friends. Every meeting. Every dinner.

The story alluded to the fact that the Outfit had tried to go into business with me to open more B.Ginnings nightclubs and use them to launder money. It was ridiculous. The only reason I ever thought about putting together a chain of B.Ginnings was because I figured it would be good for the band. The article also mentioned the meeting I had at the diner near the airport with Tony's guy. They must have been tailing him.

None of it sounded good.

As each of the guys in the band finished reading the article, they shuffled away to leave me standing alone at the newsstand. I folded my copy of the paper and let it fall down to the pile on the floor.

We sent for our attorney Ken Kleinberg and arranged a band meeting back at the restaurant in our hotel in Honolulu. Walt and Jimmy in particular were worried about the possible fallout from the article. Everyone knew we had an association with Pete, but seeing it in black and white served as a rude awakening. Chicago had always been a squeaky-clean rock band and this was the first blemish on our public record. The guys were worried and seeking assurance from our attorney. Everyone wanted questions answered: Is Pete really in the Mafia? Are we liable for anything? Could they press charges?

I was confident I had done nothing against the law. The article was trying to make me out to be guilty by association. Of course, I knew guys like Tony and Michael Spilotro and Joey Lombardo were connected with crime figures back home, but as far as I was concerned Pete wasn't a member of the Outfit. My only interaction with the Spilotros was on a purely casual level. In truth, Tony had done *one* favor for me. Big deal. I certainly wasn't in business with the guy. It wasn't as if I was hiding my association. I had eaten at Tony's restaurant a few times back home in Chicago and he and I met for dinner whenever I was in Las Vegas. End of story. But it looked bad having my name in the papers alongside guys who were known to be in the Outfit.

It was unsettling for us all, but some handled it better than others. Throughout dinner with our attorney, Jimmy pounded mai tai cocktails one after another. In the middle of the discussion, he reached his threshold and suddenly puked all over the table and our attorney. Needless to say, that concluded the afternoon meeting.

As a result of the *Wall Street Journal* article, the IRS decided to audit my finances. I was now on their radar screen. They were looking for the smoking gun in order to link Pete and me together in some type of illegal activity. I stayed confident and saw the whole ordeal as only a shot in the dark to try to uncover something criminal. Even after all of their detective work, the only violation the IRS found in my records was an invalid deduction on one of my tax returns. They may not have found what they were looking for, but the entire process cost me a lot of money in penalties and fines. Still, at the end of the day, they found I had engaged in no criminal activity whatsoever.

I'll be the first to admit I brought all of the heat on myself. My business associates were impressed with my supposed affiliation with the Outfit. Having a little bit of fear in people's minds gets them to want to know you. You become mysterious. As far as the age-old question is concerned—Is it better to be feared or loved?—you need a little of both, especially in the music business. I had used the perception that I was connected for benefit and now it had come back to bite me in the ass.

The *Wall Street Journal* article had already cast Chicago in a negative light and linked the band with organized crime. The last thing we needed was to be further associated with Tony Spilotro. I still hadn't gotten back to him about Chicago playing his benefit in Nevada. When I told Jeff Wald about Tony's request, he was convinced he would be able to book a substitute act to perform in Chicago's place. I called Tony in Las Vegas personally to give him an update, but he wasn't interested in what I had to say. He interrupted me in midsentence.

"You shouldn't be calling me right now, Danny," Tony said.

"What do you mean?" I asked.

There was a long pause on Tony's end of the line and then he spoke carefully. "I can't talk about it, but I think you know what I mean."

And with that, Tony hung up and the line went dead. It was the last time I ever spoke to him. I hung up from our short phone conversation confused by his behavior. A few days later, however, everything became clear when the FBI contacted me.

"You've called in to a legal government wiretap on Anthony Spilotro's phone line, Mr. Seraphine," a voice said on the other end. "We'd like you to come down and have a conversation with us."

There wasn't anything to hide, so hiring an attorney never crossed my mind. I was determined to prove everything was on the up-and-up. When I got down to the Federal Building on Wilshire Boulevard, however, I began to reconsider my decision not to bring counsel. The FBI guys ushered me into a room and grilled me hard. Agents crowded me on either side. It was like being interrogated in stereo.

"What's your affiliation with Tony Spilotro?"

"How do you know Pete Schivarelli?"

"Are they business partners in B.Ginnings nightclub?"

"You say Tony Spilotro's a friend of yours, huh? Do you know how he made a name for himself? Tony put a guy's head in a vise until his eyes popped right out of their sockets."

They also wanted information about the political benefit at the Aladdin Casino in Vegas.

"Why would your band play a benefit for this candidate?"

"Did you know they would possibly be using monies from the Teamsters union pension fund for this event?"

The whole scene at the interrogation was scary, but what worried me more was what Spilotro and his pals would think of my contact with the FBI if word got back to them. What if they thought I was spilling my guts and saying things I shouldn't? Either way, I was in a tight spot.

As it turned out, the FBI's involvement did help give me a perfect out with Tony. I got word to his associate that the FBI was all over me. Tony wasn't going to continue to push for Chicago to play a benefit with the level of heat on everyone. The real trick was walking a fine line between not pissing off the FBI or anyone who might be associated with the Outfit. It wouldn't be wise to give either side the impression I knew too much about anything. I had heard stories about guys who knew too much. It was no secret where they ended up.

Not that I had any valuable knowledge to begin with, but I basically clammed up. I couldn't make any enemies by keeping my mouth shut. Anything I said was going to be twisted and used against me anyway. My strategy seemed to work with Tony Spilotro, but the FBI wasn't as agreeable. They wanted me to know they were always watching and continued to pop up every now and then. Everywhere I went for the next few months, it seemed an FBI agent would appear from nowhere—on my doorstep, at a restaurant, or at a mall—and start asking questions. They couldn't get over the fact that someone who knew Tony Spilotro had no hand in any of his illegal activities. But it was true.

I had dodged a real bullet. Maybe even a couple of them.

16

Out of the '70s

Although there was still three years left on Chicago's contract with Columbia, Jeff went to work trying to get us a better deal. If one thing was true about him, it was that Jeff was an aggressive negotiator—a professional ballbreaker. Even though our contract still had three years remaining on it, he started dropping hints to the label that he had spoken with Mo Ostin over at Warner Brothers and might be thinking about moving the band over there once our current arrangement was done. Jeff used the possibility of leaving as leverage to motivate Walter Yetnikoff into sweetening the deal for us at Columbia. Walter made it clear he wanted us to stay on his label for the rest of our career, especially now that we had brought his boy Donnie Dacus into the band. In his mind, Donnie was going to help lead us back to the Promised Land and Chicago would be more successful than ever.

In the end, Jeff renegotiated a whopping five-record, $28 million contract with Columbia Records. We were able to secure guaranteed advances for each upcoming album. Even Jeff was impressed with what he was able to pull off. Needless to say, it was the biggest payday I ever had.

With our new deal in place, the band again went to work with Phil Ramone and started on a new album, splitting time between recording studios in New York, Hollywood, and Montreal. The musical climate of the late 1970s had changed and Chicago's signature sound of inventive jazz-fusion seemed out of place among the current trends. Disco music was all over the *Billboard* singles charts and popular radio. At the same time, punk and new wave also started to come out of the underground scene. It wasn't really a conscious decision, but whether we liked it or not, Chicago's sophisticated style changed with the times.

During the recording sessions for the new record, *Chicago 13*, I got a phone call one day at Le Studio in Montreal.

"Hey Danny, it's Mary," a woman said on the other end of the line. "I didn't know you were going to be in town. You should have let me know."

I thought I must have really been losing it. I didn't have a clue who Mary was. Nothing she was saying made any sense.

"I have to be honest with you, Mary," I told her. "I'm not remembering where we know each other from."

"What?" she asked. "We partied together in Hawaii. How could you forget?"

Okay, Hawaii, I thought. *I spend a lot of time there*. Still nothing. I couldn't put a face with the name. "I hate to be rude, Mary, but where did we meet?" I asked.

"In Honolulu, silly," she told me. "We went out to a club."

Honolulu was a dead giveaway, because I always avoided it. I flew straight to Kauai whenever I went to Hawaii. Something wasn't right with her story, but I didn't want to get into it on the phone. I told Mary to come down for a visit at the recording studio.

When she arrived, I realized we had never met before. I wasn't the only one who was surprised. Mary was mortified when she saw I was the real Danny Seraphine. My impostor had struck again. Would I ever shake this guy? I could see the pain in her eyes as Mary told me she had been hanging out with some unknown man and even slept with him. When she showed me a photograph of the guy, he was stocky and similar-looking only because we had the same Fu Manchu mustache. Oddly, the gals in Chicago and Austin had described him as thin and strung out, nothing at all like the guy in the photo.

I told Mary to bust him if he ever tried to get in touch with her again. It freaked me out to think there was some random lunatic running around the country passing himself off as me. Once again, I hoped it would be the last I heard of her or my impostor. But I wasn't going to be that lucky. A few weeks later, Phil and I were mixing in New York when I received another call from her.

"The guy contacted me and I called him out on everything," Mary said. "He told me some crazy story about how he was an FBI agent on assignment on a covert sting operation or something."

The guy was saying he was an FBI agent? It was getting weirder and weirder. A few days later, police in Toronto contacted me. Again, my impostor had pulled his scam and robbed a home during a cocktail party. The cops said he made off with thousands of dollars in jewelry. They also mentioned that he managed to get out of Canada and fly into New York City. As soon as the plane touched down they put him in Bellevue Hospital, but later that night he escaped. At first I wondered if he might be coming after me. In a way I hoped he was, because I wanted to get my hands on him.

The cops eventually tracked him down and extradited him back to Toronto. Unfortunately, the guy's court date was set at the same time Chicago was on tour in Australia and I wasn't able to make it. That was the last time I heard about him. I would have liked to give him a beating for portraying me in such a bad light. To this day, it's unclear whether it was one guy or a couple of different guys going around impersonating me. Chicago was known more for our band logo than our faces and names, so it was all too easy to pull off something like that. But thankfully, the whole ordeal was finally over.

• • •

On the band's earlier European tour, I came up the idea of rearranging a song Hawk and I had written years back called "Street Player." Hawk had gone on to record the track with his band Rufus and Chaka Khan, but I thought it might be a great tune for Chicago. I wanted to mold it into the ultimate dance song. Rod Stewart had recently released his hit single "Do Ya Think I'm Sexy" and disco was in full swing. I intended to revise "Street Player" in the same rhythmic vein, but give it a higher level of musicianship. I talked the concept over with Phil Ramone, and he loved the idea. We planned to cut it true to the new disco style, with drum loop and everything. The lyrics I had written chronicled my time on the streets of Chicago as a young corner guy. It was basically me trying to make some sense of my childhood growing up in Chicago and making the transition into a working musician:

> I'll never forget those aimless years
> Street sounds swirling through my mind
> Trouble was often in the air
> So we fought to forget our despair
> I'm a street player
> And I'll play you a song
> 'Cause you know, my heart and soul
> Will carry, carry on
> City life's the only way
> Street corners and billiard halls was our home away
> Lessons learned still help me today
> I'm a street player
> I've seen it all
> Hit men, thieves, and many a brawl
> But as you see I still stand tall

Once again, Peter perfectly laid down the lead vocal in the studio and the song grew into a monstrous piece of music, clocking in at over nine minutes long. After giving the finished mix a listen, the record company thought the track would be perfect for Chicago's next album. It was a hot new sound for the band

and everyone felt it was going to be a smash hit on the dance charts. I was convinced it would give me an opportunity to deliver my first mainstream hit single.

But it didn't play out like we thought it would. Despite our hard work, "Street Player" came out and absolutely stiffed. To add insult to injury, it was burned along with a mountain of other disco records in Chicago at a Comiskey Park promotion called "Disco Sucks." Admission to the event was $.98 and a disco record. Fifty thousand people showed up and our album was one of the featured demolitions. By then, the disco trend was dead and buried. Chicago had missed the party. Our stylistic departure left a lot of our fans scratching their heads. In the end, we were trying to be something we weren't.

We had grown into big pop stars over the years and in some ways had trouble holding ourselves accountable for our recent lack of success. As a result, we came to the conclusion that after recording two albums with Donnie Dacus, it wasn't working out. Someone had to shoulder a majority of the blame for the lull in our career. Overall, at that time our group didn't have the patience to work out our problems. That's not to say our scrutiny of Donnie wasn't warranted, but we probably placed more importance on his shortcomings than we needed to.

However, there were red flags right out of the gate. Back at one of the first big concerts the band played with him, Donnie had put up his own T-shirt stand down in the concession area. We told him to take it down immediately, which he did, but it still left a sour taste in our mouths. Donnie was used to being a solo artist and had a different mind-set about the situation. He never fully understood why the band made him take his merchandise stand down. Chicago had always been the faceless band of devoted musicians, and it wasn't too reassuring to deal with image issues right off the bat with our new guitarist.

It was impossible on so many levels for Donnie to come in and try to fill Terry's enormous shoes. He was probably destined for failure from the start since we found it difficult to give him the support he deserved. Peter had also gotten into it with Donnie over a songwriting credit issue and had absolutely no interest in working with him after that. For the rest of us, it was an accumulation of incidents. I was nominated to make the call and deliver the bad news. Donnie insisted he would do whatever was necessary to make it work, but the band had made up our minds. It wasn't my finest moment as a human being. I was becoming colder and more calculated like the business executives I was regularly mixing with. I had the power to go back and lobby for Donnie with the band, but chose not to. What was done was done.

Getting rid of Donnie didn't do us any favors with the record company. After the chilly reception to *Chicago 13*, our relationship became even more strained. Walter Yetnikoff began taking a lot of heat within the record company. He always wanted Chicago to stay on CBS Records and he repeatedly went to bat for us. But the backlash wasn't because the album was stiffing. The main issue was that it sold around 700,000 instead of a million and a half or two million. The record was successful, just not *successful enough*, especially to justify the lucrative deal we had signed. Overall, the label was losing money on us.

Walter was furious when he found out the band had let Donnie Dacus go. CBS soon started scrambling for ways to get out of our recording deal. Back when we had negotiated our contract, Columbia wanted to include what is known as a "leaving member clause." It meant that the deal would be voided if any of the band left or were fired. When they insisted that that clause include Donnie, we said no way. Ultimately, Walter had agreed not to put it in the contract. Well, we turned around and fired Donnie without even checking with him. Bad move.

Walt, Peter, the band's attorney Ken Kleinberg, and I flew to CBS's New York offices for a meeting with the top executives. We needed to clear the air in order to get everyone back on the same page. I believed that the company realized it had gotten into a bad business deal and was trying to void our contract any way they could.

The office receptionist led us into a big conference room and we waited until Walter Yetnikoff and executives Dick Asher and Bruce Lundvall eventually joined us. Walter closed the door behind him. He always had an abrasive style, so the meeting wasn't going to be easy.

"We don't understand why you are acting this way and trying to void our deal, Walter," I told him. "Everything we did was right there in the contract. The band didn't break any clauses."

Walter looked up and made eye contact with me. "Well, frankly, I don't give a shit," he announced to the room.

I traded a quick glance with Ken Kleinberg, who looked almost as surprised as I was. Walter *didn't care* about the terms of the contract? What was he talking about?

"Why did you guys fire Donnie?" Walter asked, leaning back in his chair.

We told him that Donnie had an ego problem and there was no way of getting around it. The band had tried to make it work, but in the end it didn't happen.

"Well," Walter said, pushing back from the desk, "I think there are some people in this room that have an ego problem. A very *big* ego problem."

"Don't forget that the band has a legal, binding agreement with the record company," Ken chimed in. "And what you're doing is breaking that contract."

Walter whipped his head around and glared at Ken. "Well, too bad. Sue me!"

Walt, Peter, and I were speechless.

Walter got up from his chair. "Sue me," he repeated. "And I will enjoin your career and put an injunction against you for five years. At that time, my successor can handle it because I really don't care anymore."

The guys and I shuffled out of the New York offices with our tails between our legs. Talk about getting it with both barrels! Walter had fought hard for us in the past and deep down I knew the band had made a major mistake.

On our flight back to Los Angeles from our meeting in New York, the plane was literally struck by lightning. *Twice.* The experience was terrifying and at one point I was convinced we were going down for good. Luckily, we made it back to the West Coast in one piece, but I was still shaken by the series of events. When I got home, I wrote scathing lyrics to a song titled "Thunder and Lightning." It gave me an opportunity to vent my frustration over the situation with Walter and the record company. After all, we were only trying to do what was right for us as a band.

I took the lyrics to Bobby and Peter, who helped compose the music and come up with a structure for the tune. In the end, Bobby did a complete revision of my lyrics and changed it around to take on the feel of a love song. Instead of being about a fight between our band and Walter Yetnikoff, it turned into a lover's quarrel. I wished I'd stuck up for my writing, because after the revision the song lost its meaning and impact in my eyes. At least some of the lyrics concerning the meeting we had with the label after letting Donnie go made it through to the final cut.

In Donnie's place, we decided to bring in a skilled guitarist named Chris Pinnick to play recording sessions and live performances. Chris had played on Herb Alpert's hit single "Rise" and reminded me a lot of Terry. They had similar mannerisms and both played guitar with plenty of fire. The band went into the studio to record *Chicago XIV* with the best intentions of rebounding after the mediocre showing of our previous record. We needed to right the ship. Although we worked well with Phil Ramone, we weren't exactly lighting up the pop charts. We made the decision to go in another direction.

We were at the low point of our career creatively and commercially. Something had to happen. In Phil's place, we brought in a legendary producer named Tom Dowd, who previously worked with Eric Clapton, the Allman Brothers, Rod Stewart, and Aretha Franklin. I had the greatest respect for Tom, but I also felt we needed a stronger-willed producer to set us straight—someone who wouldn't be intimidated by our celebrity or musicianship. Tom was an amazing producer, but not the *right* producer for Chicago at that point in time.

The band tried to move on without the dance club style that influenced some of *Chicago 13*. We wanted to streamline our sound, and for the most part we were successful in doing that. But despite everyone's best efforts, *Chicago XIV* didn't fare any better. In fact, it was even worse. The record company was shocked at how bleak the sales were. Not long after its release in July 1980, it was a certified commercial flop and became the band's lowest-selling album. Although the song "Thunder and Lightning" came close, Chicago couldn't manage to notch a hit single on the charts. The record only reached No. 70 on the *Billboard* charts before fading. I was disappointed with the outcome. No matter what we did, we couldn't break out of the hole we had dug for ourselves.

It seemed like a good opportunity for the band to take a break, and I started spending more time at home in Westlake. I decided to redecorate my house and hired Laudir's sister-in-law, a beautiful girl named Teddy, to help me. We had met a few years back at a club in Hollywood just after she moved out from Chicago to get into modeling. Teddy had been married to a good singer-songwriter friend of mine, Angelo Arvonio, but they had recently separated. She had been working part-time at Bobby's boutique Zazou and interior decorating on the side. I was absolutely taken by Teddy's gorgeous blond hair and deep green eyes. When she came over to my house to look at some of the rooms, sparks started to fly. We were somewhere in between discussing paint color for the living room and deciding on carpet samples when suddenly Teddy and I were all over each other.

I fell in love with her and that was that. A sudden and powerful attraction took hold of both of us. Teddy was an intelligent and feisty woman who came from a family of seven sisters and two brothers, and spending time with her and her two-year-old daughter Ashley was a welcome change from bachelorhood. Over the past five years since Rose and I had separated, the single-guy routine had become exhausting. I desperately needed someone like Teddy in my life.

She and I developed a strong bond over the next few months and eventually I asked her and Ashley to move in with me. Shortly afterward, Rose decided to move back to Chicago with Krissy and Danielle to be closer to her family. I wasn't too happy about the move, but I understood that Rose needed to do it for herself. I had officially moved on with my life and she had done the same with hers.

When the band played Chicago, I got an unexpected call from Elsie at my room at the Ritz-Carlton. I hadn't talked to her in ages and was surprised to hear her voice on the other end of the line. She explained that our daughter, Maria, who was now sixteen, wanted to meet me. The reunion was long overdue. Over the years, my guilt had built up to the point where it turned into a major obstacle I couldn't bring myself to overcome. I ran from it rather than turn and face it head-on.

The situation was always a major source of anxiety. I struggled to come to terms with the fact that I wasn't around in Maria's life. Over time, it became more and more difficult to find the strength to take the first step and initiate contact. To make matters worse, my relationship with Elsie had always been virtually nonexistent. I wasn't going to get any help from her. Elsie stayed very bitter toward me no matter what I did. Her behavior bordered on complete hatred.

"For some reason," Elsie told me over the phone, "your daughter wants to meet you. I don't know why, but she does. If we do this, you have to promise me you will be nice to her."

"Of course I will be nice to her, Elsie. What do you think I am?" I asked. I knew exactly what she thought I was, so it was probably a stupid question.

I arranged for Elsie to bring Maria over to my hotel in downtown Chicago the next afternoon. I had mixed feelings about reconnecting with Maria. I wanted to make amends, but I had a lot to make up for and no idea where to start.

I hadn't laid eyes on Maria in years, but with her deep brown hair and dark eyes it was obvious from the moment she came into my hotel room that she was a Seraphine. It was incredible how much she looked like Danielle. Fighting back the tears, I took her in my arms and gave her a long hug. I didn't know what to say or how to act, but just being with her was a step in the right direction. I took complete responsibility for not being in her life, and I wanted to make a change for the better. I had made some mistakes, *big* mistakes, and I alone was to blame for losing contact. I finally understood how important it was that we form a relationship.

We sat together for a little while and I answered all the questions Maria had stored up over the years. There were so many issues that needed to be brought into the open and set straight between us. We couldn't get to everything at once, but this day could at least be a starting point. I felt terrible for overlooking her and carrying on with my life. But what was done was done. I promised to bring her out to California to visit and spend time with the children. At least it was a step in the right direction.

17

Into the '80s

Everything was running on all cylinders and things were only getting better for Teddy and me. In September 1981, she gave birth to a son we named J.D. Seraphine after my father, John. After three girls, I couldn't believe I finally had a son! A few months after J.D.'s arrival, Teddy and I married on New Year's Eve at my house in Westlake in front of our family and friends. It was a glorious time.

Unfortunately, just when I had gotten my personal life back on track, Chicago was going through some hard times. *Chicago XIV* was the final album the band recorded for Columbia Records. Because of poor sales, the label finally wanted out of our deal. It wasn't producer Tom Dowd's fault by any means. He inherited a dysfunctional band and the politics he had to deal with while recording the album were ridiculous. Eventually, Tom threw up his hands and left us to our own devices, and it showed in the final product. Shortly after the record came out, the company released *Chicago's Greatest Hits Volume II* (also known as

Chicago XV) and bought us out of our contract for around two million dollars.

The band's dealings with Columbia weren't the only thing that became strained over time. Our business arrangement with Jeff Wald had also run its course. Jeff had done some great things for our band, but overall it wasn't working out. He was better suited to managing single clients as opposed to groups of artists. Chicago needed a change.

Needless to say, it was yet another tenuous period. Nobody had any idea what to do or where to turn for answers. We had always had a solid working relationship with Howard Kaufman in the past, so I reached out to him about coming in to manage the band. After being let go by Guercio, Howard had gone on to do well for himself and partnered with a successful manager named Irving Azoff. Together, they were overseeing the careers of acts like the Eagles, Steely Dan, and Boz Scaggs. It was a logical choice because Howard knew Chicago inside and out. He had been with us from the early days in Hollywood and understood what made us tick. Fortunately, he and Irving agreed to represent us and we set out to get a new recording contract with a major label. After a short round of negotiations, Irving signed Chicago to a deal with his Full Moon Records imprint on Warner Brothers.

Although Chicago's career looked like it was on its way to revitalization, some of the guys' personal lives started going in the tank. Bobby had hit rock bottom and struggled to get straightened out. His performances suffered greatly because of his extensive cocaine use. His voice was shot and his playing was inconsistent—there were nights when he had trouble just putting phrasings together on the keyboard.

My frustration with the situation finally boiled over one afternoon when we had a layover in Chicago. On the way to the airport, I glared at Bobby as we sat in the back of the limousine together. Although he told me otherwise, I had the feeling he had just scored some coke. I couldn't be sure, but I wasn't going to take it anymore. As we continued down Chicago's Michigan Avenue by the lakefront, I reached my breaking point. At a stoplight, I threw the limousine's door open and jumped out in the middle of traffic.

"Who do you think you are doing that stuff, man?" I yelled at Bobby. I reached back into the car and tried to grab hold of his jacket. I wanted to drag him out of the backseat and kick his ass right there in the middle of the street.

"Take it easy, Danny," Bobby told me. He slid across the seat out of my reach. The light turned green and cars started beeping their horns at me as I stood fuming at the intersection.

My actions may have been over the top, but we couldn't let another member of the group fall victim to the dark side of the rock-and-roll lifestyle. Our group had witnessed Terry's tragic downfall and there was no way we were going to sit on our hands and watch Bobby piss it all away. We gave him an ultimatum— either he clean up his act or he was out of the band. As expected, he didn't take the news well.

"Fuck all of you, then," Bobby shot back. "I don't need this. I quit!"

He stormed out of the room. When he came back a few minutes later, he completely broke down. I empathized with Bobby because I saw what he was going through out on the road. The band was willing to do whatever it took to help him get back on track.

"I'm sorry," Bobby told us. "I love you guys and I don't know what I would do without the band."

I certainly felt the same way about him. We had been family for over thirteen years. The band hoped a trip to rehab would help get him healthy again.

Lee's low point coincided with Bobby's trouble. Since Terry passed away, Lee had struggled to get himself together. He had looked up to Terry more than anyone else in the band and as a consequence had been drifting aimlessly since his death. But Lee witnessed what was going on with Bobby on a daily basis and it inspired him also to want to make some necessary changes to get his life back on track.

On the whole, our group was on uneasy footing. As Bobby was going through his personal crisis and Lee was taking time to focus on his health, Peter made it no secret that he was becoming more and more restless with his position in the group. Not that any of us had to look hard to see it. In a magazine interview, he alluded to the fact that he wished another band—he might have even said the Eagles—would offer him a job. He had started work on a solo album and seemed to be putting all of his attention into his personal projects. He recorded and released a self-titled solo album, which sank like a stone due to lack of record company support. Warner Brothers wasn't interested in promoting the record because they didn't want it to interfere with their plans for Chicago.

The castle was crumbling before my eyes. I hadn't come this far to see everything fall away and disintegrate into nothing. No matter what the odds, Chicago had to march on.

Despite the grueling amount of work involved to get our band back to where we needed to be, I still found the time to produce side projects once in a while. During one recording session, I came across a gifted singer named Bill Champlin. I had brought him in to lay down backing vocals with Peter on a demo I was putting together. From the moment Bill started singing, his vocal chops blew me away. His voice blended beautifully with Peter's. Bill had a diverse range and a low-end tone the band had been desperately missing since we lost Terry. The gears began turning in my head.

"What if we brought Bill in to lay down some vocals on the next album?" I asked the band. If there was an area where we were a little weak at the time, it was on R&B-style vocals. Bill was also a talented keyboard player, so he might also be able to add some dimension and support to Bobby's playing as well. The rest of the guys agreed we should give it a try.

To make room for Bill, something had to change. Since our music was becoming more pop-oriented, the band decided our journey with Laudir had run its course. We were evolving, but it was a shame to have to let him go. The group needed to streamline not only our sound, but also our lineup. It was a difficult situation, since Laudir and I had played a lot of good years together and grown very close, but the band felt we had to make room for Bill.

With our new lineup in place, Chicago needed a strong presence in the studio on our next album, someone who could give us a real kick in the ass. I had the perfect candidate in mind—a very talented songwriter, musician, and producer named David Foster. David had achieved great success and notoriety playing alongside legends like John Lennon, Rod Stewart, and Diana Ross and produced big acts such as Sonny and Cher and Earth, Wind and Fire. I had wanted to bring him in to do *Chicago XIV*, but the rest of the band and record company had voted it down. This time around the guys were more receptive to the idea of having David produce. He was a huge fan of our early material and I had a feeling he would give us a new sense of confidence we had been desperately lacking.

Our commercial appeal was dwindling and we needed to find a way to regain our audience's confidence. Everyone was convinced that David was the ideal person for the job, but as we ventured into the studio, the band began getting messages back from the marketing department at Warner Brothers, who were always our main line of communication with the programmers at the radio stations. The word was that singles with horns were a thing of the past. Radio wouldn't play any of the material. The feedback confused me. After all, we were a horn band! We always had been. It hadn't hurt us before, so why would it now?

To his credit, David helped us see there were other avenues for our music to explore. He breathed life into our songwriting and changed our signature sound to adapt to what was going on in the 1980s. David collaborated with many of the guys in the band, particularly Peter, and brought a fresh perspective and energy. He incorporated outside musicians, bringing in David Paich and Steve Lukather from Toto to write and add dimension to some of the tracks, such as the song "Waiting for You to Decide." David wasn't only there as a producer, he was a collaborator and fellow musician. He related to us on a different level than any producer the band worked with since Jimmy Guercio.

Peter bonded with David especially well because musically they shared a great deal in common. At the time, they both leaned toward adult contemporary ballads, which were becoming known as "power ballads." Their work on the single "Hard to Say

I'm Sorry" was groundbreaking. When we brought the rough mix in to Howard and Irving, they were both knocked out by it.

"That is a number one song," Irving told us. "I will guarantee it."

He couldn't have been more on the money. "Hard to Say I'm Sorry" rocketed up the charts and became our second No. 1 single in the United States. The album found its way into the Top 10. Up until then, everyone—and I mean *everyone*—thought Chicago was dead and buried. But nothing could have been further from the truth. After hitting the wall, we had rebounded once again. This was our *third* comeback. We had more lives than a cat.

David Foster deserved all the credit in the world for inspiring us. He was a joy to work with in the studio and went above and beyond the band's expectations. We might have been wandering further and further away from our jazz-fusion roots, but we were also expanding our horizons as musicians. With David's help, we opened the band up to a younger generation of fans. Together, we achieved everything we set out to do with *Chicago 16*.

While the band was in the studio working on the album, Bobby was able to find the help he needed and get healthy. Even though he barely played a lick on the record, he was paid a complete royalty and received a full credit. Some people might have wondered if it was justified, but in my mind there was no question. Bobby deserved it for all the years he had carried the band on his back with his songwriting. In the end, he came back from his stint in rehab a changed man and requested that everyone call him Robert from that day on. In my opinion, he earned that right. The old Bobby was gone and the new Robert was here to stay.

Together we set back out on the road and continued to sell out the larger venues across the country, especially arenas and civic centers. It was obvious that a major shift had taken place within Chicago's fan base. Our unbelievable commercial success added a new diversity to our shows. Suddenly, teenage girls rushed the stage screaming Peter's name. It was like a flashback to the late sixties. On any given night, I looked out over the crowd from behind my drum kit and saw couples in their forties enjoying our music as much as couples in their teens or early twenties. There were actually *teenyboppers* at our shows!

The soaring popularity of the singles changed Peter's mind about leaving the band to pursue a solo career. Besides, the success of his songs pushed him to the forefront of Chicago anyway. The once faceless band now had a distinct face. None of us had been ready for it, including Peter. His songs were showcased during our shows because they were the big hits of the time. His identity became the band's identity and there was no stopping it.

Everything aside, it was satisfying to be back on top again. Chicago had literally risen from the dead. After Terry's passing, we had struggled to find our footing over the course of *Hot Streets* and *Chicago 13* and regain our confidence. It had been a hard road, but we had made it through to the other side. A lot of credit had to be given to Howard and Irving for coming through in the clutch. Irving followed through and delivered on every promise he made. He insisted he would get our music played on the radio, and did he ever! You couldn't turn on a rock radio station in the summer of 1982 without hearing "Hard to Say I'm Sorry" or "Love Me Tomorrow." Irving also promised he would never put the band out on the road simply to get a commission for himself. He and Howard made money when the band made money. It was an even and balanced business situation.

The checks were larger than ever. As a result, I finally decided to build a house on my beachfront property in Hawaii. It had always been a place where Teddy and the kids loved to spend time. The neighborhood was full of celebrities like famous tennis player Billie Jean King, Glenn Frey from the Eagles, and Graham Nash from Crosby, Stills and Nash, to name a few. You never knew who you might bump into while you were walking along the beach. Billie Jean King's husband, Larry, even let us use their tennis court whenever we wanted to. Teddy and the kids loved the house. I flew Krissy and Danielle out from Chicago as often as possible so we could spend time together. It was an ideal setting.

When Teddy got pregnant again, I had our management schedule her due date in with the band's obligations. We blocked out a two-week period so it wouldn't interfere with Chicago's touring. Since J.D.'s birth had gone off without a hitch, I figured it would be the same this time around. Well, think again.

All seemed to be going as planned until Teddy's due date came and went. After she saw her doctor, he told us it could take up to another *two weeks* for the baby to arrive. Either way, I wasn't going to be able to join the band on the first few dates of our upcoming tour, so I was forced to bring in the well-known session drummer Carlos Vega to fill in. I gave the band the green light to leave without me.

The next morning, I was stunned when Teddy said she was ready.

"But what about the two weeks like the doctor said?" I asked her.

"I know when this baby's coming!" she yelled.

I helped her into the car and we rushed to the hospital in Westlake. Once I got Teddy settled on a hospital bed with a nurse, I wanted to go back out to get my video camera. We both wanted to document the birth just as we had for J.D.'s.

"I'll be right back," I told the nurse. "I need to go down to my car."

"You better run," she said. "This baby is *here*."

I sprinted down the hallway and back out to the car. I grabbed my video camera and raced back up the elevator. After washing my hands, I put on a mask and ran into the delivery room. Moments later, I realized I wasn't getting enough oxygen through the mask. Suddenly the room started spinning and I collapsed to the floor. I looked up to see Teddy peering over the side of the birthing chair looking down at me.

"Are you okay?" she asked.

"Yeah, I think so," I answered, staring up at her. "Make sure you push, honey," I weakly added.

I remained sitting on the floor as my baby daughter was born. I finally managed to pick myself up and hold her for the first time. Teddy and I decided to name her Taryn—Irish for "Earth Angel."

As usual, I had to leave the next day to meet up with the band on tour. It was such a sudden shift in plans that Carlos Vega didn't end up playing a single gig.

• • •

After Chicago's recent spike in success, we found we were having trouble pinning David down to produce our follow-up record. His popularity had exploded and he was in high demand within the music industry. Everyone wanted to hire him and his magic touch. In my opinion, David lost sight of what we had accomplished together and put the band on the back burner in order to focus on some of his other projects. I didn't keep my feelings a secret. We had made a ridiculously popular record together and suddenly he was too busy to return my calls? Some of it may have been my own general paranoia, but I genuinely felt slighted. Still, despite the friction, David finally agreed to produce our next album.

Not long before the band was to go into the studio, Teddy was diagnosed with what the doctors believed were the early stages of Hodgkin's disease. It was a complete surprise to both of us because there were no obvious symptoms. One of the doctors actually told her she might have *ten years* left to live if she was lucky. They said she needed to be put on medication and strongly suggested she take six weeks off to rest.

Teddy agreed on the recovery time, but had no interest in taking the medicine they prescribed for her. Being strong-minded and spiritual, she decided to pursue other homeopathic options and completely changed her diet—no more sugar, caffeine, salt, or alcohol. Teddy was determined to rely on meditation and healing herbs to improve her health. She left the children with me in Westlake and flew out to our house in Hawaii with her sister to begin the rehabilitation process.

I put in a call to David and told him about Teddy's health issues. I asked if it would be possible to hold off recording my drum parts for a week to give me an opportunity to fly out to Hawaii to support Teddy. David was understanding and said it shouldn't be a problem as long as I was back in a week or two to begin work. I told him to cut the tracks with a drum machine and then I would overdub the parts when I got back into town.

Leaving the kids with family at my house in Westlake, I flew out to Hawaii to be with Teddy. Fortunately, the rest and relaxation did her a lot of good, and in no time, her health improved tremendously. It was a relief for both of us. Ten days later, I left

Hawaii in good spirits and returned to Los Angeles. I couldn't wait to join in on the recording sessions with the band, but on my first night back in town, I got a late phone call from my buddy Hawk.

"I heard through the grapevine Jeff Porcaro is playing drums on your new record," he said. "What's going on?"

I didn't have an answer for him because it was news to me. Maybe Hawk had heard it wrong and gotten confused. At least I hoped that was the case.

The next morning I drove down to the Record Plant in Hollywood to find out what was going on. When I got there, the band was listening to a playback of a song called "Stay the Night." Hawk had heard it right. It was Jeff's drumming on the tape.

None of the guys looked too happy to see me. David's sound engineer, Umberto, met me at the door full of excuses. He insisted that David had tried to contact me to let me know they were bringing Jeff in on drums. David said he needed him because Jeff had an early set of Simmons electronic drums they wanted to incorporate into a few songs.

Did he think I was going to buy something like that?

Everyone had left me out of the loop, and I was livid. The incident came at an especially bad time in my life when there was a possibility that Teddy could have cancer. Why would David do something like that to me? Band problems were the last thing I needed. My stress and anxiety over Teddy's condition were overwhelming me, and on top of that I now had to deal with people in the band pulling shit behind my back. The rest of the guys couldn't understand my anger. David had brought in other musicians to record guitar and piano parts in the past, but in my mind this was different. Although there had been percussionists, no other drummer had ever played on a Chicago song or album.

I put my anger aside long enough to sit down behind my drum kit, but I was too distracted to concentrate on the music. My playing was all over the place and it was difficult to keep in time. The harder I tried, the worse it became. From my drum stool, I saw David frowning back at me behind the glass of the control room and discussing something with Umberto. I could only imagine what he was saying:

Jeez, what's wrong with Danny? He's lost it.

David had started incorporating electronic drum machines into the songs, and it totally threw me off. He insisted that I play along to a click track in order to stay in time. I couldn't make it work no matter how hard I tried. I'd been playing drums since I was eight years old and had never played to a click track. It was turning into a nightmare.

I called Howard later that night. "This guy is fucking with my livelihood," I shouted into the phone. "Does he know I wouldn't think twice about coming down there with a baseball bat and breaking his legs?"

The pressure was causing me to crack. I channeled all of my anxiety over Teddy's health issues into my conflict with David. Howard was taken aback by my outburst, but told me he would have a conversation with David to straighten everything out.

Whether he said it as a joke or not, Peter actually told David to be careful with me, because I'd had guys *killed* before! Can you believe it? It must have been Peter's attempt at dark humor, but David didn't take it that way. He freaked out and locked me out of the studio the next day. After his initial panic, we eventually were able to talk it out and put our differences aside. We decided he would go easy on me and I would give the click track another try.

The real problem was that my confidence in my abilities was shot. I was desperate and had no idea how to pull off any of the drum parts. I turned to our sound engineer, Umberto, for help. The band still needed drums on the song "You're the Inspiration," so we scheduled time in the studio with only the two of us so I could concentrate and lay down the track once and for all.

I went in with a positive attitude, but everything quickly deteriorated and I got caught up on the same timing issues. The song had a bass drum pattern I couldn't pull off for some reason. I literally dropped down on my knees behind my kit and tried to play the part on the pedals with my hands. It was the height of my musical humiliation. Even Umberto was embarrassed for me.

"Come on, Danny," he told me. "Get up, man."

It was a full-blown musical breakdown. In the past I could have played the parts in my sleep. The band ended up having to bring in Carlos Vega to play on "You're the Inspiration." It was a weird feeling not to be able to perform up to the best of my abilities. My mind and body were misfiring.

18

Peter Goes Solo

When *Chicago 17* was released in the spring of 1984, it shot up the charts and even outperformed *16*. Peter was at the top of his game and sang lead vocals on all four of the singles we released: "Hard Habit to Break," "You're the Inspiration," "Stay the Night," and "Along Comes a Woman." Every one of them was a radio hit and in many ways locked us in as an adult contemporary "ballad band."

The record redefined what we had considered as successful and went on to sell over *six million* copies. After everything we had gone through in our career, we were bigger than ever. Not only was Chicago still playing the massive venues like Madison Square Garden in New York City and the Great Western Forum in Los Angeles, but we were selling the places out for consecutive nights at a time.

With Peter continually assuming the lead vocal duties on our biggest hits, the disconnection between him and the band widened over time. When we held a meeting to talk about putting together an extensive world tour, Peter was the only one not in favor. He had hit the wall and was suffering from major burnout. Being the stubborn and persistent Virgo, I went to work on him. In many ways, I understood how to communicate with Peter better than anyone in the group. After all, I was the one who had worn him down early in our career and convinced him to join the band in the first place. I explained that we had made money in the past, but this was *seven-figure* money we were talking about.

And it was true. Peter's songs were up and down the *Billboard* charts. Once he saw the projected numbers in black and white, he came around. Everyone knew it was too good of a deal to pass up. The idea was to strike while the iron was hot. And we were absolutely smoking.

Peter reluctantly agreed to the world tour and additional dates, but he needed something in return—a double share in Chicago's business. From the beginning, Chicago had operated as a democracy, but that was beginning to change. Aside from songwriting royalties, we had always split everything equally. Peter was wielding a new sense of power and became frustrated by all the bureaucracy. Not that I didn't see his point, but I didn't necessarily like it. Peter got an attorney and began negotiating a new arrangement with Howard. Because of the business dealings, the distance between Peter and the band was at an all-time high. He also mentioned that he wanted to record another solo album before doing the proposed hundred tour dates. We insisted that he do the shows and *then* record his next solo album. The back-and-forth between our two sides continued and we weren't getting any closer to a compromise. We were at a stalemate.

During the break in touring, I took the opportunity to get some much-needed rest and relaxation with my family. My daughter Danielle had been acting up and giving Rose a hard time back in Chicago, so we decided that she move in with Teddy and me for a while out in Westlake. Now that she was older, being with Danielle on a day-to-day basis was like looking into a mirror. Krissy had her mother's calm demeanor, but Danielle inherited my fiery Italian temper, so we constantly butted heads. Her stubbornness brought out the worst in me. The new living arrangement wasn't easy on any of us, but at least I was helping lighten the burden on Rose. She had come to her wits' end.

My idea of home was where Teddy and my children were. I wished they could have been out on tour with me more, but Teddy was never too thrilled about that idea. I always wanted her to meet me out on the road with the kids so we could be together, but she had a different take on it.

"I'm not going to drag the kids around and sit in hotels all day while you have your band meetings and play shows," Teddy told me.

What I didn't take into account was that their concept of home was a place where friends and family were there to support them. It didn't have anything to do with planes, hotels, and concerts. The situation was hard on all of us, but we tried to do the best we could to make it work.

During the break in our schedule, I took the family out to the house in Hawaii for a short vacation. I got back from a jog on the beach one afternoon to find the phone ringing. Peter was on the other end of the line. We hadn't seen each other in a while, so it was good to hear from him. We both knew the negotiations between Howard and his attorney were at a standstill. Initially, I thought Peter might have been reaching out to me to put my mind at ease over the situation, but as our conversation continued, I wasn't so sure. "You know, Danny," Peter said, "we've been through so much together over the years. I care for you and your family and want to say that I hold you in the highest regard. I've always considered you one of my best friends."

"Thanks, Peter," I said slowly. I didn't know what to make of his demeanor.

"Listen, no matter what happens in the end, I don't want you to overreact," Peter told me. The seriousness in his voice was unnerving. Whenever someone mentioned "don't overreact" in a conversation, there was usually something coming up that I was going to overreact to.

"Of course, Peter," I said.

And with that our awkward call came to an end. I walked out onto the back porch of the house scratching my head. What had gotten into him?

The questions didn't linger in my mind long. When I switched on the television the next morning, the news ticker on the bottom of the screen caught my eye: "Peter Cetera announces his departure from the band Chicago."

Peter held a news conference to let everyone know he was leaving the band to pursue a solo career. I sat in silence staring at the television set. Peter and I had known each other for eighteen years and it broke my heart that he couldn't take the time to explain his decision to me. His odd behavior on the phone should have tipped me off, but I still expected more from him. Not long after the press conference, he tried to call me a couple of times, but my anger prevented me from speaking to him. I bad-mouthed him at every opportunity. Much of the band did the same thing.

We had finally climbed back to the top of the mountain, and now we had just had lost what everyone was calling the "voice" of Chicago. How could we replace someone like Peter? I wasn't convinced we had another comeback left in us. We had overcome so much as a group over the years and part of me wondered if it was the end of the line. Any other band would have buckled and called it quits. But none of us were ready to pack it in yet.

Once again we were forced to try to replace someone who was irreplaceable. We made offers to Mickey Thomas from the band Starship and Richard Page from Mr. Mister, but they both turned us down. Then the president of Warner Brothers, Lenny Waronker, suggested we consider a young, twenty-three-year old bassist and singer named Jason Scheff. Lenny sent us a demo tape of Jason's material and we liked what we heard. When we auditioned him, we noticed that Jason had the uncanny ability to sound very similar to Peter. They shared the same inflection and vocal range. Although the band was convinced that Jason would be a good fit, David Foster wasn't nearly as certain and had other singers in mind . . . that is, until I started working on him. Sure, Jason suffered from some pitch problems, but that wasn't any reason to cast him aside. He was the best option the band had for Peter's replacement. To David's credit, he gave it a try, and together with Umberto he worked to help Jason develop.

In retrospect, we should have treated the situation with Peter the way Genesis handled their dealings with Phil Collins. We could have scheduled in breaks for Chicago to allow Peter the opportunity to go do his solo albums and tours. But things didn't go that way. What was done was done. None of us were strangers to overcoming adversity, and Peter's departure was yet another opportunity for Chicago to show what we were made of. Although Robert still handled vocal duties now and then, the band relied on our two newest members, Bill and Jason, to carry the bulk of the singing.

As a result of the chart-topping success we achieved with David Foster, we decided to collaborate once again and went back into the studio to record the follow-up to *Chicago 17*. The band was coming off of our most successful record, so we had a tall order ahead of us.

At that time in the mid-1980s, electronics had all but taken over in the studio. Playing had been replaced by programming, especially with the drum arrangements. There was an overall feeling among many producers and studio techs that drummers were becoming obsolete. If they didn't like what you were playing, they would simply cut you out of the loop and perform it electronically on their own. Producers loved drum machines because they played in perfect time and didn't have the ability to talk back. Like most drummers of the time, I was intimidated by them and reluctant to embrace them in the studio. But it was no use putting up a fight. I grew tired of banging heads with David over the same drum issues. In the end, I figured if you can't beat 'em, join 'em.

I couldn't stand hearing songs on the radio with drum parts programmed by a keyboard player. Damned if I was going to let someone else arrange drum parts on Chicago's records. From the beginning, the drums were my job and would always be my responsibility. To educate myself, I purchased an E-mu SP-12 drum machine sampler and learned it inside and out. In the process of exploring the new technology, I came up with an elaborate setup of digital drum pads. It was necessary to make sure that anything done in the studio could be played live in concert. My acoustic drum set grew to incorporate electronic pads and triggers to deliver the new sound. Now I not only had to be a plumber, but also an electrician to set up my kit. In the end, I went on to program all of the drum parts on *Chicago 18* and David was satisfied with how they turned out.

Peter had also been busy in the studio. He put out his second solo effort, *Solitude/Solitaire*, in the early summer of 1986, and we weren't able to get our album out until the early fall. The late showing really hurt us. *Chicago 18* was lost in the wake of Peter's record. His single "Glory of Love" from the *Karate Kid II* soundtrack tore up the charts while our album clunked along looking for airplay. Our previous album had gone platinum six times over, and the new record, despite the success of the single "Will You Still Love Me?" only managed to reach No. 35 on the *Billboard* pop charts.

Peter's solo success with *Solitude/Solitaire* overshadowed Chicago's album. In fact, a case could be made that it swallowed us whole. The band was still successful, but we slipped down a few notches in overall popularity. Because of his huge success and the chilly reception to our album, I was even more pissed at Peter.

Late one night, I was watching the evening news when a breaking news report came on. A black-and-white photograph of Tony Spilotro flashed onto the television screen. I hadn't had any contact with Tony for quite a while and his mug shot photo was a little jarring. The reporter started his voice-over:

> The bodies of reputed mob figure Anthony "Tony the Ant" Spilotro and his younger brother Michael Spilotro were found in a Newton County, Indiana, cornfield today. Police say the two brothers were beaten to death and placed in a shallow grave clad only in their underwear. So far, police say nobody has been charged with the murders.

It made me sick to my stomach to find out someone I had known was murdered in such a brutal way, but Tony existed in a different world than the rest of us. He and his brother associated with a violent and unforgiving breed. I had always heard that Tony was notorious for pissing people off and getting under their skin. I guess his wild ways finally caught up with him. (Little did I know that he would one day be the inspiration for Joe Pesci's character Nicky Santoro in the Martin Scorsese movie *Casino*). It's like they say: you live by the sword, you die by the sword. And that is exactly how Tony and his brother Michael went out. Still, there was a part of me that felt sad for them.

After all I had gone through in life, those days back in Chicago seemed so long ago. Everything was much more complicated now. At one time our band was a tight brotherhood that could do no wrong. But all of a sudden our new lineup were still getting to know each other and trying to do something, *anything* right. Jason Scheff and I clicked from the start. I found him easygoing and likable, and we grew close over a short period of time out on the road. Bill Champlin, on the other hand, wasn't the easiest guy to get along with. He may have been a talented singer and musician, but I found him to also be overly insecure and abrasive. He had a horn band in the seventies called the Sons of Champlin that never managed to take off, and it seemed like Bill held on to some jealousy of Chicago over the years. It was as if he was bitter that our band had made it and his had not. He and I clashed much more often than we saw eye to eye. Over time, he started making comments here and there about my drumming, which really got under my skin. He said I constantly overplayed and that he wasn't crazy about my style. There was no way I was going to sit back and take it. I was the one who brought him into the band in the first place. Who was he to criticize?

"Well, don't talk to me about overplaying until you stop over-singing," I told him. He used to oversing the shit out of "Colour My World" every night and it drove me nuts. It was as if Bill was trying to cram every vocal lick and run he knew into one song. As time went on, he proved to be surprisingly controlling. To be honest, we were very much alike in some respects. But where we differed was that Bill was not the type of person who would do things simply for the good of the band. He did things for his own benefit, and I had never operated that way. The group always came first with me.

Whether I was still the elected head of the band or not, I continued to take charge of the day-to-day duties of a leader. Whenever anybody wanted to talk business with the band, even our own management, they came to me first. It was just the way things worked.

One tremendous positive change in the band was that the guys were putting a lot of effort into maintaining their sobriety. On many nights out on the road, I came back from the hotel gym to find them on their way out to an Alcoholics Anonymous meeting. I'd pinch myself sometimes and wonder, *Is this really our band? What is going on?* Back in the day, everyone would have been hiding out in their rooms getting high and staying out till all hours of the night. But now they were determined to concentrate on their personal health and well-being. I never thought I would see the day. Despite any distance that may have been developing among some of us, I still thought Chicago was playing as tight as ever and putting on great performances.

Jimmy Guercio at
Caribou Ranch

Clowning around with Jimmy
at Caribou Ranch studio

New B.Ginnings

With Pete Schivarelli in Rome in 1976

With Howard
Kaufman on tour
in England in 1977

Howard Kaufman and Pete Schivarelli at Westminster Abbey in 1977

With Danielle and Krissy at the Caribou Ranch

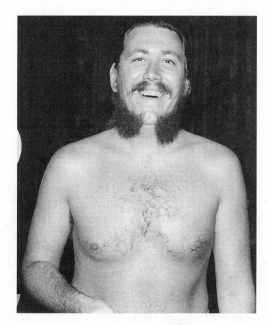

Terry healthy and happy during a pool party at my house in Encino

My birthday party in 1979: (left to right) Hawk, Marty Derek, Pete Schivarelli, Angelo Arvonio, me, John "J.R." Robinson, and Lee Loughnane and his son Bryan (front)

Double-bass drum action on the *Chicago 13* tour

Performing with
Laudir de Oliveira

My daughter
Maria

At a fund-raiser for the Terry Kath scholarship fund in 1982: (left to right) me, Robert, Marty, Lee, Walt, and Jimmy

I made quite a fashion statement covering up my hair transplant scars

With Hawk entertaining the troops at Le Studio in Montreal, Canada

On tour in Europe
in the '80s

On top of the world during the band's third comeback in 1988

The *Chicago 16* "Hard to Say I'm Sorry" comeback

With my young son,
J.D., in Hawaii

It was always comforting spending time with Mom and Dad in Colorado

The proud papa with Danielle and Krissy at Krissy's wedding

Daddy with his little girl Taryn

J.D. growing up
in Evergreen

With my
daughter
Ashley

Today I'm back where I belong

19

The Hairpiece That Saved
My Life

Image has always been an important part of the entertainment industry. Not that Chicago relied that much on our appearance over the course of our career—if anything we purposely leaned away from pushing an overall look. The only image we promoted was of our recognizable band logo. Aside from that, we let our talents do the talking. That being said, Chicago was constantly in the public eye and appearance had an effect on how many people thought of us as a group. There was no getting around it.

My hair had been thinning since I was in my early twenties, but over the years I tried everything possible to fight it. My decision to get a perm at one point back in the seventies to look like Jimi Hendrix didn't do me any favors. The procedure burned the hell out of my scalp. I had a respectable Afro for about two seconds before the hair on the front of my head started falling out.

I had been putting it off for years, but my baldness couldn't be ignored any longer. I started feeling tremendously self-conscious about my appearance. Though I tried every method of concealing my hair loss, nothing worked. Nobody was going to be fooled by the traditional comb-over technique. Hats were always an option, but they got annoying after a while. Since the band was the center of attention wherever we went, there was even more stress involved. There were appearances on press tours, photo shoots, and nightly performances in front of packed houses. The world was watching, and whether I liked it or not, I had an image to protect as I grew older.

One of the most sensible options was hair transplantation, so at one point I tracked down the top Beverly Hills doctor and started the procedure. At first it looked like the process was going to work, but as I continued to lose hair in other areas on my head, the transplanted strands started to look out of place. The other guys in the band occasionally ribbed me about my hair, joking that I looked like a human Ken doll. To tell you the truth, I couldn't disagree with them. It wasn't a pretty sight.

I always needed to wear something while out on tour to cover up the scars left by the hair transplantation process. When I went without anything on my head, there were a lot of odd looks from people since my scalp was heavily rutted from the surgery. Back in the seventies, I took to wearing a turban, of all things. It may have seemed like an odd choice, but it went well with my Fu Manchu mustache. Besides, we all were entertaining some pretty wild fashions in those days. My turban seemed to fit right in.

After I realized the hair transplants didn't work, the only option left was investing in a quality hairpiece. *Who has the best hairpiece in Hollywood?* I asked myself. To me, the obvious answer was Burt Reynolds. I consulted my good friend Marty Derek, a hairdresser in Los Angeles, and he was able to refer me to Burt's hairpiece maker, a guy named John Evans.

When I reached out to John, he insisted I come down to his shop. He assured me he had exactly what I was looking for. His clients entered through one door of his hair salon and exited out another in the back of the building. It was like going to an appointment at a psychiatrist's office. The whole process was very discreet because nobody in Hollywood wanted the word to get out that they wore a hairpiece. It was as if I was becoming a member of a protected Hollywood society. Everyone wanted to be sure their secret was safe.

John made two hairpieces for me so there would always be one to wear while the other was being cleaned. My jaw hit the floor when I found out the things cost *seven hundred dollars* apiece! It was a tough pill to swallow, but if they were going to be the answer to my hair dilemma I didn't have a problem parting with the cash. I routinely left the hairpieces at the back desk of John's salon like I was dropping off my weekly dry cleaning.

At first I was relieved, because the hairpieces looked wonderful. People began telling me I looked ten years younger. But my new accessories came with a powerful weight of narcissism. I couldn't walk by a mirror, or any other reflective surface, without stopping to check myself out. My appearance may have improved, but psychologically nothing had changed. My anxiety was at an all-time high. Once I made the decision to wear a piece, I was a slave to it day in and day out. I couldn't go out and be seen with a full head of hair in the morning and then be bald in the afternoon. I was horrified to let anyone see me without my hairpiece.

It took a ridiculous amount of effort to keep up the charade. I kept the hairpieces on plastic styling heads, which I lugged around in large storage cases whenever Chicago was out on the road. It was a hassle dragging them through airports and into hotels. Every time room service came to my door, I scrambled to stash the plastic styling heads out of sight in the bathroom or hide them in the back of the bedroom closet. Quite a workout.

The hairpieces may have been doing the trick overall, but the situation was a joke on so many levels. Most of the time, I wished I had never started wearing the things in the first place. But once I committed there was no changing my mind. I was stuck.

Since our prior run with the Beach Boys had been so successful, we did another package tour together in the fall of 1988. We put on some great shows, but some of the outdoor venues proved to be tough. Playing out in the elements didn't always make for our best performances.

I certainly experienced a "wardrobe malfunction" or two along the way. Anyone who has ever worn a hairpiece will tell you that, above all, *the wind is your worst enemy*. In the pecking order of toupee hazards, it comes right before exposure to water and crazed lovers wanting to run their fingers through your hair. Typically, double-sided tape was enough to hold my hairpiece down, but on a few rare occasions I had to break out super-strength glue. It was supposed to be made especially for use on skin, but it was a real pain in the ass to remove. At the end of the day, I had to use acetone on my scalp to get the damned thing off.

I wasn't too happy when I found out we were set to play an outdoor show at a racetrack in Nebraska. The weather forecast said there were going to be gale-force winds and terrible thunderstorms. Once we got to the venue, outside Omaha, our management sent word that the storms were going to be on top of us before we knew it. They wanted both bands to do short sets, then get off the stage. In other words, take the money and run.

The Beach Boys hurried through their performance and left. By the time Chicago was halfway through our first song, the weather was atrocious. Darker storm clouds rolled in and the wind began violently whipping around. The stacks of sound columns teetered back and forth, threatening to collapse at any minute. Our stage crew did their best to keep them steady, but the gusts were becoming too strong. The rows of lights above swayed precariously over our heads, clanging against the supporting trusses.

I looked out over the faces of the crowd as they held anything over their heads for protection against the driving rain. The skies had opened up and it was a full-on downpour. Thunder clapped and lightning flashed over the audience.

Suddenly I felt a fluttering sensation coming from the front of my scalp. Earlier that day, I had decided to go with the tape and not the glue. Well, the double-sided tape was beginning to lose its hold and detach from my hairpiece. An almost debilitating fear came over me. I tried to throw a hand up to my head during a drum fill to press the tape back down, but I couldn't do it. I tried a second time, but still didn't solve the problem.

Alert the control tower, I thought. *My beloved hairpiece is preparing for takeoff.*

It got to the point where I was basically playing drums one-handed with the other hand holding my hair in place. I envisioned the nightmare of my hairpiece flying off of my head in slow motion and being carried out into the audience by the wind. I imagined the stunned faces of the crowd, people pointing up as it hovered overhead. I could hear someone asking, "What the hell is that up there?" right before it was whisked away by a burst of wind and disappeared up into the storm clouds.

I couldn't deal with it anymore. Right in the middle of "Saturday in the Park," I suddenly put my drumsticks down, stood up from my stool, and jogged off the stage. Without hesitation, the other guys turned and trotted off after me. Apparently we were on the same wavelength, but nobody wanted to be the first one to make a move. What a relief. We hopped on our tour bus and barely made it out of the racetrack, because there was zero visibility.

The next morning, we found out from our stage crew that most of our equipment had been destroyed by the storm. Even worse, a few minutes after I left one of the lighting trusses came loose and collapsed onto my drum set, completely crushing it.

I never once was concerned about my safety. The only thing I cared about was how embarrassed I would have been to have my hair go flying off into the air. I wasn't mature enough to realize that I should have just been who I really was. There aren't many things in my life I regret, but deciding to become a slave to those things is definitely one of them.

Thinking back, I should have framed the hairpiece I wore that day and hung it up on a wall somewhere with the caption, "The hairpiece that saved my life." Thank God I wasn't still sitting at my drums when the lights fell. Without a doubt, it would have been the last show I ever played.

20

The Beginning of the End

There was a phrase I heard my buddy Pete Schivarelli utter many times over the years: "Lose your head and your ass will follow." I never put much thought to it, but eventually I understood how right he was.

On the last leg of our tour with the Beach Boys, I invited my mother; my sister, Rosemary; my niece, Colleen; and my two nephews, Michael and Bryan, to a gig the band played at Notre Dame University in South Bend, Indiana. My son, J.D., was out on tour with me for a few dates as well, so it was a nice opportunity for all of us to spend time together. Typically, friends and family were ushered into the backstage area of the venues in the time between the final song of the set and the encore. My family stood off to the side of the stage watching the band wind down our performance for the night.

When we had finished the show, I walked backstage to towel off and was confronted by our stage manager, Jimmy J. Together, he and Jack always made sure everything went smoothly at our shows, but on this night he looked concerned. I noticed he had trouble holding eye contact with me.

"What's wrong?" I asked him.

"I had a little misunderstanding with your family, but I straightened it out and everything is cool," he told me. There was no reason for me to think everything *wasn't* all right, so I left it at that.

When I came out of the dressing room to say hello to my family, my mom's face was flushed with color and I could see she was upset. She was already talking to me before I reached her.

"How dare that man speak to us that way!" she said.

"Wait, Ma. Slow down," I told her.

She went on to tell me that Jimmy J. had run up like a maniac to where they were standing during the last song. For some reason, he swore at them and demanded to know not only who they were, but also what they were doing on the side of the stage. When my mom explained they were with me, Jimmy J. told them to get out of the way and find some other place to stand. Scared by the commotion, my young niece, Colleen, started to wander away. My mother said Jimmy J. grabbed Colleen by the arm and yanked her in the direction he wanted her to go.

"How were we supposed to know where to stand? He doesn't have to swear at us like that, Danny!" my mother concluded.

I had regained my breath after our performance, but I sensed my heart rate steadily increasing again. There had to be a logical explanation for what had happened, but my mother was talking so fast that I had trouble understanding the details. However, soon it didn't matter to me anymore. My sense of reasoning went out the window the moment she lifted my little niece's sleeve and showed me her arm. There were dark, blotchy red marks from where Jimmy J. had grabbed ahold of her.

"I need to take care of something," I calmly said to my mom. "I'll be right back."

Without another word, I tore off to find Jimmy J. How dare he manhandle my young niece? Someone said he was in the main dressing room with the rest of the band, so I made a bee line through the crowd. I was overcome with uncontrollable rage. Although I knew what was going to happen, I couldn't do anything to avoid it. I flew in through the dressing room door and absolutely unloaded. I grabbed him by the hair and started punching him in the face. I did everything I could to inflict pain. By the time the guys pulled me away, Jimmy J.'s shirt was torn to shreds and there was blood coming out of his nose and ears. Everyone in the room looked on in complete shock. The band knew a violent side of me existed, but they had never been around to see it rear its ugly head. When I realized the scene I had made, I backpedaled sheepishly from the room.

I rode in silence to the airport with my young son, J.D., and boarded the flight that was to take us to the next leg of our tour. I brought him into the front of the plane and tried my best to keep out of sight. It was important to give everyone a chance to relax and calm down.

A long table was set up in the middle of the plane with a full spread of food for everyone during the flight. After the rest of the guys had run through the line, I made my way up to grab a couple of sandwiches for my son and me. A sinking feeling set in the moment I noticed Jack approaching. It wasn't as if we had ever been the best of buddies on the road. There had always been an undercurrent of animosity between us, but we had learned to live with it. It wasn't a problem keeping my dislike for him beneath the surface because our time with one another was usually limited to touring.

Given what had gone down backstage earlier, Jack should have left everything alone. I hoped he was going to fix himself a plate of food and go back to hang out with the others. If there was something he wanted to say, he could have vented somewhere else. But Jack was set on confronting me then and there.

"You know, Danny, Jimmy J. didn't curse at your mother," he suddenly piped up. "I saw the whole thing and he didn't say anything like that."

Our eyes met. "After eighteen years together, you're going to stand there and tell me to my face that my mom's a liar?"

"I was right there, and it didn't happen that way," Jack answered.

He was starting to piss me off. "Why are you sticking up for someone who's been with the band for two seconds?" I asked.

Apparently Jack was convinced I was going to swing on him, because all of a sudden he lunged forward and sucker-punched me. His fist felt like a sledgehammer, and I thought I might have broken my jaw.

"You wanna throw hands with me? Then come on!" Jack yelled.

The rest of the band must have heard the commotion from the lounge, because when I lunged for Jack, Lee and Robert were already there to grab me.

"You've done enough damage for today," Robert told me. "Go out back and cool out."

"What is it with you fucking guys?" I shouted at everyone. "Don't you ever back anybody up?"

After Jack and I were separated from each other, I spent the rest of the flight in the back with J.D. There was no excuse for violence, but Jack had taunted me at a time when he should have let it go and avoided a confrontation. He had worked for the band for eighteen years, and in my mind he should have known better. Why did he have to go and push my buttons?

The band gave me the deluxe silent treatment for the last ten days of the tour. It was like I was invisible. They blamed me for everything that happened that day backstage and on the airplane. Meanwhile, Jack didn't take heat from anyone. Overall, I felt a deep and painful sense of betrayal. How dare Jimmy J manhandle my young niece and treat my family like that? Who was Jack to call my mom a liar? What had happened to the tight-knit brotherhood of our band? Nobody had taken my side or tried to console me during any of it.

I attempted to explain the situation to J.D., but it was difficult. He knew I was troubled and upset. "What's wrong, Daddy?" he kept asking me for the rest of the tour. I didn't have a good answer for him.

Not long after we arrived back in Los Angeles, the band called for a meeting at my house. We needed to drag everything out into the open in order to move on in the right direction. They were just as worried about what had happened.

"Are you okay, Danny?" Walt asked me. "The guys and I are concerned."

"What's going on with you?" Lee added.

I wasn't going to let the conversation center around me. There were other issues on my mind. I sat down at the table and explained that Jimmy J. had to be let go. There was no way he was ever going to have any connection with the band again. They didn't like what I was telling them, but none of the guys had a problem with it. Aside from that issue, there was one more thing to get off my chest. I cleared my throat and took a deep breath.

"I'm sorry, guys, but Jack has to go too," I said. "There's no way around it."

The guys' faces dropped. There was no way they saw a bomb like that coming. Sure, Jack had been with the band since the beginning, but there was no excuse for him to sucker-punch me. I had already talked the whole matter over with Howard and he had agreed to back me in my push to get rid of Jack. In principle, there was no way we could let an employee, no matter how valued, hit a member of the band and still keep his job. The guys knew it was the right thing to do, but they didn't like being put on the spot. They were shell-shocked and sat around my kitchen table trading glances for what seemed like forever. Walt was especially stunned because Jack was his brother-in-law—it wasn't only a business decision for him. He would have to answer to his wife. Everyone pleaded with me to reconsider, but I couldn't bring myself to do it. Hindsight being twenty-twenty, I should have given Jack another chance, but in that moment I was determined to make a power play on someone who had over the years gotten on my bad side. I saw my shot and I took it. In the end, the guys reluctantly agreed and we handed Jack his walking papers.

As the guys filed out of the room, I saw Bill turn to Jason and mutter something along the lines of, "I guess violence got its way today." Not that I cared. I had gotten what I wanted.

Six months after the band fired Jack, we received some bad news. We were told he had suffered a major heart attack and died. Nobody came right out and said anything, but I got the feeling some of them placed a large part of the blame for his passing on me. Some people, particularly his sister Jackie, believed being fired from the group had brought a high level of stress and anxiety into his life. Apparently they disregarded the fact that Jack, who was in his early forties, wasn't exactly in the best of shape. He was a type A personality who often drank to excess and constantly smoked cigarettes. That being said, some of the resentment was warranted. I never argued that the firing didn't add more stress and strain on his life, but it was heavy-handed to place a large part of the blame on me for his passing. Because of his family's bitterness, they wouldn't allow me to attend Jack's funeral service. No matter what had gone down between us, Jack and I had known each other for twenty years. I should have at least been given a chance to pay him my final respects.

All of the other issues aside, the real question was: after falling short with *Chicago 18*, did our band have what it took to climb to the summit one last time? Our recent lack of success didn't give us the motivation to continue working with David Foster. I was grateful to him for giving us back our self-respect, but it was time for both sides to move on.

One night, I was talking to my buddy Hawk on the phone when he mentioned that Peter and his producer Pat Leonard had decided to take a few months off from recording the much-anticipated follow-up to *Solitude/Solitaire*. A lightbulb went off in my head and I called a band meeting to plot our next move. I thought we should write, record, and release a new album before Peter was able to put his together. We had six weeks to get into the studio and get it done. I didn't want to let Peter beat us to the punch again. I saw it as a golden opportunity, but the rest of the band weren't as eager to spring into action and took some convincing from Howard and me.

Howard suggested we bring in outside talent to help with the band's songwriting. He recommended Diane Warren, who was one of the hottest writers on the scene, and producer Ron Nevison, who had a great deal of success working with the band Heart. Diane wrote the first two singles, "I Don't Want to Live Without

Your Love" and "Look Away," and Ron ended up coproducing the album with Chas Sanford.

Ron was a hard-ass in the studio, but an *effective* hard-ass. He understood what needed to be done and pushed the band to deliver. Chas, on the other hand, was more of a feel-good, positive-vibe type of producer. He let me reestablish my confidence in my abilities in the studio and I played drums on the entire album.

Walt, Jimmy, Robert, and Lee weren't as thrilled with the recording process. Toward the end of our studio sessions, they called a band meeting to vent their frustrations with *Chicago 19*'s final song list. The guys actually wanted to take the songs Diane Warren had contributed off the record. I wasn't thrilled about the idea, and Bill didn't like it either. He had sung lead vocals on both tracks and considered them his first real moments to shine in the band. Ron and I had fought for him to sing on those tracks. The songs were definite hit singles and there was no way we could let them be pulled. Bill's voice gave us a departure away from the Peter Cetera sound. It was going to be the new direction for our band. Walt, Robert, Jimmy, and Lee's real beef had to do with the fact that there weren't any horns on either of the songs. I understood how they felt, but those songs were essential to having a commercially successful album. Though the guys eventually gave in, I could sense a deep resentment developing. Maybe I had pushed it too far, but we needed hits to get Chicago's career back where it should be.

As a whole, the record showcased Bill's vocal talents. He sang lead on three of *Chicago 19*'s singles. "Look Away" went on to become a number one hit, while "I Don't Want to Live Without Your Love" and "You're Not Alone" broke into the Top 10. The album went platinum and had five Top 10 singles.

Once again, we had fought our way back tooth and nail. Who would have believed a group would be able to recover from the loss of talents like Terry Kath and Peter Cetera and come out on top? The record proved once again that the band was the true star—not one particular member, not one manager, and not one individual producer. Despite the infighting and lineup changes, we always found a way to make it work. And in my mind, that is what great bands are able to do.

21

Bad Moves

Gradually, Pete Schivarelli worked his way into a business relationship with the band. When Howard got busy with other projects, he needed someone to help him with the day-to-day operations of Chicago. Although Pete had gained a good deal of music industry experience managing B.Ginnings for me, his solid personal relationship with the guys in the band, especially me, was what made him Howard's first choice. So Pete was offered a partnership to help manage us.

I had mixed emotions about the decision to bring Pete in. We had been close friends since back in the early days, but I never envisioned him as Chicago's manager. As much as I loved Pete and trusted him (after all, I named him godfather to my son J.D.), I wasn't sure what effect it would have on our relationship.

At the time, I was going through a personal awakening of sorts. As the 1980s came to a close, I reached a point where I was consumed by guilt and anxiety as a result of my running around with groupies on the road. I had stayed faithful to Teddy for the first two years of our relationship, but eventually old habits crept back in. They had exerted a strong hold on me for years and I was finally sick of the charade. It was another situation between Teddy and me where if we didn't talk about it, it wasn't happening.

It was time to get out of Los Angeles and rededicate myself to my marriage and my children. I needed to grow up and concentrate on my role as a father and a husband. Besides, life in Los Angeles was getting strange and unsettling. There were nightly news reports of stabbings, shootings, and gang violence everywhere. It was too similar to the life I had left behind on the streets of Chicago, and I had no intention of allowing my young ones to grow up in such a dangerous environment. My plan was to do another five years with Chicago and then retire. It was time to set that idea into motion.

Over the years, I had enjoyed the time spent up at Caribou Ranch in Colorado experiencing the peacefulness of nature and the overwhelming beauty of the Rocky Mountains. I'd also taken up skiing and fallen in love with the lifestyle, so I couldn't think of a better place to relocate. Teddy wasn't as interested in the idea, and I had to work hard to convince her it was the right choice for our relationship and our family. After we considered locations like Telluride, Aspen, and Steamboat, a few friends recommended the town of Evergreen. It was a stone's throw from Denver, so I had access to a major airport to fly out of whenever I needed to. It seemed like the perfect fit.

When I approached the band, they gave me their blessings and supported me completely. But Howard had a different perspective on the situation.

"I'm not sure why you're doing this, Danny," Howard told me. "It's going to be the three-million-dollar move."

My guess is there were already rumblings from within the band and this was his way of warning me. Maybe I should have listened more closely to what he was saying, but I forged ahead anyway.

In the late summer of 1989, Teddy, the kids, and I packed everything up and moved to the beautiful town of Evergreen, Colorado. We spent the fall enjoying the outdoors—hiking, mountain biking—and I took up the beautiful sport of fly-fishing. Being out in nature with my kids was a welcome change of pace from the hustle and bustle of Los Angeles.

After some quality time off to adjust to my new life, the band and I began putting together a plan to record our next album. To warm up, we scheduled a batch of upcoming tour dates, booking gigs at the world's largest rodeo in the Houston Astrodome and also a show at Mardi Gras in New Orleans. We were set to be the co–grand marshals that year with actor John Goodman.

I needed a few weeks to shake off the rust, so I called in to our management's office in Los Angeles to schedule rehearsal time with the band. After the long layoff, it was going to be hard work on my part in order to be ready for our gigs. A few days later, I got a strange phone call back from Bill, who said the band had decided they wanted to go ahead and rehearse without drums.

"*Without* drums?" I repeated.

"We just want to go over vocals and horns for a while and drums will get in the way," he told me.

The whole thing sounded odd, but I tried to put my suspicions aside. I figured I could woodshed the material on my own and play along to the live tapes of our music. I continued with my practicing, but something about what Bill said didn't sit right. I had never gotten ready independently from the band before an upcoming tour, so why would I now? It was like a football player practicing without full contact before the season started. What was going to happen when I got out onstage and was face-to-face with a live audience?

There was an uneasy feeling the moment I met up with the rest of the guys at our hotel in Houston a few weeks later. It was the first time I ever felt like a complete outsider in my own band. The guys were distant when I joined them for breakfast on the first morning. Before long, they each got up one by one and excused themselves from the table. I suddenly glanced up and found myself eating alone.

The trip didn't get any better as the day wore on. I was in trouble the second we hit the enormous stage at the Houston

Astrodome in Texas. For starters, the sound was awful and I had trouble hearing in my monitors what the guys were playing. And just like I feared, my chops weren't in game shape. The hours spent practicing on my own for the show didn't do a thing. The band was out of step and the responsibility rested on my shoulders.

After the inconsistent performance, we went back to the hotel to listen to the playback of our show in one of the rooms. Once again, the rest of the guys eventually excused themselves and I was left sitting alone. I couldn't tell if they were pissed or just not interested in hearing the tapes. None of them gave me any indication.

Even though we played better at our next show at Mardi Gras in New Orleans, there wasn't much time to talk it over. Teddy flew out from Los Angeles to meet me and we jumped on the Concorde to travel to our next gig in England. When Chicago performed at the Hammersmith Odeon in London, I was unbelievably jet-lagged. My drumming chops were even worse than at the Astrodome. On the whole, our band was downright awful.

After the show, Teddy had an interesting take on the weak performance. She knew things weren't right. "I don't know, Danny," she said. "It's like when you stay at a party too long. All the ashtrays are full, the drinks are empty, and the smart people are long gone."

Teddy always told it straight, and in many ways she was right. Terry had left us way too early. We had parted ways with Jimmy Guercio. Peter had set off on a solo career.

"I watched the entire show tonight," Teddy continued. "It was like eight individuals onstage playing the same song, but there was no band in sight." It wasn't only because of my playing. All of us were on a different page. A distance was setting in that never used to be there.

Later that night, Teddy pulled me aside and told me the other wives were beginning to whisper about my playing. They were asking what was wrong with my tempos and alluding to how I was "all over the place." Being in a band, you know that if the wives are discussing something, the husbands are *definitely* talking about it. My playing was made the main topic of conversations. The guys wouldn't let it go. It allowed them to lay the responsibility on me and take the focus off of them. Not that they weren't partly right. My playing was truly out of synch.

I should have made an effort to stay in and rest at the hotel each night to get my strength back, but I felt obligated to spend time with Teddy and accompany her sightseeing in between shows. I was constantly on the go and never regained enough focus on my playing. My performance was slightly better at our gig in Ireland, but I was never able to get back on track.

As soon as we returned to the States, I put a call in to Howard. There was no overlooking that something was wrong. I desperately wanted to get to the bottom of what was going on behind my back. When Howard finally got around to returning my call, he had some disturbing news that only validated my fears.

"Listen, the band feels you take too long to record and decided they want to use a studio drummer on the next album," Howard said.

A studio drummer? Who did they think they were dealing with? I played on every track of our last record, which had gone on to sell over a million and a half copies!

"What the hell is going on?" I asked him. "They're trying to push me out of the band, aren't they, Howard?"

"No, Danny. Don't overreact," he told me. His tone made it seem like I was the one being unreasonable. "I promise you. That's not going to happen. Your royalties will remain the same and you'll still be listed as the drummer in the credits."

"This is complete bullshit. There's something more to all of this," I hissed into the phone before hanging up.

Deep down, I figured they knew what I meant to the band. They understood what went on behind the scenes day to day. Sure, I could be difficult to deal with, but I was also a major driving force in Chicago and an original member. Who had the foresight to recognize Bill's talents and bring him into the band? Who had supported Jason and pushed everyone to give him a second chance at taking Peter's place? Who had brought in Howard and Irving Azoff to manage us? For perhaps the first time, I understood why Peter had left the band.

That's not to say I wasn't suffering from major burnout. I occupied myself with the business side of being in Chicago twenty-four hours a day, seven days a week. The band came before everything else that was precious and dear to me in my life. Everything I did, I did for the group. I had carried the load for long enough and it finally caught up with me. Maybe my playing wasn't up to par for the European tour, but was I performing any worse than Robert when he had reached his lowest point years earlier? Or Jimmy when he had gone off the rails and hit rock bottom with his drinking? The same thing went for Walt. All of us had struggled at one time or another. Now that it was my turn, they were casting me aside.

I jumped on a flight to Los Angeles and went down to the recording studio where the band had already begun rehearsing with a new drummer named John Keane. I was done getting my information secondhand through Howard. We sat down in the control room and the band let me have a few minutes to speak my mind.

"I don't understand," I told the guys around the table. "We just notched five top-selling singles. I played on every one of them."

Jason cleared his throat. "Yeah, we talked about that, Danny. But we think the success was in spite of your playing," he told me.

I shot him an incredulous look. I wanted to slap him. His words tore at my insides, but I wasn't going to give him the satisfaction of acknowledging his statement. I stared down at the floor and shook my head in disgust.

"We just want the old Danny back, man," Jimmy sincerely said after the silence. "You've gotten too deep into the business side of things and your mind isn't on the music anymore."

I took his words to heart and mulled them over. Maybe I had overstepped some of my bounds and gotten too involved in the business issues. In all honesty, it was only because I was looking out for our best interests and trying to protect us from ever falling into a poor business agreement again. Nobody wanted history to repeat itself.

No matter what I said, the band was going to do the album without me. The guys wanted me to rededicate myself to my playing and come back with a new outlook. Walt went a step further and called me on the phone a few weeks later.

"Look man," he said. "I want to put your mind at ease. Do you remember that oath we took at my house back in 1967?"

His question brought back some good memories. I thought of the six of us sitting around that kitchen table in his mother's house talking about the vision we had of the band and the things we wanted to accomplish. I remembered Terry sitting next to me at the table. God, I missed him so much. I also thought back to Peter and me driving through the Mayfair parking lot stealing those Christmas trees. What a scene. Who would have ever thought in their wildest dreams that we would have made it this far?

A smile found its way on to my face. "Yeah," I answered. "I remember that oath, Walt."

"Well, it still stands true for me," he said. "We're not trying to fire you or push you out."

I appreciated Walt's honesty. The band's feedback was a wake-up call to straighten out my priorities, and I was man enough to take my medicine. It was time to get my playing back in shape and come back as strong as ever.

I returned to Evergreen and started practicing with a well-known local jazz drummer named Bart Mann. During the next six weeks, Bart and I put in long hours out in my garage. By the middle of the following month, my chops were at an all-time high. My technique might have been different, but I looked at myself as similar to an aging pitcher who'd lost his fastball, but replaced it with a wicked slider. I even called Howard one afternoon to tell him how great my playing was sounding.

It was decided I would rejoin the band for a corporate gig for Shearson Lehman Hutton at the Phoenician Hotel in Phoenix. Unfortunately, my return was not as celebratory as I had imagined. Again, the guys didn't seem happy to see me. But I was determined to let my playing speak for itself. I had worked too hard woodshedding in Colorado to let anything get me down. At the soundcheck, my drum tech Mike Murphy was impressed with how much I had improved since he last heard me.

"You sound better than ever, man!" Mike told me between songs. "Your timing is great and your chops are blazing!"

The vibe backstage before the show was bizarre and awkward. There was the feeling that everyone was whispering behind my back. The guys passed a headset back and forth as they listened to the new tracks the band was working on in the recording studio. Not one of them offered me the headphones. They gave them to Pete before me!

This is my band? I asked myself. *Where did it go wrong?*

Despite the band's treatment of me before the show, I played my ass off that night. All of the guys commented that I sounded great and how good it was to have me back, even Jason. But after returning home to Colorado, I was still overcome with anxiety. I had an awful feeling about my status in Chicago. Everything felt like it was slipping away and there was nothing I could do to stop it. My fears were further fueled by a late-night call from Pete a few days later.

"Something's going on," he explained. "The other guys, Jason and Bill, were talking on the plane back to Los Angeles. I didn't hear what was being said, but they're up to something."

I figured Pete had my back, but I still hadn't felt as helpless in a long time. It killed me to know there were people scheming against me two thousand miles away and I didn't have a voice in the matter. All I could do was hope for the best.

Mother's Day in 1990 is a day I will never forget as long as I live. I spent the weekend with my family at my brother-in-law Graham's house in Denver. Later in the afternoon, I got an unexpected call from Howard. He sounded very shaken up.

"I feel really awful about having to do this to you, Danny, but I have some bad news," Howard said. "Without my knowledge, the guys got together and held a meeting."

Howard let out an extended sigh. I knew what was coming next.

"They voted you out of the band, Danny."

The world came to a complete stop. I let my hand holding the receiver fall away from my face and stared vacantly at my joyful relatives standing in the room. They immediately knew something was wrong and got quiet. I gradually brought the phone back up.

"What?" is all I managed to ask.

"You have to believe me when I tell you this is the last thing I wanted, but the guys got together and made the decision. There was nothing I could do about it. It happened behind my back," Howard explained. "I am so, so sorry, Danny. We both know this has nothing to do with your playing."

So this is it? I devoted my entire life to Chicago and this is how they repaid me? A phone call from Howard?

My shock was soon replaced by anger. "Are you saying you didn't know any of this was happening?" I yelled.

"I am telling you the truth," Howard answered. "The whole thing is as much of a shock to me as it is to you."

"I find that hard to believe, Howard," I said quietly.

Around the room, my family stood around watching me. I leaned back against the wall and blankly looked up at the ceiling.

When I recovered from the shock of Howard's call, I dialed Walt's number. Jason and Bill had probably engineered my whole firing, but the other guys in the band would have still had to vote in favor of getting rid of me.

"What the fuck happened, Walt?" I yelled as soon as he answered the phone. "So much for our oath, huh?"

"I'm sorry, Danny, but things changed," he told me. "I feel really bad, but there was nothing I could do."

I hung up before he said another disgusting word. The Walt Parazaider I knew wasn't on the other end of the line. It wasn't the same guy I had played with since I was sixteen years old. What was the use of staying on the phone and listening to him harp on the same tired excuse that my playing had slipped? The end result was still going to be the same. I was out.

Part of me wondered whether Walt's wife, Jackie, had prodded him into his decision because she always held me responsible for her brother Jack's death. In my heart, I couldn't truly believe that Walt wanted to fire me, because there was too much history between us. Over the years, we had our differences, but there was always a deep sense of love and respect. Sure, Walt didn't like that I was responsible for getting Jack fired. But did he also blame me for Jack's death? I suppose it is a possibility, but I don't think it's true.

My phone call with Jimmy was an absolute joke. He sat on the other end of the line and tried to rationalize the band's decision. Jimmy explained that everything had come as a result of my poor playing and shaky live performances. Was my playing worse than his when he was on a drinking bender? Not a chance. But Jimmy didn't want to hear any of what I had to say. He had no idea that I had saved him from getting thrown off our last tour and being put into rehab. Jimmy's drinking and partying had gotten way out of hand and the guys were disgusted with his antics. I had stood them down because I knew Jimmy's father was about to have major surgery. Being booted from Chicago at that point in his life would have killed him. In the end, I thought he would stand behind me, but I was wrong.

By the time Robert got in touch with me, I was sick and tired of everyone's double-talk and petty excuses.

"Do you want to know how it all really went down?" he asked me.

"You know what? It doesn't matter," I told him. "Why don't you go fuck yourself! You guys are a bunch of chickenshit motherfuckers!"

I slammed the phone down and went out onto my porch to take in some fresh air. To this day, I regret not letting Robert speak. He was trying to be honest with me, but I refused to listen. I felt sick to my stomach. It was the worst scenario I could have imagined.

And where had Pete been when all of this went down behind the scenes? Trying to understand his role in the situation left me scratching my head. Pete and Howard always insisted that the other members got together and made the decision to fire me without their knowledge, but that explanation didn't sit right. It was tough to believe that Pete had no idea what was going on. He prided himself on having eyes in the back of his head. Needless to say, our relationship would never be the same.

As I wallowed around the house in Evergreen, I received an interesting envelope in the mail one day. It was a legal document announcing a Chicago Corporation board meeting in two weeks to make my firing official. By law, Chicago was obligated to notify me of the proceedings.

"You should go back there and make each and every one of those guys look you right in the eye," Teddy told me.

I agreed with her. There was no way I was going to miss out on a chance to confront the band face-to-face. It was important to make sure they knew what I thought about the gutless way they had fired me. I flew out to California for the meeting at a law office in West L.A. I wanted to be the first face the guys saw when they walked in, so I arrived early and carefully snuck past the receptionist and into the conference room. Then I sat down and waited. As the band filed in, they looked like they had seen a ghost. Their jaws nearly hit the floor. They probably weren't sure that I would take the time to fly out to Los Angeles and attend the meeting. When Lester Kaufman walked in with two of the band's attorneys, he wore the same expression.

I asked to have a minute alone with the band. Once Lester and the attorneys left the room, I closed the door and sat back down at the table. One by one, I looked Walt, Robert, and Lee dead in the eye. Jimmy turned out to be a no-show.

"Did you ever, in your wildest dreams, imagine it would come to this?" I asked them. "What did I do that was so bad?"

There was a silent moment before Robert spoke up. "Listen, Danny, you lost your focus," he told me.

"I lost my focus?" I repeated. "Did I lose my focus any more than you when you were so strung out on coke you could barely play?"

Then I looked at Lee. "Any more than you when you were drinking yourself into an early grave?"

And then Walt. "Any more than when you lost your mind and had to be put into a psychiatric ward?"

The silence in the room was broken when Lee finally spoke up. "Well, this isn't about us, it's about you," he said.

What a bunch of hypocrites. I had said my piece and was done talking. It was obvious nothing would ever change in their minds. The time came to finally put forth the official vote, so Lester and the attorneys came back into the room.

Lester stood up at the head of the table. "All those in favor of Daniel Seraphine remaining as drummer in the band Chicago, raise your hand," he said.

I raised my hand.

"Duly counted," Lester said. "All those in favor of dissolving Daniel Seraphine's association with the band Chicago, raise your hand."

When Walt, Robert, and Lee raised their hands, I glared at them from across the table.

Lester turned toward me. "Could you please excuse us, Danny? The band has pending business matters to attend to."

Without a word, I got up from my seat and walked out of the conference room. I left the building with my head held high. I wanted those guys to look me dead in the eye when they pulled the trigger. And they certainly did.

22

Evergreen Daze

A tornado had just torn through my life and left behind a wake of utter destruction. For the first time since I was sixteen, I was without a band and scrambling to find shelter from the harsh reality that was setting in.

I couldn't keep it together and sank like a stone into a deep depression. The life had been sucked out of me and it was difficult to find the strength to get out of bed in the morning. Even therapy had no effect on my state of mind. Not that I gave it a chance. I went to an appointment or two, but shut down once things became too painful.

Luckily, my family and a few good friends were around to support me. I flew my parents out to Colorado regularly to visit and spend time with their grandchildren. Sometimes they stayed at my house for months at a clip. My mother was having health problems, so I had an elevator installed to help her get around. I was grateful that my relationship with my parents improved as we got older. Despite what had happened throughout my teen years, my father and I were finally able to develop a deep love and understanding of each other. He was always there to talk things out with me.

One afternoon, we were out driving along a backwoods road not far from my house. "You know," he said looking out the passenger-side window at the rays of sun pushing through the trees. "It should have been so perfect."

His statement rang true. I had moved my family to a beautiful area in Colorado and should have been enjoying the fruits of my labor during the twilight of my career. Instead, everything had imploded. Many people say that when one door closes in life many more open, but that couldn't have been further from the truth in my case. Every one of them had closed at once. Most of the friends I thought I had in the music business soon disappeared and my phone stopped ringing.

My father understood what I was going through and saw how dissatisfied I was with the way everything had turned out. My identity, my heart, and my soul were directly tied to Chicago. Over the years, I had fought for the band tooth and nail. I would have done anything for the guys. Chicago came before everything in my life—my wife, my children, and at times my own well-being. In the end, maybe that intense devotion was my downfall, but it was the only way I knew how to operate. As far as I was concerned, it was all or nothing.

My dealings with the band weren't completely over. Walt called me one day to try to settle some of the lingering business issues. He wanted to know if I would be willing to sell my rights to the Chicago name for $200,000. I was so insulted I hung up on him. They were offering me a paltry settlement for my entire life's work. Not a chance. I hired an attorney named Mike Rosenfeld and filed a lawsuit against the band.

I halfheartedly opened a small recording studio under my Street Sense Productions moniker in a space in downtown Evergreen and tried to develop local talent. But nothing ever came of it. I was going through the motions, trying to sort through the pieces of my broken life.

After almost a year, Teddy had finally reached the end of her rope. We had been drifting away from each other for years, and now that I was out of the band and at home the distance was painfully obvious. One night she told me that our marriage was over and I needed to move out. I don't blame her for leaving me and wanting a divorce, but the timing couldn't have been worse. I was already hanging on by a thread and her leaving put me over the edge. For the first time in my life, I was convinced it was the end of everything. The bottom of my world had dropped out. My band was gone and my wife was leaving and taking the kids.

In the beginning, I had moved out to Colorado to start a new life. Boy, I had started a new life all right!

My lawsuit against Chicago proved to be ridiculously expensive. The courts froze all of my band royalties. The guys were trying to wait it out and starve me off. Once they caught wind that Teddy was seeking a divorce, they seized the opportunity to come after me with another settlement offer. I didn't want to budge, because they had a tough case to build. I was a founding member of the band and held a full share in the corporation we created. They would have to prove that my playing had fallen off so drastically in the end that it was impossible for Chicago to continue performing. No matter what they claimed, that obviously wasn't the case.

As time wore on, however, I lost the will to continue the fight with the band and with my wife. I was tired, depressed, and wanted everything to be over and done with. The stress and the financial strain of fighting a war on two fronts was overwhelming.

Over the course of the process, I regretted my choice. I discovered I had hired the wrong attorney to help me with my legal fight. I repeatedly asked him to track down the contracts that detailed when Chicago's recording masters would revert to the band, but for some reason Mike never found them. The masters were the most important issue because I understood how valuable they were going to be in the future. I decided to take the case into my own hands and directly negotiated with Howard to reach a settlement.

"I don't want to give up my rights to those masters, Howard," I told him over the phone.

"Well, Sony's never going to let those masters go," he quickly answered. "So consider that a nonissue and let's not make them a deal breaker."

I thought of Howard as a close friend and believed what he was telling me. He knew what kind of state my life was in. Besides advising me on the settlement, he even offered to help me get back into the music business to start managing and producing bands. It was a small consolation, but I certainly had no interest in playing drums anymore. That part of my life was over.

In the end, I reluctantly agreed to settle with the band and flew out to Los Angeles to put an end to the madness. I met Mike at a café in Santa Monica to sign the papers.

I was officially out.

It may have been legally over, but the pain had just begun.

What is left to live for? I wondered to myself.

I considered anything that would cure my heartache—even suicide. It seemed like I had already been left for dead by everyone who knew me, so what was the difference?

When a buddy of mine from back in my time living in Westlake, Bill Denton, called from California to check up on me, I was inconsolable.

"Listen to me carefully," I told him. "Don't *ever* let me get married again."

Bill was there for me in a real period of crisis. He was doing a real estate project in downtown Denver at the time and visited me whenever he could. I was a wreck and Bill gave me his unconditional support every step of the way.

After Teddy and I settled our divorce, she decided to stay in Evergreen for a while so I could be close to the children. Good friends of mine, Kit and Beverly Bradshaw, lent me a pop-top trailer that I moved into on forty acres of land I had purchased from the Coors family, on top of a nearby mountain. Originally, I had bought the lot in hopes of one day building a large house with a full recording studio similar to Caribou Ranch, but that dream was a thing of the past. I retreated up into the woods into an area called Soda Creek and kept to myself. Although there had never been much religion in my life, I started saying a Hail Mary and an Our Father whenever I felt down and out. I must have said thousands of them.

I became, for all intents and purposes, a hermit. My beard grew long and I wore the same clothes for days on end. I no longer had an important image to uphold. There were no more media and fans to impress. I wouldn't have to show up to a photo shoot anytime soon. The hairpieces were tossed into the trash. That life was a hundred years ago.

The pop-top trailer had no running water, so I did all my bathing at a local health club or a friend's house. For electricity, I ran a power cord from a nearby abandoned caretaker's house that was operated by the Colorado School of Mines. I kept a large cooler to store food in and dug a fire pit so I could cook. At night, the strong mountain winds violently shook my small trailer. Many times I wished they would sweep me up and carry me off somewhere, *anywhere*.

My young son, J.D., knew I was hurting and constantly wanted to stay with me out in the trailer. We both had a great deal of pain to deal with from the divorce, and it was good to have J.D. out there in the forest to keep me company. But overall I wasn't thrilled about him seeing me in such a condition. Who knows what kind of effect the whole scenario was having on him.

Interestingly enough, during that dark period my thoughts also turned to the young daughter Terry had left behind, Michelle. It always broke my heart to think of her growing up without her father around. And then a thought hit me—I remembered the black satin Caribou Ranch tour jacket I took from Don's house the night Terry died. I decided the time had come to pass it on to Michelle. I had kept the jacket folded up in a trunk for years and it wasn't doing anything but collecting dust anyway. Through her mother, Camilla, I managed to get it to Michelle for her sixteenth birthday. In the end, it's what Terry would have wanted, and it felt very rewarding. In my mind, the jacket was finally with its rightful owner.

The following days were spent out on my land replaying the years of Chicago back in my mind. When I wasn't skiing or fly-fishing, I reclined in a chair outside my trailer and listened to old CTA records on a cheap stereo system. The music brought me back to the golden years—the traveling and touring, the sense of brotherhood, and the overwhelming success we achieved together. But for the most part, the memories remained on an endless loop and constantly tormented me.

I was living out in the harsh elements of the Colorado winter with little shelter. The weather turned and the snow season descended upon me. Some local friends offered me a place to stay, but I couldn't bring myself to accept. The peace and tranquillity of being alone high up in the evergreens was calming. I saw why God had led me to such a beautiful place.

One morning I was sitting in the middle of the trees on a makeshift toilet when I heard a rustling from over the hill. I looked up to see a group of elk come wandering out of the woods. They stopped and stared curiously at me sitting half-naked with my pants at my ankles. The absurdity of my situation finally hit me. Everyone believed I had gone off the deep end, and now even the elk were looking at me like I belonged in the nuthouse.

I chuckled to myself. A second later, I guffawed again. Then uncontrollable laughter gripped me until tears began running down my cheeks. The outburst frightened the elk and they trotted back up over the hill.

"What a life!" I cried out into the treetops overhead.

That ridiculous moment alone out in the woods marked a turning point for me. If I didn't begin the long road back to recovery I would remain up on that mountain and wither away until there was nothing left. After a great deal of soul-searching, I was ready to take the first step, but it wasn't going to be easy.

I thought back to the lyrics I had written for the song "Birthday Boy" that lonely night in my hotel room in New York City. They perfectly fit the situation: "Good days are coming, Once you stop running."

It was clear the time had come to stop running.

Besides, the weather had gotten too cold for me to keep living in such a way. I wouldn't have lasted much longer. After eight months of sleeping in my pop-top trailer, I decided to go ahead with the construction of a house on the land. I rented an A-frame home on nearby Blue Creek Road and threw myself into my music studio in hopes of once again trying to develop local talent.

I may not have had the desire to play, but I found that my interest in the creative process of making records was still strong. During my career, I had collaborated with some of the most talented music producers in the business: Jimmy Guercio, Phil Ramone, Tom Dowd, and David Foster. I had learned something from each and every one of them and felt I had a great deal of knowledge to offer up-and-coming artists.

Although I might have taken a step in the right direction by coming down off of the mountain and getting back into producing, I still wasn't out of the woods. My identity was so closely tied to Chicago that it was difficult to find myself. *Who are you?* I thought. I was always proud of my legacy with the band, but now it haunted me wherever I went. Every time I turned on a radio one of our songs was playing. Whether I was in my car, in a restaurant, or at a shopping mall, Chicago's music was everywhere.

People often came up to me and explained how my style of drumming inspired them to learn to play, but I never knew how to answer. Their praise was flattering, but at the same time the comments served as a painful reminder of my past—of who I *used to be*.

The months of living in Colorado eventually turned into years. I reveled in the peace and tranquillity of life in Evergreen. It's as if nature was a drug I took every day to ease my pain and suffering. Over time, I began to open myself back up, and eventually I met a beautiful young girl named Rebecca. We hit it off and soon began dating. It had been six long years, but I was finally able to open my heart back up and have a meaningful relationship again. Rebecca is the most beautiful woman, both inside and out, that I have ever been with. She is a true gift from God, because I believed it was his way of letting me know the best was still to come. For years, I had been convinced my best days had passed me by. Suddenly there was a bright light at the end of the tunnel.

With Rebecca's love, I came out of the darkness a much better person. The scars were still there, but I was able to start dealing with my intense feelings of resentment for the band. I didn't want it to consume me any longer. No matter what, my heart was and always will be with Chicago. Whenever Pete called me from Los Angeles for advice, I helped in whatever way possible. As much as I tried to stay tight-lipped, I couldn't help myself. Part of me didn't have anything to say to Pete, but another part desperately needed to know how the band was doing. The vindictive side wanted to see them fail on every level, but deep in my heart I hoped they would continue to succeed. It would have been like rooting against one of my children, and there was no way to bring myself to do it.

I desperately wanted to put the past with the band to rest, so I decided to call Pete in the hope that he could arrange a meeting with the guys. It was time to clear the air between us and let them know there were no more hard feelings on my end. Pete said he would check with the band and get back to me.

It didn't sound too promising, but I accomplished something by at least offering to meet and mend the fences. When Pete finally called back, he told me the band had an upcoming show booked in Denver and it would be the best opportunity to get together with the guys. Unfortunately, he also told me he wouldn't be able to fly in for the show. Pete's not being able to be there wasn't too reassuring, because he was the middleman in the whole line of communication. But I decided to go through with the trip anyway. I had no intention of holding on to my resentment any longer.

I was a ball of nerves as Rebecca and I drove down to the show at Fiddler's Green Amphitheatre in Denver. Half of me wanted to turn around and retreat back to the safety of Evergreen, and the other half couldn't wait to get to the place. For the most part, I was looking forward to reconnecting with Walt, Robert, Jimmy, and Lee. It had been years since we had seen each other and I hoped it would turn out to be a cathartic experience.

Rebecca and I arrived at the venue and the band was kind enough to leave tickets to the show at the will-call area out front. As we settled into our seats, I put in a call to the road manager, Steve Braumbauch, to let him know I was in the audience.

"So we'll meet up backstage after the show?" I asked him.

Steve paused before answering. "I don't think the band is comfortable with that, Danny," he said.

It was laughable. Was this some type of cruel joke? After I realized I wouldn't be meeting with the guys, I wanted to do nothing but leave. But I ended up going against my better judgment and stayed to watch the set. When Chicago took the stage, I was stunned. I couldn't believe some of the changes they had made to the songs. When the band played "Does Anybody Really Know What Time It Is?" they cut out the 5/4 section of the song altogether. In my mind, it was the unique part that gave the tune its identity. Then the guys transitioned into a medley of the band's greatest hits. A *medley*? Since the beginning, we had always insisted we would never do a medley of our songs. Now here I was watching them tear through one with my own two eyes. It was an all-time low in terms of the band's performance, and it wasn't because I wasn't up onstage with them. The bottom line was that the band had become unrecognizable.

The group's refusal to meet with me was a real letdown. What was it going to take to put this whole ordeal behind us? I'm not sure whether they feared I would flip out on them or that they simply had no interest in seeing me. I guess I'll never know. I went into the situation with the best of intentions and instead old wounds had been reopened.

My trip to Denver might have been a bust, but in a way the negative experience motivated me to reach out and write to Peter Cetera. In the years since he had left the band, he had tried to contact me on more than a few occasions, but I could never put my anger aside long enough to have a conversation with him. After the failed attempt to mend the fences with Robert, Jimmy, Lee, and Walt, my interest in reconnecting with Peter increased. I tracked down his e-mail address and sent him a message explaining that I was interested in meeting. Fortunately, Peter replied back a few days later and we agreed to get together. It was a genuine relief.

We decided I'd drive out to Sun Valley, Idaho, to meet him. Over the course of the weekend, Peter and I played a few rounds of golf and had dinner. We reminisced about all the good and bad times we had been through. I apologized to him for the way I had acted over the years, but explained that I was very angry that he had never said goodbye to me when he left. Peter accepted what I had to say, but he had a different take on what happened. He said that in his mind he had been *forced* out of the group. I and the rest of the guys were always under the impression that he had elected to leave Chicago to pursue his solo career. In that moment of sitting with Peter at dinner, I realized that all it would have taken was a simple phone call on my part. Instead, we had allowed other people on the business side of things to interfere with our relationship. It was too bad all those years had to go by with each of us not knowing what the other had been thinking. We could never pick up where we left off years earlier, but at least in the end Peter and I were able to clear the air.

During our conversations, Peter could tell I still had a great deal of resentment toward the guys in the band. He offered his support and provided me with some helpful insight.

"You just need to move on and not let the situation bother you any longer," he told me.

"Yeah, I know, man," I said. "I need to move on."

Although I agreed with Peter, saying it and actually doing it were two very different things.

My career might have been long over, but at least some of the music I had written continued to remain relevant. A few of my songs turned out to have tremendous staying power, especially "Street Player." In late 1995, a band called the Bucketheads had sampled the song in a dance track called "The Bomb!" that was tearing up the dance charts in Europe. *The Bomb?* I asked myself. And then it dawned on me—"Street Player" had turned out to be the biggest *bomb* of Chicago's career. Very funny. I was surprised when I got a call from the Bucketheads' manager in London, who said he had been trying to track me down for months. He explained that he had already spoken with Hawk, who had agreed to license the rights to the song for fifteen hundred dollars.

He wanted me to agree to the same terms. There was no way in hell I was going to accept an offer like that.

The Bucketheads had gone ahead and released the song without checking with either Hawk or me and now they were scrambling to tie up the loose ends. In the end, we negotiated a third for them, a third for Hawk, and a third for myself. Everyone ended up making a ton of money on the track.

A few months later, I got word that "The Bomb!" had been nominated for an ASCAP (American Society of Composers, Authors, and Publishers) Award for Dance Track of the Year. "Street Player" had gotten killed when it was released, and now all of a sudden it was proving to be the most successful single of my career. Talk about poetic justice. In the end, it turned out to be the dance hit I always wanted it to be, just not in the form I'd originally written it in. Go figure.

I flew to New York City with my buddy Bill Denton to attend the awards ceremony, but received some terrible news shortly after we checked into our hotel—my father had suffered a stroke and had been rushed to the hospital back in Chicago. I left Bill in New York and hopped the next flight out of the city. Rebecca flew from Colorado to meet me.

My dad hung on for about another month or so. Fortunately, it was enough time for all of us to say our goodbyes. On July 4, 1997, we got a call that he was close to dying and that we had better come right away. We rushed down to the hospital, only to find he had passed literally seconds before we got to his room. As I walked up to the bed, a single tear still glistened on his cheek like a diamond. I dabbed his face with a tissue and put it in my pocket for safekeeping. My dad was the sweetest and most beautiful man I had ever known. He had a smile that captured your heart and he didn't have a mean bone in his body. It was heartbreaking to see him go, but I knew he would be in a better place.

I gave my mother the tissue with his last teardrop on it. I actually wrote "Dad's last tear" on it. I felt like he left it for her as a gift.

With my father gone, it seemed in many ways like my mother was only waiting for her time to come. She had lost her soul mate and life would never be the same. When her health started to decline, the prognosis wasn't good. They admitted her into the hospital back in Chicago and found she was suffering from congestive heart failure, diabetes, and leukemia. I constantly flew back and forth to Chicago to be with her. I begged God to take away her pain, because it was too much for either of us. I wanted to be able to do something, but felt powerless over the situation. Day after day, I felt as if a large part of me was dying with her. She was the strongest person I ever knew and fought to the end. In a way, it was a relief when she passed away, because I couldn't stand to see her suffer any longer. But in my heart I understood she was finally at peace and together again with my dad.

It was difficult to see my parents go. They had given me so much over the years. I would not have been able to do the things I did without their love, support, and guidance. I wished they were still around to talk to about the ongoing identity crisis I was going through in my life day to day. But I guess God was letting me know the time had come for me to continue on my own path.

23

Full Circle

My new life in Colorado with Rebecca was amazing. I was living off what was supposed to be my Chicago retirement money and enjoying everything the outdoors had to offer. The transition into a "normal" way of living wasn't easy, but at least I was making an effort to try to enjoy myself. My days were spent skiing with my kids, mountain biking, and fly-fishing. I also became the defensive coordinator for J.D.'s football team so we could have more time together.

I realized I was getting older. It was hard not to. I became a grandfather when my daughter Danielle gave birth to my first grandchild, a girl she named Katie. I was more at peace than I thought I would be to assume my role as a grandfather. It didn't mean I had to feel old. If anything, it gave me a renewed sense of excitement about life.

The time had come to take the next step and ask Rebecca to marry me. She said yes and we were married in a small ceremony in Denver on August 26, 2000. My kids were all able to fly in for our special day. Even Maria came in from Chicago. It was nice to have all my family and friends in the same place because it didn't happen as much as it used to.

A couple of days before the ceremony, my friend Bill Denton called me late one night.

"Listen, Danny," he said. "You told me *never* to let you get married again."

"I changed my mind," I told him. "Never say never, right?"

We both had a good laugh over the whole thing. Bill had spent enough time with Rebecca to know she was the one for me.

A year into married life, Rebecca and I decided the time had come to get out of Evergreen. She was tired of seeing me wasting my effort and money trying to make it in the music business long-distance from Colorado. Over the years, I had had a string of near misses trying to get some very talented artists signed to major labels, but it just wasn't happening.

"It's now or never, Danny," Rebecca told me. "You have to be in Los Angeles."

Rebecca was right, but I hated to leave the new life I had found so much comfort in. At the time, I was trying to develop a talented local singer named Shilah Phillips, and we both needed to be in the Hollywood mix if there was going to be a chance to bring her to the next level. In my eyes, Shilah was like a young Whitney Houston and had the talent to get signed. She only needed a legitimate opportunity at exposure. Her mother entrusted Shilah's career to me and allowed her to move out to the West Coast with Rebecca and me. It was an honor to have someone put so much faith in me, but also a ton of pressure to deliver a record contract.

I broke my forty-acre plot of land overlooking the Continental Divide into three separate pieces and sold them off at a sizable profit. As bittersweet as it was to say goodbye to the land that had brought me so much solace and tranquillity, the sale of the property saved my ass. It gave me the cash necessary to make the move to the West Coast. Eventually we relocated to a nice home in Northridge, California, and I went to work trying to get Shilah a deal.

Initially, many of the major labels were interested, but the buzz around Shilah eventually cooled off. She was a smart and sophisticated young girl and the labels didn't think she was "street" enough. Despite my contacts within the record industry, a record deal didn't come together. Regretfully, I had to send Shilah back to her mother in Texas. It was tough for me to accept that we hadn't achieved what we set out to do. I added the experience to the growing list of near misses. It was time to look for another avenue.

As I tried to figure out my next move, an old friend from Chicago's early CBS Records days, Ron Alexenburg, called me and suggested I take a meeting with his son-in-law, a guy named Scott Prisand. Scott was helping finance the Broadway theater business in Denver and Ron thought I might be able to use some of my past business contacts in Colorado to help him out. We arranged a meeting and Scott told me he was helping develop a play called *Brooklyn*, which the producers wanted to test in a theater in the Denver area. They asked if I might be interested in helping raise money for the production. Shortly after we got together, Scott sent me a videotape of the workshop, and it was amazing. From my time living in Colorado, I was well connected and knew many wealthy people. Why not give fund-raising a try?

I delved into my book of contacts and called everyone I thought might be interested in investing in the production. Once I was able to put together a decent-sized group, I flew to Denver to make the necessary introductions between the producers and potential investors. Many of the people I contacted ended up putting money into the development of the play. For my part in the deal, I was given an associate producer's title. The work was rewarding because I was helping find funding for a project I truly believed in.

Suddenly I found myself with a new career and started fielding calls from other productions looking for financial backing. It wasn't long before Anita Waxman and Elizabeth Williams contacted me and gave me an opportunity to help raise money for an Andrew Lloyd Webber play called *Bombay Dreams*. They told me one of their main investors had pulled out of the production at the last minute and they were scrambling to find more money to finance it. Scott and I saw this as a great opportunity, as Waxman/ Williams were very successful producers; Elizabeth Williams helped produce some of the biggest hits ever on Broadway, such as *The Phantom of the Opera, Les Misérables,* and *Miss Saigon.*

As always, to make the right decision it was important that I hear the soundtrack before picking up the phone and calling anyone. If the music didn't blow me away, I wouldn't be able to devote myself to the project. When they sent me a tape of the orchestration, which was written by the great Indian composer A. R. Rahman, I was thrilled and couldn't wait to get started. I called many of the same investors I had approached to back *Brooklyn.* I figured if it worked once, it would work twice. And in the end it did.

I regularly traveled to New York City to meet with the show's producers and possible investors. I was still running away from my destiny in many ways, but my Broadway work was serving as a good tonic. It kept me close to music. I needed new projects to occupy my time so I wouldn't have to confront the larger personal issues looming over my head. Just because I was avoiding my problems, however, didn't mean they couldn't somehow find me.

One morning I came walking out of a restaurant during one of my trips to New York City and suddenly found myself face-to-face with Robert outside on the sidewalk. Needless to say, I was caught completely off guard. We had run into each other once at a benefit for Beach Boy Carl Wilson shortly after I moved back to California, but there were a lot of people around and we hadn't said much to each other. Before I knew it, Robert and I were giving each other a friendly hug.

"How are you doing?" I asked, trying to hide my nervousness.

"Pretty good, man," Robert answered. "It's great to see you, Danny."

"Yeah," I told him. "It's nice to see you too."

Our small talk was painful. I sensed my emotions building and my heart rate picking up. I don't know what was coming over me, but I had to get out of there right away. The levee was going to break.

"Listen, why don't I give you my cell phone number?" Robert said.

My hand was already beginning to shake as I typed his number into my phone. "Okay, man, I've got to go," I told him quickly. "Good seeing you."

Robert could see there was something wrong. A concerned expression swept across his face as we parted ways. I took off walking in the opposite direction as fast as I could. At the end of the block, I rounded the corner and ducked into an alley. Suddenly my legs buckled and I collapsed against a section of chain-link fence. All the emotion I held back over the years flooded to the surface. I hadn't cried that hard since my mother had passed away. I clung to the fence tightly until I was able to regain my balance and stand back up on my feet.

The outburst left me shaken. It took me another few minutes to get my head straight. I called Rebecca and told her about what had happened. She said she had never heard me that distraught before.

Will I ever be able to put this behind me? I wondered. There had never been any type of resolution. Every time I put some distance between the band and myself, all my pain popped back up again. There would never be any relief until all of us could get together and put the past behind us. But I didn't know if I would ever see that happen.

A few days before Thanksgiving in 2005, I was talking on the phone with my close friend Peter Fish when he brought up a topic I hadn't thought about in a long time.

"Listen," Peter told me. "The other day I was thinking about how amazing the early Chicago Transit Authority material is. What if we put a band together?"

I mulled Peter's idea over.

"Don't say yes and don't say no right now," he continued, "but I've been thinking that before I die, I want to be in a band with you. You are too talented a musician not to be playing."

I was more than flattered by Peter's words. I told him it meant a lot to hear that level of praise coming from him. Over the years, there were many friends and business associates who'd started asking why I wasn't playing drums anymore. A vague interest in putting together another band had been floating around in the back of my mind for years, but my heart was never into it. I told Peter I needed to woodshed to see if I could whip my drumming chops back into shape. I didn't want to be seen as a guy who should have stayed retired. Over the course of the next two weeks, I practiced tirelessly in the garage at my house in Northridge and studied with a renowned teacher and old friend, Joe Porcaro (father of the late founding member of *Toto* and drumming legend Jeff Porcaro). My family and friends gave their unconditional support. Everyone was happy to see me playing drums again. When I was physically and mentally ready, I called Peter back and told him I was in.

We hatched a plan to do a rock/big band album covering some of the best songs from the early years of CTA. Now we only had to find other talented musicians who were as excited about doing the project.

At the same time, Don Lombardi, the owner and founder of DW Drums, had also been urging me to get back to playing again. Don was always a close friend and a big advocate of my drumming style. I had been endorsing his company's drums and equipment since the mid-1980s. He couldn't understand why I wasn't at least traveling around the country doing drum clinics.

When I told Don about the project idea Peter and I had come up with, he was very supportive. He arranged a jam session with a group of other musicians at drummer extraordinaire Gregg Bissonette's house in Thousand Oaks, not far from where I lived. Gregg is a world-class drummer who has had a successful career playing with big acts like David Lee Roth, Toto, Don Henley, Carlos Santana, and Ringo Starr. That evening in his rehearsal space we were joined by bassist Bob Birch, who had been playing with Elton John for thirteen years, and a tremendously talented guitarist named Marc Bonilla. They had all grown up on Chicago's early music, so I spent the first few hours sitting around telling them band stories about being out on the road. For the rest of the night, we jammed together. We didn't worry about arrangements or sound levels; we simply let the music flow. There was no denying the immediate musical connection between Marc and me. I hadn't experienced anything like it since my days of playing with Terry. The rehearsal was an awakening. Playing with highly talented musicians stirred up emotions and feelings I hadn't experienced in years.

At the end of the day, Marc and I talked about a plan to put something serious together in order to play some rock clubs in Los Angeles. As soon as I got home, I called up Peter Fish in New York to see if he wanted in on what we were putting together. He told me to let him know as things developed. It was building inside of me—the same sense of expectation I experienced when Walt and I were putting the Big Thing together back in the early days.

A few weeks later, Marc called to ask if I wanted to participate in a fund-raiser that was being put together in Phoenix to help a photojournalist who had worked for *Modern Drummer* magazine. When the organizers, close friends Danny Zelisko and drummer Troy Luccketta from the band Tesla, also called to ask if I would perform at the benefit, I couldn't say no.

Later that day, Marc called me. "Why don't we get the guys together and learn 'Make Me Smile,' '25 or 6 to 4,' and 'I'm a Man'?" he told me. "I've got a bunch of ideas about playing the horn parts on guitar and synthesizer."

With Marc, Peter, and I in on the project, we needed to round out our lineup. Marc recommended a friend of his, an exceptional bass player by the name of Mick Mahan, and had another musician, Ed Roth, in mind to play keyboards. After we ran through a few rehearsals to learn the arrangements of the old CTA songs, we felt we were ready.

The fund-raiser in Phoenix was packed with talented musicians from all over the country. Luckily, we ran into Larry Braggs, lead singer of the outstanding group Tower of Power, who was there performing with another drumming legend and friend of mine, David Garibaldi. Larry volunteered to sing lead vocal on

"I'm a Man" and "25 or 6 to 4" for us. Part of me was horrified to take the stage in front of the full theater, and the other part couldn't wait to get up there and play. Fortunately, our rehearsals paid off.

After finishing "25 or 6 to 4," we walked to the front of the stage and took a quick bow. When I picked my head back up, the entire place was standing and applauding. The audience's wild reaction hit us hard. After being lost for so many years, it was as if I had come home again.

I fell down into a chair back in the dressing room and toweled off. I was dripping with sweat and my heart was still racing. My thoughts flashed back to the first big show I played with Jimmy Ford and the Executives at the Civic Arena in Pittsburgh. I began laughing and couldn't wipe the grin off of my face.

And then it hit me. For the first time in as long as I could remember, *I had gotten off on the music.* I was high.

At that exact moment, I knew what I needed to do; put a band together of the same cloth as the original CTA—a skilled group made up of the best musicians around.

After getting back to Los Angeles, we locked in our lineup: Larry Braggs on vocals, Marc Bonilla on lead guitar, Mick Mahan on bass, and Ed Roth and Peter Fish on keyboards. We had the bases covered musically. *But what will we call ourselves?* I wondered. And then it came to me . . . *CTA.* But it couldn't stand for Chicago Transit Authority. All of us were living in California . . . what about *California* Transit Authority? The name made sense to everyone.

The group name was a fitting acknowledgment of the original CTA days. Besides, I was starting over again like I had when I moved out to Hollywood in the summer of 1968. The group is a revisiting of the old Chicago Transit Authority music, a sound that has always defined me. It's a fresh beginning and another opportunity to prove myself.

We continued to rehearse and eventually put together a seventy-minute set that included a variety of early CTA tracks like "Colour My World," "Make Me Smile," "25 or 6 to 4," and "South California Purples." Marc came up with an innovative rock/big band arrangement of an old Cannonball Adderley song called "Something Different," doing a faithful interpretation with guitars instead of horns. Finally, the band played our first official gig at the Canyon Club in Agoura Hills, California, in January 2006 and never looked back.

When I found out I was set to be one of the featured drummers at the 2006 Modern Drummer Festival at the New Jersey Center for the Performing Arts, I was absolutely thrilled. The organizers explained that I would be joining a lineup of legendary drummers like Stewart Copeland, Steve Smith, and Thomas Lang on the bill. The band and I played a powerful set in front of every major drummer in the world. We received a standing ovation and I considered the performance one of the defining moments of my life. The drummers of the world had welcomed me back with open arms. A great weight had been lifted off of my shoulders and an overwhelming sense of redemption had set in. And to think I was supposedly let go from Chicago for my poor playing. From that point on, I vowed never to take my talent for granted again.

Next, the new CTA recorded on and off for nine months at the Green Room in Van Nuys in hopes of putting an album together. Going back into the studio was a strange experience. Although I had produced other artists on and off over the past seventeen years, I hadn't played and recorded my own material. There was a high standard set in my mind and I initially put a lot of unnecessary pressure on myself. Luckily, I settled down very quickly. Once we hit our stride, the band started killing it in the studio. The sound engineer, Marc Greene, helped us get the old-school type of sound we were looking for.

I leaned on many friends and business contacts in order to come up with the money to finance recording the CD. People came through in the clutch and invested out of their deep respect for me. I didn't come to them as a fast-talking car salesman type of guy. I gave them the honest truth, and people could feel my passion for the project. I will be forever grateful for their support.

In the end, the hard work paid off, and on August 14, 2007, California Transit Authority released our first studio record, fittingly titled *Full Circle*.

Since the day we started, every day has been an uphill climb to try and establish the new band. I may have initially come back to music to play drums, but I have found myself wearing many other hats: manager, promotion man, road manager—you name it and I'll do it. It's certainly another case of "be careful what you wish for." I wanted to get back into playing in a working band again, and boy did I ever! *Working* is the key word! At the same time, I also realize the band can be a big part of my life, but I will not let it *become* my life. I've already made that mistake once and don't intend to do it again.

It isn't realistic to compare the current status of the new band with the astonishing success of Chicago, but unfortunately it is my natural tendency. I can't overlook what I have been accustomed to throughout my career. The days of overwhelming popularity and international superstardom are over, but California Transit Authority still has the ability be successful in its own way.

Fortunately, we have gotten a great response for *Full Circle* and there's a buzz building about our live performances. Robert Lamm even called me shortly after we released our album to tell me he was thrilled we were doing reworked versions of his songs "25 or 6 to 4" and "South California Purples." I was thankful for Robert's support, because not many bands would take the risk of redoing those songs. I enjoy being around all the fans again. Actually, I consider them more like friends than fans. Many of them have been with me since the early days and have told me how happy they are to have me back playing. That alone makes it all worthwhile.

Epilogue

Looking back, I realize I had a problem with my temper, and I am probably more paranoid than I should be. But I will never apologize or make excuses for following my instincts over the years. They are all I have had to rely on since my days of running the streets of Chicago. Act first and ask questions later. Hesitate for a moment too long in the old neighborhood and you would pay for it. I didn't make it as far as I did by being passive and docile. I've never been a yes-man for anyone. The rest of the guys in Chicago had a difficult time understanding my behavior sometimes, because none of them came from a background like mine. They grew up in the quiet suburbs outside of the city and never ran from shotgun-wielding members of gangs, eluding bullets and buckshot.

From the beginning, I was always the drummer, the backbone of the operation. It was my job to keep everyone in time and in balance. I set the pace and carried it through until the end no matter what. It may have not been the right way, but it was the only way I knew. Over the course of my life, I will be the first to admit I have been guilty of being overly aggressive in dealing with people. It's something I still struggle with today. My fiery Italian personality has made me in certain situations and broken me in others. I believe in karma and I could have handled things differently when the band got rid of Laudir de Oliveira and Donnie Dacus. I could have approached my power play against Jack Goudie a little differently. It's taken me a long time to understand that I've been the master of my own destruction.

As I've grown older, I have made major strides in my life, but I am still a work in progress. Like Pete always said, "Lose your head and your ass will follow." It's true. I have always been more of a lover than a fighter, but it took a long time for me to get it through my head. Luckily, I had great teachers to guide me along the way, like Bob Tilles, Chuck Flores, and both Papa Jos—Jo Jones and Joe Porcaro. I learned as much about life from them as I did about drumming.

At sixty-two years old, I can still see the flame out there in the distance, but instead of running, these days I *walk* toward it.

Above all, I couldn't be more proud of my music career and the legacy Chicago left behind. I'm honored to have been part of a truly golden era in music and lived to tell the story. So many people didn't make it along the way. More than anything, I'm happy to still be playing the music that has been inside of me since the afternoons of banging on my mom's pots and pans on our kitchen floor back in Chicago.

Many nights, I lie quietly in bed and thank God for the tremendous good fortune I have had throughout my life. I know my mom and dad are up there somewhere rooting me on. And Terry is up there too, smiling down on me as I play in a band he helped inspire. He's a big part of the reason I go out there and perform night after night. I do it for Terry and all the fans who still remember the early days of CTA and our contribution to music. I also do it for my family, who have always been there to support me. They give me the strength to get out of bed in the morning and try to enjoy every moment of life. And I want to continue to make them proud.

Even though the cowardly way I was fired from the band has hovered over me like a black cloud since 1990, it was merely an unfortunate end to an unbelievably joyful period in my life. It doesn't erase the remarkable life I've led. There isn't a person in the world who can take my achievements away. Hopefully, one day my former bandmates and I will be able to reconcile and put our differences behind us. Until that time comes, I can only remain optimistic and go about my business.

Whenever fans today come up and ask, "Hey, are you guys ever going to get back together again?" I look at them and say, "If there is one thing I have learned, it's never say never."

Acknowledgments

First and foremost, to My Sweet Lord—who has given me such an incredible and interesting life. You have always taken care of me, no matter what.

I'd like to acknowledge the following people for the profound impact they've all had on my life, whether positive or negative. They helped shape who I am today.

To Adam Mitchell, thanks for your patience with my ADD and crazy lifestyle. You made writing this book an incredibly positive and cathartic experience.

To Alan Nevins—this book would not have happened without your persistence and belief in my story. Thank you.

To Bill Denton, Don Lombardi, Ken Kleinberg, Danny Zelisko, Rich "G-man" Goins, Jimmy "the Count" Pacifico, Jim and Stevie Cummings, Kirk and Grace Eberl, Bill Grimes, Iris Smith, Larry Walker, and Larry Thomas for their undying friendship and support with my current and hopefully future endeavors.

To Rose and Teddy, thank you for your love, tenderness and devotion to me in our years together. Just know that I loved you, no matter what my actions said. I'm still working on that husband thing but can't seem to master it.

To my bandmates in California Transit Authority—Peter Fish, Marc Bonilla, Ed Roth, Mick Mahan, Larry Braggs, Eric Redd, and Walter Rodriguez—for being my new musical soul mates and following me on this sometimes perilous journey that we now call the new music business. You've all enriched my life more than you will ever know.

To my former Chicago bandmates: Walt Parazaider, Peter Cetera, Jimmy Pankow, Robert Lamm, Lee Loughnane, Bill Champlin, and Jason Scheff. Thanks for the ride of a lifetime—though it was a bit bumpy toward the end—and the amazing legacy of music we created together. I hope someday we can put all that silliness behind us and once again share some laughter, friendship, and, who knows, maybe even some music.

Very special thanks to Pete Schivarelli for being such a good godfather to my son and educating me on the ways of the street; to James William Guercio for showing us the way and how to always treat our music; to Howard Kaufman for continuing what James started and passing on your amazing business skills; to Larry Fitzgerald for being the voice of reason in a sometimes insane world; to David "Hawk" Wolinski for being such a generous friend and creative songwriting partner; to Irving Azoff for always taking my calls and being the best in the business; to Coleman Gibson, Bill Cosby, Gavin Christopher, and Grady Tate for teaching me to be color-blind. Also special thanks to Jeff Munger, Howard Asher, and George Jones. To all my Evergreen friends, you know who you are: I can't thank you enough for embracing me and my family. You were there during some of our toughest times and not only helped us forge a new life but also inspired us to become better human beings.

To all my friends: Jennifer Mesa, Pete Hayes, Bob Weise, Jerry Vaccarino, Rick Cooper, Mike Unger, Brian Stratton, and John DeChristopher. To my baseball buddies: Tony and Elaine La Russa and Phil and Carol Garner. To my friends at Zildjian, Eric Smith and Auralex Acoustics, Remo Belli, Matt Connors, Steve Smith, and Gregg Bissonette for helping me back into the saddle. To Gwen Riley for helping me keep it together, Scott Prisand (the Hebrew Hammer) for introducing me to Broadway, the Lonely Street Crew—Jay Mohr, John Gerit, and James Brown (the King)—for helping keep Elvis's memory alive in a positive uplifting movie, and Bruce Lundvall and Phil Ramone for being the classiest men in the record business.

To Wiley: Thanks to my wonderful editors Tom Miller and Dan Crissman for their hard work and dedication to this project.

Credits

Photos

Pages 89, 90, 91, 92 (bottom left), 93, 94 (top), 95, 96, 98, 102 (top), 218 (bottom), 219, 220, 221 (top), 223 (bottom), 224 (bottom), 225 (top), 227, 228, 229 from Danny Seraphine's personal collection; page 92 (top) Maurice Seymour; page 92 (bottom right) Colin Underhill; page 94 (bottom) © Ron Werntz 1971 reproduced with permission; pages 97, 222, 223 (top) Patty Buscemi Molloy; pages 99 (top), 221 (bottom), 224 (top) courtesy of Martin Derek; pages 99 (bottom) and 100 (top) Peter Duke © 2010 all rights reserved; pages 100 (bottom), 101, 102 (bottom), 103, 104, 217, 218 (top) courtesy of James William Guercio/Caribou Ranch; pages 225 (bottom) and 226 Teddy Newton Seraphine; page 230 Tim Ellis.

Lyrics

TAKE ME BACK TO CHICAGO Written by David Wolinski and Danny Seraphine. Copyright © 1977 BIG ELK MUSIC, HAWKNASH, SPIRIT CATALOG HOLDINGS, S.À.R.L. All Rights for Big Elk Music and Hawknash Controlled and Administered by Spirit Two Music, Inc. (ASCAP). All Rights for Spirit Catalogue Holdings, S.à.r.l. Controlled and Administered by Spirit Two Music, Inc. (ASCAP) in the United States, Canada, UK and Eire. All Rights for Spirit Catalogue Holdings, S.à.r.l Controlled and Administered by Spirit Services Holdings S.à.r.1 for the World excluding the United States, Canada, UK and Eire. International Copyright Secured. Used by Permission. All Rights Reserved.

Index

NOTE: Page numbers in *italics* refer to photos.